THE DISPOSAL OF LIBERTY
AND OTHER INDUSTRIAL WASTES

The Disposal of Liberty
and
Other Industrial Wastes

by EDGAR Z. FRIEDENBERG

DOUBLEDAY & COMPANY, INC.
GARDEN CITY, NEW YORK
1975

ISBN: 0-385-08249-5
Library of Congress Catalog Card Number 73–9028

To Roger Mosher and Terry Todd, who in quite different ways have done so much to make this book possible; and to Stephan Regina-Thon, who kept my life interesting while I was writing it. Comes now, likewise, Ross Waters and his sister, Susanne Manuel; and her children of course.

And Sespe, and so to the limits of the *karass*.

CONTENTS

INTRODUCTION
Ressentiment

My central purpose in writing this book has been to examine a paradox that has troubled me for as long as I have dealt with general ideas, and that has steadily become more and more important in politics. This paradox is the peculiar incapacity of the democratic, populist national state to deal generously with the less fortunate members of its population. In North America, especially, we have been taught to believe that generosity was not only economically feasible, but that it might reasonably have been expected. Our high state of technological development, it has constantly been supposed, could produce goods and services enough to provide all our people with leisure and affluence; and it has been only recently that the mounting problems of pollution and overpopulation have led us to doubt that this could ultimately be done for the entire world. Our populism was supposed to insure that the people could insist on an equitable distribution of this abundance, so that none should go in want of what they needed for a satisfying life—or at least a life filled with all that money could buy.

We now know that these were empty clichés; indeed, to say that they are has itself become a cliché. Technological development has led instead to greater concentration of wealth. All over the world, the poor become more numerous and even objectively poorer as their level of expectation rises on the waves of television. Quite adequate and convincing explanations have been offered as to why the democratic political process is unable to countervail against these destructive developments. My own thought on these issues has been molded by, and coincides most closely with, that of Jacques Ellul, especially in *The Political Illusion*.[1] But there has been no dearth of explanation as to why democratic politics does not produce democratic results; of these, Robert Heilbroner's recent book, *An Inquiry into The Human Prospect,* is surely among the most stimulating.

Yet none of these recent analyses of contemporary world politics deals directly with what seems to me the most remarkable, persistent and disgusting characteristic of democratic political life. This is its peculiar mean-spiritedness. "In our times, from the highest class of society down to the lowest" John Stuart Mill observed in his essay "On Liberty," "everyone lives as under the eye of a hostile and dreaded censorship." In *his* time, over a century ago. He should see us now, as millions of hard-hats and other middle Americans maintain their not so silent majority vigil against blacks, poor people on welfare, pornographic books and textbooks that picture God as polyglot and the United States as one nation among many, all with problems. Middle America experienced a chastening setback in 1974, with the fall of their standard-bearer and his suite. But this is unlikely to improve their dispositions, or alter their political attitudes. In Canada, their counterparts likewise flourish, directing their efforts to the restoration of capital punishment and the repeal of the Official Languages Act.

The nineteenth century, which had not yet accepted as orthodoxy the view that the cause of egalitarianism is likewise the cause of liberty, was more critical of society's increasing rancor than the twentieth century has been; however, our century did produce one indispensable and seminal volume on these issues, by the neglected Danish classicist Svend Ranulf, whose *Moral Indignation and Middle Class Psychology*[2] finally became available in English after its author's death and twenty-six years after it had been published in Copenhagen. The old regimes that were so widely, if at the time unsuccessfully, challenged throughout Europe in 1849 thought of themselves as defenders of liberty as well as of privilege, even though their insurgent adversaries usually claimed liberty as a slogan first. But there were many nineteenth-century voices to question the claims of the spokesmen for equality that they were likewise spokesmen for liberty; though these were by no means enthusiastic supporters of *anciens régimes*. Tocqueville is most familiar to North Americans, though Burckhardt based his arguments on firmer theoretical grounds than Tocqueville's *ad hoc* observations; and Henry Adams, who came a little later, saw, with peculiar clarity and bitterness, the special threat to freedom inherent in industrialism itself.

But it was Nietzsche, pre-eminently, who understood the importance of the growth of spite and rancor among the lower-middling functionaries of modern society. He gave this phenomenon the name

Ressentiment, choosing a coinage from a foreign tongue to avoid the misleading connotations already inherent in any German word he might have used. English-speaking readers still tend to see the word as "resentment," but this is crucially wrong. Ressentiment is to resentment as climate is to weather, in places like the Aleutians. Ressentiment is a free-floating disposition to visit upon others the bitterness that accumulates from one's own subordination and existential guilt at allowing oneself to be used by other people for their own purposes, while one's own life rusts away unnoticed. Rebellion, which directs the rancor at the people or institutions that actually aroused it, reduces ressentiment sharply, though at the cost of invoking further sanctions if the rebellion is unsuccessful. Acquiescence makes it worse.

One of the purest examples of ressentiment in action I have ever seen—shocking, despite its triviality—was shown me by a cashier of the Nova Scotia Liquor Commission, a gentle-seeming, deferential middle-aged man, wearing the jacket of authority required of him by the province, which controls all sales of beer, wines, or spirits in Nova Scotia. On this particular morning, there was no one else in the store when I entered it, and the cashier was scrutinizing intensely a small object that he held lightly between his thumb and forefinger. "It's an earwig, sir," he explained with real interest in his voice. "You don't see many of those around here."

He held the little creature out so that I could see it. It was, indeed, odd-looking, though its chief distinction, which the dictionary describes as "a pair of large movable pincers at the rear of the abdomen," might, if we had them, do much to keep us safe on the streets of New York. Completing his scrutiny, the cashier tossed the insect toward the open door of the store with, I thought, the intention of freeing it. It fell short and landed in a patch of sunlight on the terrazzo floor.

"Where did it go?" he asked eagerly.

Stupidly enough, I pointed it out to him. He rose calmly from his counter, walked over to the doorway, and crushed it under his foot. So it goes.

Ressentiment is the inescapable consequence of exploitation, which is why Nietzsche saw it as central to "slave mentality." It is therefore the moral responsibility of elites even more than of their victims. In a democratic state, however, ressentiment assumes a striking political importance, in which the victims of ressentiment are far more fully implicated than they would be if they had not so insistently—if mis-guidedly—assented to the formal definition of themselves as the titular source of political authority. However manipulated or misled the electorate in a democratic state may be by those who manage its industry and means of communication, the hand that pulls the lever on the voting machine also releases the bombs on the helpless villagers in the bombardier's path. To claim otherwise is simply to insist at the outset that the democratic process is a mammoth en-terprise in political mystification. One cannot simultaneously claim political rights as one of a sovereign people and disclaim respon-sibility for the atrocities committed in the people's name.

In practice, unfortunately, ressentiment evades this issue, since a mass electorate in which ressentiment prevails finds it much easier to accept atrocities than public generosity. It is far less controversial po-litically to spend billions destroying Indochinese homes than to spend millions providing homes for unwed mothers and their children. No Indochinese victim was ever required to fill out complicated forms and wait hours to be interviewed by a bored clerk so that the bombs and napalm he could not afford to provide to his children would con-tinue to be delivered. Though it is true that both domestic welfare-mothers and Indochinese women had reason to dread nocturnal visits by agents hoping to surprise their husbands at home. If only the American peace movement could successfully have floated a rumor that the Vietcong were *getting something for nothing*—like by selling unexploded bombs to the government of India at an immense profit and making more money than a teamster picking grapes—the war would have been over in months. The American people wouldn't have stood for it.

A ressentiment-ridden policy thus faces peculiar difficulties in dealing with the pressing needs of its less fortunate members. Though a substantial proportion of the relatively better off may be moved by compassion and by fear of revolt—in whatever combination—they cannot prevail against the ill-will of those who are outraged by the proposal of a direct subvention of the poor. Every proposal for a guaranteed annual income is met by querulous objections that, if the income granted were large enough to insure a decent life, it would no longer be possible to get people to accept the worst and most poorly paid jobs; they'd live off the government instead. Since large entre-preneurs can easily pass rising costs on to their customers, especially if that customer is another entrepreneur or the government, they are not usually frantic about having to pay higher wages. These objections are more urgently voiced by persons who are themselves economically marginal, either as employees or as employers. And the proper answer to their objection seems to me to be "Yes, that is the intent. Nobody should have to do lousy work for lousy pay; and nobody should know that better than you, who have had to do it all your life. Avoid envy; it's a cardinal sin."

Since this answer is not politically possible; and since it is likewise impossible to ignore the plight of the disadvantaged, whose increasing alienation and desperation make them a social threat, our society has evolved an uneasy and increasingly unpleasant compromise. It defines as a social problem the poor, the young, the deviant and anybody who seems to be unable to cope—especially if other people find them disturbing. And instead of dealing directly with their difficulties and, whenever possible, giving them the money to deal with their lives themselves, our society sets up bureaucracies to rehabilitate and control them. This circumvents ressentiment; or, rather, gives it expression, since the people on whom the money is thought to be spent receive very little of it themselves; and that little under circumstances that insure that they will get no satisfaction from it. Instead, they become welded into what I call *conscript clienteles,* who provide the *raison d'être* of the cadres of professionals who are supposed to serve them; and whose services they are no longer free to refuse. It is the school children who support the school, whether or not they learn anything there or whether or not it is destructive to their self-esteem. It *could not* exist without them; they are *not allowed* to exist without it. The Canadian Penitentiary Service depends absolutely on the involuntary custom of some eight thousand prisoners to justify an expenditure of over 100 million dollars per year, making the per capita cost of wretchedness in prison greater than the average Canadian family income.

It is not much of an exaggeration to say that the modern industrial state can spend big money only on making people miserable; to spend it on making them happy would tear it apart in jealous rage. And in this respect, the egalitarian industrial state may be more vicious than its imperious predecessor, untroubled by democratic pretensions. It has always been profitable, almost by definition, for the more powerful to enrich themselves at the expense of the weaker. But greed, pure and simple, is a relatively genial vice, and need not be insatiable. The rich and mighty enjoy what they gain at the expense of the poor; but they do not resent the poor and think of them as gaining what little they have at *their* expense. They do not ordinarily think of the poor and outcast as exploiting *them,* and fear that the poor may get a little more than they deserve. If they could, the rich would like to forget the whole thing, since it tends to spoil their day. They do not enjoy the fact of the poor's humiliation; *that,* in itself, is not the source of their wealth or prestige.

But if it is true that behind every great fortune there is a great crime, a great many more lesser fortunes are derived from the definition of certain persons as criminals and from the services and industries intended to maintain the definition and control them. It is usually true that crime does not pay, since actions that consistently do pay are redefined as lawful when their practitioners gain wealth and power; *vide* the liquor industry. And it certainly does not often pay as well as a federal judicial appointment or an executive position with a firm that provides security guards and hardware. Policemen and prison guards are not very well paid, though the former have become quite adept at making other arrangements. But they are well aware of their ceremonial function in society, not only to maintain order, but to dramatize the outcaste character of the criminal. Police do many other more useful and benign things—they are often more skilled and humane at working out the domestic troubles of the poor than professional social workers are—but they are also the visible and ceremonial expression of the ressentiment felt by the frustrated law-abiding citizen including, especially, themselves.

The prevalence of ressentiment seems to me to make it absurd and sentimental to suppose that liberty will ever be a popular cause in a modern industrial society, whether that society be socialist or liberal-capitalist. Most citizens despise the very idea of idiosyncratic and personal self-expression as the very essence of privilege, and expect the bitter disciplines of adult life to stamp such tendencies out if the schools fail to do so. And, of course, they are right.

I, too, as a middle-class American, was indoctrinated early in life with the belief that personal liberty was the fruit of democratic polity and that the freedoms that Americans enjoyed, or at least talked a lot about enjoying, could only flourish in a land whose people were hostile in principle to rank and privilege. Yet it seemed to me, even as a child, that the actual freedoms that our family enjoyed were, in fact, derived primarily from our upper-middle-class position in the community we lived in—Shreveport, Louisiana—and owed little or nothing to the Constitution of the United States, which had been forced on us in Louisiana, seventy years earlier, anyway. It was, though, very clear indeed that those freedoms were not overvalued; they were what made life worth living. The important freedoms were a mutually reinforcing combination of material and spiritual advantages: good food and leisure, which meant servants you felt comfortable having around; books, travel, and the sense that the law would rather be on your side than not, if a controversy should arise. In that sense the Constitution really did form the basis for our freedom; it protected our property rights and provided social class bias we needed to keep us safe. "Life, liberty, and property," Locke had urged, were very important. *"Liebe und Arbeit,"* Freud added even more urgently; "love and work!" It remained for Marx, who was not usually favorably cited in Shreveport during the 1930s or even later, to show how all these were related, but I did come to understand at an early age that if you were going to have to do without any one of these five things for any length of time, it had better be the one Locke listed first. Provide, provide; though the Frost lie heavy.

It is an article of common faith among liberal Americans that this recognition that one was leading a privileged life among a majority of persons far less fortunate ought to have made me feel guilty. No doubt at some level of consciousness it did, as, according to Robert Jay Lifton, merely being alive made the survivors of Hiroshima feel guilty. But the guilt of survival, and the even greater guilt of prosperity and good fortune, are among the fardels men must occasionally bear cheerfully. At any rate, I prefer those who do.

Moreover, the very severity of the Depression made it less effective in inducing guilt in those who were spared its ravages, while driving home its lessons about the significant advantages of class. Its impact was like that of a natural catastrophe, which brings its victims great suffering but no personal discredit; and inspires little smugness or sense of personal responsibility in its survivors. It did produce the odd middle-class hero, like the putatively rich Shreveport real-estate man, doughty as Captain Scott in the antarctic, who stepped outside his lovely home one morning, still clad in pajamas, and shot himself so that his insurance would spare the family ruin. This was clearly the only thing he could have done; it established his family's social position firmly.

The Depression, in short, was nothing to mess around with. The great stock market crash came just two and a half years after the greatest flood in living memory hit the Mississippi and its tributaries. Those who happened to live on high ground survived intact; those who lived on middle ground carried some insurance; those in the lower areas did not. Flood relief was an immediate necessity; and the Atchafalaya spillway system was speedily constructed for flood control so that this particular disaster need never repeat itself. But nobody, so far as I know, apologized for not having drowned. The Army Corps of Engineers and America's captains of industry should each in their turn, no doubt, have shown greater diligence and foresight; the negligence and incompetence of individuals, and in some cases the malfeasance, contributed to the disaster, and people were glad when the Insulls crashed and later the president of the New York Stock Exchange, Richard Whitney, was sent to jail for fraud. But I don't think anybody who escaped injury in either disaster felt his good fortune to be an indignity. And even those who understood the social system well enough to perceive that they were *not* saved by good fortune but by their relatively privileged position were inclined to remain grateful for, rather than embarrassed by, the provisions that had protected them.

In the twentieth century, social class has replaced sexuality as the fundamental source of really dangerously confusing hypocrisy. We are now quite ready to admit that there are tensions and conflicts of interest between the sexes that are no less real because we also recognize that some people may—and should—become naturalized into a sex different from the one they were born into. And we are all surely healthier for this candor. But, today, there are barely even closet aristocrats; and those who occasionally flaunt their upper-class tendencies and feelings face severe social sanctions. Elites in democratic countries usually seek to maintain their advantages by mystification and obscurantism. They conceal their pretensions even from themselves in the hope of keeping those who are relegated to more exposed and deprived positions in society from understanding how the system that allocates privilege works, and works so unevenly and so reliably. Nor is this obscurantism left to chance; a major function of the compulsory public school system, which now costs about $1,500 per pupil per year in the United States, is to conceal the functioning of the social class system by spuriously purporting to equalize economic opportunity; conveying, in the meanwhile, a false model of the workings of the political and economic systems, and humiliating the

children of the poor into believing that they are too dumb to do anything effective to change society anyhow.

Yet, if they are not really that dumb, they can clearly be made so,
and with their parents' advice and consent. Nothing could be more
depressing than the ressentiment of the poor-white miners of the area
around Charleston, West Virginia, screaming in rage and burning the
few textbooks that were reasonably honest and comprehensive in
their treatment of the society that was screwing them. Except, perhaps, the white folks of South Boston, hurling rocks and abuse at
blacks who didn't much want to be there in the first place, in defense
of the school system that had done so much to make them what they
were. It does no good, and is quite irrelevant, to assert that the ressentiment of the outraged and vindictive *lumpenbourgeoisie* is understandable in terms of their own fears, marginalities, and deprivations.
Of course it is understandable. It is also intolerable, especially in a
society that still employs a democratic rhetoric and imputes to the
people of south Boston a dignity—and with it a responsibility—
equal to that of their black victims and anybody else. If God really
did create Louise Day Hicks the equal of Martin Luther King, Jr.,
then she ought to be thoroughly ashamed of herself. So, perhaps,
should She.

To understand is not necessarily to forgive; but I still find it hard
to understand why it has proved consistently so easy to conceal the
fact that different social classes have crucially conflicting interests
from members of the underclasses, when it was perfectly obvious to
me even as a youth in a provincial city of north Louisiana. I understand *why* this is done—to make exploitation easier—and *how* it is
done; but I have never understood why the process works. How can
it be so easy to get people systematically and continuously over a
period of decades to blind themselves to the meaning of their own
life experiences? Even a dog, Mr. Justice Brandeis once observed,
knows the difference between being stumbled over and being kicked.
But an underdog, apparently, can be persuaded to deny that there is
a difference or at least to bite another underdog rather than the men
who are kicking him.

I have gradually come to understand that the basic component of
this mechanism of obfuscation is the nation-state itself. It is this
which provides the pretext of a common interest that transcends
social class. A community can, of course, have interests that transcend those of the individual; or, more accurately, an individual may

have an interest in the preservation of his community that transcends his other interests—though if this happens too often, he might consider moving to a more congenial community. But a nation-state is not a community. It is what Kurt Vonnegut calls a *granfalloon:* an association of individuals who have very little in common under a common banner. A social class, though still no community, approximates one a little more closely. A major executive transferred from New York to Brussels by his firm is unlikely to have to make much of an adjustment. Not as much, certainly, as if he lost his job and found himself reduced to living in central Newark or Yonkers.

The Great Depression—should it now be called Great Depression I?—might have provided an ideal opportunity for Americans, among others, to be jolted out of their patriotic reflexes and into an awareness of their conflicting class interests. It was Franklin Roosevelt's peculiar genius to forestall this development, institute measures designed to effect a degree of social and economic reform with a minimum of real transfer of political power, and thus preserve the nation, such as it is, for the next fifty years. These are now about up. There appear to be several possibilities for the near political future: none of them, to a bourgeois like myself, very attractive. The nation-state may undergo revolutionary change or at least drastic political realignment in response to altered world economic and social realities. High schools in Dallas and Houston will certainly soon be offering Arabic instead of Spanish as a second language in their college-preparatory track, if they aren't already. But this may not be enough to restore American supremacy. On the other hand the state may, indeed, wither away, to be replaced *de jure* as well as *de facto* by the intercontinental corporation. The inscription on the base of the Statue of Liberty, never in especially good taste in its characterization of prospective immigrants, may be replaced by a simple declaration: "Welcome to North America, a wholly-owned subsidiary of Litton Industries." A similar notice, conspicuously placed on the heights overlooking the St. Lawrence near Quebec, would presumably be written in French. I should like to be optimistic about the prospects for America's survival, but am perplexed because I'm not sure which position would, indeed, be optimistic. It would, in any case, be out of character to expect Gerald Ford to announce, in paraphrase of his Bourbon predecessors, *"Le déluge; c'est moi."*

THE DISPOSAL OF LIBERTY
AND OTHER INDUSTRIAL WASTES

CHAPTER ONE

The Conscript Clientele

A large proportion of the gross national product of every industrialized nation consists of activities which provide no satisfaction to, and may be intended to humiliate, coerce, or destroy, those who are most affected by them; and of public services in which the taxpayer pays to have something very expensive done to other persons who have no opportunity to reject the service. This process is a large-scale economic development which I call the *reification of clienteles*.

The reification of clienteles is novel. It can only occur in a society that possesses the technological means to afford abundance, but cannot deploy those means to meet the felt needs of its poorer members because this would be politically intolerable to the marginally affluent, work-oriented mass of its constituency. When the demands of the deprived cannot be ignored, the funding that might have been directly used to provide for them is diverted into bureaucratic structures whose major function is to control them, though minimal provision for their subsistence will be made in the process as necessary to keep them going and maintain the *raison d'être* of the service organization.

The most obvious example of this process is the development of the huge public-welfare apparatus, so much of whose time, money and energy is devoted to trying to police possible chiselers and, indeed, to find the means of channeling a trickle of assistance through the maze of its own regulations to those compelled by circumstances to accept the bureaucracy's meager bounty on the bureaucracy's terms.

But poverty is not the only condition that may lead to impressment into a reified clientele. All politically powerless persons are subject to redefinition as members of a social group requiring the administration of services they may not refuse, on terms they are powerless to alter. Youth of school age, persons defined as criminal or mentally ill, native populations of Latin-American or Asian countries who are about to slip into insurgent socialism unless rescued by American intervention; all share this experience.

Although they are called "clients," members of conscript clienteles are not regarded as customers by the bureaucracies that service them, since they are not free to withdraw or withhold their custom or to look elsewhere for service. They are treated as raw material that the service organization needs to perform its social function and continue its existence. It does not take many hours of observation—or attendance—in a public school to learn, from the way the place is actually run, that the pupils are there for the sake of the school, not the other way round. Pupils whose idiosyncratic requirements make special demands on the school—unless there are enough of them to be reified as a special subclientele of "exceptional" children requiring a new kind of counselor or therapist—are regarded as miscreant. Students who try to discuss in class readings beyond those that were assigned, and that call for greater or subtler insights than the teacher stands ready to accept; or even those who respond to one another directly in discussion instead of addressing their responses to the teacher's question; those who want to use the facilities of the school after hours except as members of a recognized club, or to attend on a different schedule in order to pursue some compelling interest of their own; all such students usually find this impossible and are likely to be punished for even trying.

Ultimately, bureaucracies with conscript clienteles become real clients of one another, mutually dependent for referral of cases. They create conditions in one system that generate clients for another: the continued stigmatization of the children of the poor as stupid by the schools certifies them out of the job market and into welfare or crime-in-the-streets.

A third or more of the population at any one time—and all of us at certain times in our lives, especially toward the beginning or the end—are assigned to conscript clienteles. This is obviously a development with the most profound implications for liberty in a mass society, but its significance has been obscured, I believe, by a parallel and much more obvious set of socioeconomic developments characteristic of latter-day capitalism. The modern bourgeoisie has come to believe that it has sold its birthright of liberty for a mess of packaged breakfast cereals, all fundamentally alike though marginally differentiated to provide the illusion of choice, and none as nourishing or satisfying as a mess of genuine pottage. Social critics as different as Vance Packard and Herbert Marcuse, along with others less familiar, have pointed out again and again that the consumer choices offered by the mass market are not really choices; and that they serve to bind the consumer to the economy and distract him from the fact of his exploitation and from the economic constraints that channel him. Not only are the goods offered so lacking in real variety that automobile companies seek to differentiate their pseudo-sports imports by extolling the virtues of genuine corduroy or genuine pigskin upholstery. Even worse, the demand for goods is generated through advertising campaigns designed to create a market for items suited to inexpensive mass production. At no point in this process is there any spontaneous demand for the product to be offered, or foisted off on, the public.

This process has become so familiar and so irritating as to convince most of us that we are all members of conscripted clienteles. Freedom of choice has come to seem illusory, the mechanism by which we are chained to the economy like Prometheus to his rock, at the mercy of the vultures of production who have proved to be more punctual than compassionate. But I think the case against mass delights has been overstated. Only mass technics, with their built-in limitations on genuine stylistic diversity, could support the present population of the world, much less provide the simulacrum of luxury upon which most members of industrial society must depend for a little comfort and, especially, self-esteem. Those phony Olde Englysshe steak houses evidently do help a little to make people who want to feel British on the basis of inadequate ethnicity to do it—as a real pub certainly would not. And being nearly identical throughout the industrial realm, they present few problems in orientation. Often they serve pretty good steak.

Within their own context, the delights of mass society must surely be conceded a certain face-validity. Few things afford people more pleasure in life than a well-stocked supermarket; pleasure is not joy, but don't knock it. And Las Vegas surely provides as true a reflection of life in the age that built it as the cathedral of Chartres. Both are misleading if taken as evidence of what life must have been like for all their contemporaries, and neither is a work of art in the sense of being the creation of an individual designer or an expression of disciplined personal vision. But both are revealing collective expressions that have evolved under the pressures of their respective times in ways that now seem inevitable. And, both tell us a great deal—in the case of Las Vegas too much, perhaps—about what the people who built them valued.

In any case, the most blatant advertising campaign, promoting the most meretricious product, must still concede something to the individual human will; it must still attribute to each prospective purchaser some of the dignity of the classic bourgeois, making a free choice in the market place. Indeed, it is the triviality and irrelevance of the choices offered that make the advertiser's pitch so irritating. Nevertheless, his sales effort represents—even as it violates—his concession to the concept of human freedom that would have been acceptable to Adam Smith or John Stuart Mill. It is quite true, of course, that the tastes of the customers might actually be much better than the array of costly trash the market offers them.

The reason why nothing better is offered is at least as likely to lie in the fact that the profit margin in quality goods would be smaller as the possibility that the demand would be less. This is obviously so in the construction industry, where the value added by decent craftmanship may not even become visible for years, while ornate style can be made to appeal instantly at far less cost to the builder. But there are enterprises in which it is cheaper to spend marketing money to convince customers that they want a cheap faulty product than it would be to spend it on trying to design one that would meet their needs as well as was economically feasible, for the same price. And that includes most enterprises for which a large demand can be generated. Undeniably, the industrial market-mechanism degrades and manipulates the customer. But it does, even at its worst, treat him as a customer and solicit, in every sense of the word, his acceptance of its transactions.

This last vestige of dignity is lost to the client, however, when he becomes defined as a passive member of a reified clientele.

Certain specialized markets, of course, possess this characteristic inherently, or by virtue of cultural assumptions so deeply rooted as to appear almost innate. Because of their marked irresponsibility in fiscal transactions, one does not sell dog or cat food to dogs or cats; the merchandising appeal must be directed toward their owners, but the fact that such animals are regarded as property attests to the lack of dignity accorded them. It is probably not too much to say that, in modern industrial societies, anybody who cannot, or who is not permitted to, participate in the economic transactions presumed to provide for his needs will find, in fact, that he possesses no other defensible civil rights either. Children's books and toys, which are bought by and designed to appeal to parents, provide a more striking example, since children could, in fact, choose these for themselves, if their social roles and the institution of "shopping" were designed to permit it.

Pets and children, however, do retain a secondary veto power; pet food that is not eaten and toys that no one will play with are taken out of production. And television advertising is, notoriously, intensively directed at children. This practice seems to me desirable rather than objectionable, since it at least acknowledges their presence and their right to participate in the small decisions that affect their lives—which may be more than their parents do (most of the advertising is, itself, objectionable—but so is that aimed at the adult market). Consider, however, the actions of the U. S. Department of Defense, which, during the consumer boycott of grapes maintained by the supporters of Cesar Chavez's efforts to unionize the workers in the vineyards of California during the late sixties, began purchasing, for the first time, huge quantities of grapes to be shipped to Vietnam and served in Army messes. Whether American soldiers like grapes, or wanted grapes, or ate the grapes provided them, or whether those grapes rotted in shipment or in storage we do not know; such questions were not relevant to the decision to purchase them and go on purchasing them, in quantities sufficient to compensate the growers for the difficulties they were having with the domestic market. The consequence was to free them from any constraint related to consumer attitudes at all; they were marketing a political abstraction to a government agency that feared and hated social groups that opposed the war and knew well enough that these were likely to be the same people who supported the grape pickers. The soldiers, then, without expressing an opinion, raising a hand, or peeling a grape found themselves drafted into service again—this time as strikebreakers (though in this, the Army was no more successful than in the rest of its Vietnam operation).

Enlisted members of the armed forces have, of course, long been issued their allotments of food, clothing and shelter without regard to their tastes or their own conception of their needs. However, the fact that this is indeed a form of status-stigmatization as well as a way of rationalizing distribution is shown by the fact that officers, who are also governed by uniform regulations, are issued allowances for the same purposes and presumed to exercise discretion, even though their range of choice is limited. And quartermasters' contracts have been regarded as valuable political prizes by merchants for as long as there have been merchants and armies. But not only is the scale of operations different today; the range of careers and enterprises dependent for their success and continuation on the decisions of persons who will never consume the goods and services provided, and who are not responsible to those who will, has grown truly enormous. When the Congress finally cut off the funds necessary for the bombardment of Cambodia, the bombing, the heaviest in history, ceased. Even though many American jobs, including some in the Pentagon itself, were jeopardized, the Pentagon launched no advertising campaign to induce the people of Indochina, whose poverty is recognized, to support its resumption by popular subscription. They do not have this option; they will receive American bombs and napalm at the option of the American government—though if possible at the request of their own—or not at all.

The clientele for public education—which costs the American taxpayer about as much each year as the Vietnam War did at its height—is almost as involuntary. In many small towns, especially those from which the country doctor has fled, the school staff are the highest paid professionals and their payroll the biggest in town. This, too, is money spent providing goods and services to people who have no voice in determining what those goods and services shall be or how they shall be administered; and who have no lawful power to withhold their custom by refusing to attend even if they and their parents feel that what the schools provide is distasteful or injurious. They are provided with textbooks that, unlike any other work, from the Bible to the sleaziest pornography, no man would buy for his personal satisfaction. These are, precisely, not "trade books"; rather, they are adopted for the compulsory use of hundreds of thousands of other people by committees, no member of which would have bought a single copy for his own library.

The population of pupils in school has, of course, increased much more rapidly than that of the nation as a whole. In 1940, only about half of all Americans of high school age were in fact attending school; today, nearly all are. Whether one regards the change as

THE CONSCRIPT CLIENTELE   7

providing greater economic opportunity to children from social
classes the school formerly excluded—the evidence is against this
proposition[1]—or as intended to further restrict the movements of all
young people, it has resulted in the creation of an education industry
whose captive clientele consumes, willy-nilly, one of the largest single
slices of the gross national product in North America.[2]

A comparable, though less obvious and less frequently vaunted,
expansion has occurred in the area of law enforcement, which, with
its increasingly horrendous technical paraphernalia, has become one
of the most rapid growth industries in North America as Americans
and Canadians have become more and more concerned with "crime
in the streets," drug addiction, and other putative urban problems. I
say "putative" because it is impossible to be sure how much of this
concern reflects an actual increase in the crime rate, and how much it
reflects the resentment and anxiety fomented by the greater salience
and visibility of blacks in large cities. There is really no way to tell by
examining existing statistics, because every datum reported is affected
by anxiety and political pressure. More publicity stimulates police
activity, leading to a larger proportion of crimes and alleged crimes
reported and much larger arrest rates. Suspects, many of whom are
never charged with the offense that led to their apprehension, are frequently maltreated. "Cover" charges are, however, almost certain
to be laid against them to reduce the vulnerability of the police to actions for harassment or false arrest, especially if the victim has been
maltreated in custody—and this, too, artificially inflates the crime
rate. All bureaucracies tend to emphasize their own importance by
exaggerating the seriousness of the conditions they are supposed to
control; and police departments tend to respond to public concern
about crime by triumphantly capturing as many criminals as they
can, even if they have to conscript them from mere loiterers. A
recent and scrupulous report on violence to and by New York City
police[3] also reveals that police, though inclined to dramatize the
risk of attack by criminals, are frequently shot by other police
officers. Of five police killed in the line of duty in New York City in
1972, Logan reports that "one was certainly killed by another policeman and one very probably was." Another officer was shot and killed
by a colleague in a quarrel following the funeral of a fellow policeman who was shot while firing at two men who were trying to rob a
butcher shop. New York City police themselves killed sixty-six people in the line of duty in 1972—one a ten-year-old black boy, who

was shot accidentally when he fled from a stolen car with a fourteen-year-old friend whom the police were aiming at. In 1971, they killed ninety-three persons in what the chief medical examiner of New York City calls "legal interventions." The force obviously maintains a high level of activity; yet, during the six-day police strike in New York City in 1971, no appreciable rise in the crime rate was reported.

Whether or not the police prevent more violence than they contribute, it is certain that there has been a remarkable rise in the relative and absolute costs of police protection provided by already over-strained municipal budgets—and, of course, by a mushrooming growth in the private protection agencies as well. The sociologist Theodore M. Becker notes in a recent article[4] that private security forces are useful to their employers precisely because they are even less hampered than official police by the requirements of due process. "The private police retain the privilege but not the obligation to arrest and detain and also are not obliged to provide the suspect with his full measure of constitutional rights. Scott and McPherson[5] elicited these statements during the course of their Minnesota interviews:

" 'We can rough a guy up if we want to,' 'we can get a confession in cases where the police can't because we don't have to worry so much about a guy's rights,' and 'we can use every means possible to secure information.' "

In the evolution of the contemporary police state, there appears to be a trend toward the creation of special cadres to evade constitutional restrictions that would otherwise make it harder to control members of the population who cannot be convicted of crime and confined by ordinary legal process, but whose activities threaten more powerful members of the population. Moreover, a very large proportion of the personnel of private security forces are either currently employed as policemen and are moonlighting—which must make it confusing for them as they try to remember just what rights their detainee enjoys on this occasion—or are former policemen.

Some readers may object that my definition of those apprehended as the clientele of the police is biased if not wrongheaded, and that the real clients of the police are the citizens who do not receive the service for which their taxes pay, and not the small minority of wrongdoers. A disagreement on this point, though it has serious moral implications, cannot however affect the present argument as long as my meaning is clear. By clientele, I mean the persons to whom goods, services and hardware, if any are involved, are delivered; those on whom the praxis gets practiced, whatever its theoretical justification may be.

A case for the proposition that the true client of the penal system is the law-abiding citizen who chooses to pay for and expects to receive protection from criminal acts could be made only if there were evidence enough that the imprisonment of convicted offenders provided such protection, or at least that those of the public who support imprisonment as a means of social control believe that it does. Under some conditions, which hardly exist in the modern state, it may; an absolute monarch with the power to throw traitors into a modestly equipped but strong dungeon after an inexpensive minimum of due process probably does derive a certain degree of real protection from doing so. But there is no evidence that in a complex society the imprisonment of criminals acts as a deterrent to crime; it seems more often to breed further crime and certainly adds a legitimate and extremely serious grievance to whatever hostilities the offender may have felt—and criminals are selectively recruited from among the aggrieved.

The question whether prisons breed crime or deter it is probably impossible to answer by research; there are too many variables that cannot be controlled. What is clear is that law enforcement is an industry that depends on the definition of a certain proportion of the population as criminals to keep it going. It is a rewarding industry for its executives, in power, money, and prestige. At the moment, a proposal to raise the salaries of Members of the Canadian parliament by 50 per cent is stalled, at least temporarily, by widespread popular derision. A bill simultaneously introduced that would raise the salaries of Canadian judges up to 72 per cent, although equally publicized, has excited little public comment. In this industry, people are processed, sometimes in response to their probable overt acts, but nearly always, in any case, in keeping with their status characteristics; and adeptness in dealing with the aggression of social institutions is one of the most important status characteristics. Justice is a very unwelcome product that is dumped on people who are unable to defend themselves successfully. I do not mean to imply that the courts often convict innocent people—I do not know whether they do or not. But I am pretty certain that they seldom convict anyone (if indeed there is anyone) who is both innocent and rich. In law, innocence is a technical rather than a moral distinction, and the crimi-

nal code is most importantly a way in which existing power and
status arrangements in society are defended and maintained.

The recent insistence of more militant prisoners that all convicts
are political prisoners regardless of their guilt or innocence, or of the
offense of which they have been convicted, seems to me manifestly
true. I hardly see how they, or the public, could have supposed otherwise. The issue of equal protection of the laws, which the United
States Constitution guarantees, seems to me a minor if not a false
issue. Even if all Americans *were* treated equally before the
law—and they certainly are not—they would still not receive the
equal protection of the law, since in any society, whatever the structure of the law, it ends by serving as a safeguard and an instrument
for perpetuating the existing distribution of interests and power. This
does not mean that the law cannot be changed so as to help maintain
a more moral and just society; it can and should be and quite often
is, as with recent civil rights legislation. But such legislation does not
so much promote the cause of greater justice for blacks as it recognizes and consolidates the actual political and economic gains made
by some blacks—and for those who remain poor and powerless, it
does little or nothing. The law cannot, I think, ever form the
spearhead of any movement for social justice, though it is an indispensable tool for defending and retaining power once won.

Law enforcement, imprisonment, and, of course, capital punishment are different aspects of the same particularly clear example of
an industry whose clientele is entirely reified. In fact, it produces its
own clientele as it goes along. This is what makes the reasoning of
the U. S. Supreme Court, in selecting the grounds it did for its 1972
decision declaring capital punishment unconstitutional, so deplorable
and ironical. The Court chose to do absurdly and ineffectually—the
death penalty has already been restored by about half the fifty
states—what it ought to have done nobly and permanently. Its
reasoning was based on the fact that the death penalty is administered in a discriminatory way; that it is virtually never carried out except against poor, usually black defendants, among those convicted
of capital crimes.[6] But the whole prison population in the United
States is predominantly poor and black; in any society it will be composed of the powerless, although in the wake of a successful revolution or an unsuccessful revolt, they may have been powerful before.
If the poor and black are to be protected from the public executioner,
it must be through a just recognition that his function is obscene and
his services abhorrent to the dignity of the state, however much they

may be cherished by a majority of its fearful and resentful citizens. The Court's position, instead, merely condemns capital punishment as, in effect, an abridgment of the rights of the white and affluent who are taxed to provide a costly and highly specialized service that is presumably public but which is in fact never made available to them. Hanging people is constitutional as long as it is integrated.

Only the destitute and despised are, however, truly eligible for capital punishment, the ultimate in service to an involuntary clientele. Essentially the same conclusion applies to imprisonment.

Criminal proceedings, and the imprisonment following conviction, are costly, though profitable to the purveyors of these social services. One would suppose that a rational society, faced with the prospect of keeping a man in prison at a cost of $5,000 to $15,000 per year, would long ago have decided to handle what are now classified as crimes against property on an actuarial, no-fault basis. Some jurisdictions have adopted programs for paying damages to the victims of crimes; but I know of none that has yet taken the step of freeing itself from the costs of attempting to identify the perpetrators as criminal and to punish and control them in ways that deprive them of their dignity and sense of worth as people. There are, to be sure, experimental programs that make imprisonment less total by giving prisoners occasional leaves to visit what remains of their homes or attend worthwhile cultural events; some of the more advanced of these even allow prisoners to leave the prison during the day to take a job, and charge him correspondingly for his room and board in the prison. But these programs do not eliminate the stigma of imprisonment or much reduce the cost to the state, and they are especially vulnerable to the ressentiment of the more moralistic among the law-abiding, particularly the prison guards made anxious and angry by their loss of authority and prospective loss of employment. Prison custodial staffs have repeatedly proved to be the most serious and intractable obstacle to prison reform or even to the humane treatment of convicts—at Attica in 1971; in Canadian prisons where early in 1973 a rash of escapes provided a pretext for strikes and protests by guards' organizations against "permissiveness"; and most seriously, in the State of Massachusetts, where their agitation finally resulted in the ouster in June of 1973 of John O. Boone, a middle-aged black with years of experience in penal administration and the most enlightened director of the state penal system Massachusetts had ever had.

Prison reform, indeed, seems to me to be an almost meaningless

concept, because the actual function of imprisonment is contra-
dictory to its expressed purpose. The actual function is vindictive and
moralistic; and if—as seems clearly the case—the expressed purpose
of the prison to rehabilitate the offender and reduce crime can only
be achieved by treating prisoners with the same respect and openness
accorded to other people, the expressed purpose will be sacrificed to
the popular demand for moralistic vindictiveness. Consider what
would happen if the state, on convicting a defendant of crime,
awarded to him and his family freely the sum of money now spent on
confining and punishing him. This would eliminate the wretched circumstances that account for much crime; it would also give the criminal an income approximating the national average. Families would
not be deliberately broken up and might be preserved; the burden on
the taxpayer would not be increased and would be markedly decreased if the grants given to convicts were treated, like other income, as taxable. But the rage of the law-abiding citizen would be
boundless; it would probably drive him to crime himself—if only to
collect the income. It would also dreadfully undermine the law enforcement industry, which is a source of employment as well as of
feelings of righteousness. Towns like Attica, New York, or Kingston,
Ontario, whose economics depend on the prisons located there, also
lead in their fear and hatred of convicts and their opposition to
recognizing them as people, which would threaten the town's whole
way of life.

Prisons are not maintained because anyone really supposes that
they provide society with substantial and reliable protection against
criminal acts. They are maintained to ventilate the anger of those
who have always kept to the lawful path at the paucity of their rewards for doing so; and to assert the validity of social norms that
criminal acts call into question. The *deprivation* caused by crimes
against property would be more rationally dealt with by treating them
like acts of God or industrial accidents, and using state funds to insure and indemnify the victims rather than to punish and humiliate
the perpetrators if they can be identified. Crimes without victims
could—and but for the political weight of ressentiment clearly
would—be handled by decriminalising the acts so defined altogether
and regarding them as the private business of those who engaged in
them: the state, as Prime Minister Trudeau once observed, has no
business in the bedrooms of the nation—nor I would add in its
smoking rooms either.

Crimes against other people present a more difficult category, since indemnification of the victim of kidnaping, assault or, obviously, murder is not really possible. Imprisonment or execution, however, cannot be justified simply on the grounds that "something must be done." Hard-liners who argue that the advocates of "permissiveness" always have compassion for the criminal but never for his victim have failed signally to demonstrate how condemning the assailant to misery or death would constitute or demonstrate compassion for the victim. I might, conceivably, derive a certain wholesome satisfaction from attacking or even destroying a person who had severely injured me or someone I loved: revenge *is* sometimes sweet. But it is also personal. Any man who derives his satisfaction from having the state punish his enemies has been, to say the least, oversocialized. I do not mean to suggest that life in a complex, overcrowded society would be better if men "took the law into their own hands"; it would doubtless be somewhat worse—though the worst events in modern times occur when the state "takes the law into its own hands," as the Indochina war and the "destabilization" of the Allende government in Chile have made perfectly clear. I mean rather that violence is an inescapable fact of modern industrial life, and condemning those who commit it to suffer violation themselves can hardly be expected to reduce the total amount of violence we all experience. On the contrary, it effectively doubles the violence to which crimes of violence lead.

The citizenry who support the law enforcement industry cannot, therefore, be regarded as its clientele. They do not in fact demonstrably receive any objective benefits from its existence. They do receive considerable psychological relief from the vicarious expression of their hostilities and the confirmation of their fantasy that the most serious threats to their welfare are external. But this psychological satisfaction does not depend on or derive from any detailed awareness of what life in prison is like any more than it does on any verifiable social consequences of imprisonment. Ordinary citizens do not raise questions about what goes on behind bars unless they begin to suspect that it is less unpleasant for the convicts than they had assumed, or that there has been some misuse of public funds. Convicts, therefore, do indeed constitute an example, and a fairly egregious one, of what I have been calling a reified clientele: a group of people who, without their consent and in this case against their will and their power to resist, have been made the putative beneficiaries of a service that costs enough to have great economic significance to the total society, but whose terms and quality they cannot affect by their response to it. The architects and administrators of prisons have to satisfy the legislature and the people it represents; they have to come to terms with the conflicting social service and custodial bureaucracies they depend on to keep the place running. But they do not have to satisfy the people who constitute the raison d'être for the prison's existence and their own professional status.

There are few, if any, institutions that serve so exclusively involuntary a clientele as prisons, schools, and invading armies. These, moreover, have always served involuntary clienteles, although they have played increasingly prominent and costly roles in history in modern times. Indeed, none of the three existed in anything like their present form before the end of the eighteenth century; they are wholly characteristic of the modern national state. Prisons, in earlier days, were quite different places with different social functions; as Michel Foucault made clear in his work *Madness and Civilisation*,[7] preindustrial societies did not conceive of prisons as instruments for reform or rehabilitation of prisoners, and made no attempt to affect the character or motives of those confined in them. Prisons were merely places of sequestration for persons deemed to be dangerous, miscreant, or public nuisances. Minds innocent and quiet might take them for hermitages. This is not an attitude the behavior modifiers on the psychological staffs of modern prisons would be likely to accept. The novel and implausible idea that imprisonment might improve human character provided, indeed, the occasion for Alexis de Tocqueville's visit to America, which was undertaken to study, in the interests of the government of France, the first prisons that undertook to do so. By seeking to alter their prisoners, the authorities converted what had previously been passive captives into an involuntary clientele.

Permanently established cadres of professional police are similarly peculiar to modern times, as shown by the derivation of the British term "Bobby" for a police officer, from the nickname of Sir Robert Peel, under whose government the force was organized. Sheriffs and magistrates, as well as secret police whose function was to protect the sovereign from opposition, are of course far older, as old as government itself. But a publicly recognized profession of specialists whose function is to enforce public law impersonally against all offenders is a modern idea. Unlike criminal law, civil law, some form of which is practiced in all societies, does not make the community or the sovereign a party to the process; it merely provides the apparatus by which litigation brought before the magistracy by interested parties is adjudicated and decisions enforced. Until public indignation becomes institutionalized as a political force, the only actions punishable as crimes by the state are treason or sedition, in which the state is really and not just ritually involved as adversary; and contempt of court. Svend Ranulf in his evocative work *Moral Indignation and Middle Class Psychology*[8] indeed traces the emergence of ressentiment or moralistic, punitive rancor, as a social force from just such indices as the development of cadres of law-enforcement officials. Earlier on, the establishment of codes of criminal—as distinct from civil—law, had marked, in Ranulf's view, the growth of an alienated and resentful middle class intent on having the state assume the function of stigmatizing and punishing wrongdoers and upholding public morals.

The public school system, likewise, is by any criterion a modern institution. Though compulsory schooling—intended to frustrate the "old deluder, Satan" by enabling people to read the vernacular Bible—was introduced into the Massachusetts Bay Colony, it was not until 1874 that the city of Kalamazoo won an appeal from a lower-court decision forbidding it to use tax money to support a high school. Though Kalamazoo was not the first city to do so, the decision is usually regarded by educational historians as a landmark that established the right of the state to maintain an institution then widely regarded as serving only the children of the rich. The legal school-leaving age has risen through the years till several states now require attendance until the age of eighteen or high school graduation, whichever is earlier; and exemptions by granting "working papers," a previously common practice for working-class youth, have grown rarer with the declining market for unskilled labor and the reluctance of employers to give serious employment to young men still subject to the draft. By 1971, about 90 per cent of Americans between five and seventeen years of age were enrolled in school; more than 80 per cent were in average daily attendance. What proportion of these would have attended school if not compelled to by law is impossible to state and probably not a meaningful datum, since the social policy that has made schooling compulsory has also eliminated most other possible alternatives like employment, wandering, or actually educating oneself, which might appeal to young people as they do to older ones.

School children certainly fulfill the principal criterion for membership in a reified clientele: being there by compulsion. It is less immediately obvious that they serve as raw material to be processed for the purposes of others, since this processing has come to be defined by the society as preparing the pupil for advancement within it. In just this way might a socially conscious sultan have defined castration as service intended to prepare young men for administrative advancement in the imperial household. Whatever the needs of young people might have been, no public school system developed in response to them until an industrial society arose to demand the creation of holding pens from which a steady and carefully monitored supply of people trained to be punctual, literate, orderly and compliant and graded according to qualities determining employability from the employers' point of view could be released into the economy as needed.[9]

Though the public schools as we know them are institutions that developed primarily within the past century, armies, surely, have been with us throughout history: certainly, throughout history as taught in school, with its heavy emphasis on military events. Conscript, citizen armies are another thing, however, wholly characteristic of the industrial era. Tyrants of the past have, of course, impressed into involuntary service such hapless men as they needed to fill their battalions; but these victims were not perceived and were not led to perceive themselves as fulfilling a universally shared military obligation. Only a small proportion of the population actually saw service; and their morale did not depend on their identifying themselves with the national cause. It is this aspect of the military experience which is most alienating, since it requires the conscript not merely to risk his life, but to lie continually to himself about its value, in relation to the value of the national purpose. The effect is so shattering to integrity that people who have been put into this position cease to make sense. Witness the hatred of American GIs for the war resisters and protesting students who were risking their freedom in order to end the war which the soldiers themselves saw as brutal and purposeless.[10]

One would expect the most prominent examples of reified clienteles to be created by agencies which, like those so far discussed, have been granted the authority to coerce their clients in the putative interests of the larger society. But the obvious and enormous economic advantages of dealing with masses of cases defined by social category, rather than with individuals seeking to satisfy their own felt needs, has also led to the increasing reification of clienteles of institutions with a long and honorable tradition of service to—usually privileged—individuals. The most prestigeful and lucrative professions, medicine and law, have adapted themselves in large measure to ministration to increasingly reified clienteles. If they had not they would hardly have remained as lucrative as they have. Only on television does the family doctor continue to preoccupy himself with the affairs of whole people as patients, one at a time. One reason, seldom cited, but possibly more potent than is realized, for the recent rise in interest in Satanism and diabolical perversions of religious ritual may well be simply that the devil, too, still makes house calls when summoned, and responds only to the expressed free will of his clients. Only individual choice can lead to damnation; there are no packaged, corporate excursions to hell.

Although a large proportion of the practitioners of even the classical professions, medicine and law, never see a client; many of these physicians and attorneys may nevertheless be serving real clients, individual or corporate, in a highly significant way, as specialized professionals on the staff of large firms. The work they do, in other words, is still a part of a professional service performed at the behest of a client and intended to serve his interests even though they never meet him. But many do work that is not. The physician who examines prospective draftees or who serves a school board or prison or mental hospital by authorizing the use of drugs to control pupils or inmates who would otherwise be troublesome to handle; the lawyer who becomes a cog in the squalid machinery of a public prosecutor's office, getting clients to plead guilty to lesser charges without concern for their assumed innocence of greater ones or who makes his career by devising means whereby that exceptionally vindictive edifice, the White House, may harass its opponents—these, like prison guards, have captive and involuntary clienteles. They do not represent or serve their clients; they are not judged by professional criteria of competence, but by how effectively they use the authority vested in their profession to induce or compel people who would not voluntarily have consulted them to alter their behavior in ways that may not even involve the profession they represent.

The most notorious examples of this perversion of professional function still come from the military, and are epitomized by the witty title of Robert Sherrill's book, *Military Justice Is to Justice as Military Music Is to Music.*[11] But the military may yet be outstripped by the accelerating growth of the "helping professions," which often have to catch their clients before they can administer help to them. Social workers, probation officers, school counselors and the like spend their whole professional lives in a double bind created by the way their jobs are organized and defined and their agencies funded and controlled: they *do* perform genuinely valuable services for many persons on their usually abundant case loads, and may be genuinely concerned for the welfare of people on welfare; but their security and advancement within the agency also depends, and often in larger measure, on their willingness to call on a client in the early hours of the morning to see whether a husband, repentant and returned, has disqualified her for Aid to Dependent Children; or to return a paroled convict to prison because he has been found to have applied for a driver's license, or bought a bottle of whiskey.

Below these professionals both in status and in the moral quality of their function is a much larger number of people who fill jobs and fulfill roles that are simply a part of the hassle. At best these can claim that they do no harm to those who receive their services; at their worst, they are patently malignant: private investigators, often former law enforcement officers for detective and insurance agencies or credit bureaus, electronic technicians engaged in spying with or without a warrant and the assistance of the telephone company; junk-mail and telephone canvassers, etc. Taken altogether, a large proportion of the labor force employed in modern society is engaged in processing people according to other people's regulations and instructions. They are not accountable to the people they operate on, and ignore or overlook any feedback they may receive from them, as the nurses in the famous Rosenhans experiment ignored the sanity of their patients.[12] The dehumanizing effects of such treatment on those who experience it—and all of us do at various times in our lives—are probably too familiar, important as they are, to need further discussion here. But there are two other social consequences of the reification of clienteles that are less obvious and familiar, which are nevertheless devastating and which do require further comment.

The more apparent, if somewhat less serious, of the two is the process of institutional symbiosis, by which institutions with reified clienteles become dependent on one another for referrals, so that a person who has been enrolled as a client of one such institution finds himself being batted from one to another like a Ping-pong ball. Those of the children of the poor, and there are many, who find the school insufferably hostile, alien and oppressive in its language and folkways, and who refuse to accept its routines are themselves quite routinely classified as behavior problems, or hyperkinetic, or delinquent. They are referred to clinics for professional judgments to support the position the school has taken or to the police or juvenile authorities for judicial disposal. In this process the pupil is treated as an object; his own wishes and purposes are not considered except as symptoms. Children who respond idiosyncratically to drugs given them to keep them in line in school and are sufficiently injured by them to require hospitalization are likely, if the damage is critical, to be falsely recorded as victims of an overdose, with the implication that this was self-administered.[13]

By the mere fact of being enrolled in school, a child becomes, willy-nilly, the recipient or victim of an array of paraeducational services, whose major function, whatever their ostensible purpose may be, is to create a dossier on him for the use of schools or employers to which he may subsequently apply and, perhaps even more important, a justification for employing the functionaries who provide the services. The classic study of this process remains Aaron Cicourel's and John I. Kitzuse's *The Educational Decision-Makers*,[14] which concentrates its attention on "educational counselors"—at the time, in comparison to "psychological counselors," a relatively new echelon in the schools—and finds that they conduct, in effect, a "talent farm" for problems among their students, with those who claim to have no problems being regarded as the most afflicted of all. This particular example is only symptomatic of the process itself, in which a new professional cadre is created as a spinoff from the schools which could not conceivably have come into being or maintained its existence as a corps of independent professionals offering its services to those who desired them; this new cadre feeds its clients back into the school that sent them, this time with records that further delimit their range of choices and increase their dependence on the schools for the implementation of their future plans.

The most sinister institution to take part in this Ping-pong game is the mental hospital. The metaphor may, in this instance, seem too optimistic, since for many of the "patients" the huge, overcrowded state institution is a final resting place of no return. Most inmates seldom see a psychiatrist, never receive treatment other than sedation or restraint to make them easier to handle, and will never be free to be defined as a client by any other social agency. They are, however, so defined even while confined in the mental hospital, and they support numerous cadres of attendants and social workers, none of whom is required simply to attend to the client's expressed needs and wishes.

The mental hospital is the ultimate example of the institution with a reified clientele, since its "patients," having been diagnosed as insane and thereby deprived of most of their civil rights, have been for-

mally judged incapable of knowing what their own needs and interests are. It is this which makes mental hospitals, in principle and
often in fact, more repressive than prisons, whose inmates are denied
gratifications at the order of the state for logically indefensible
reasons, but who are not held to be incapable of knowing what they
want and need. Yet, as R. D. Laing and Thomas Szasz, among
others, have argued—powerfully, though from different premises—
throughout their work, mental illness is essentially a political, not a
medical classification, to which persons deemed incurably threatening
or troublesome to others are assigned. The hospitalization of the mentally ill is a service to those others, not to the patient; a presumption
which is almost self-evident when commitment is involuntary, but
which is likely to remain true even of patients who commit themselves voluntarily, since this is usually done only under intense social
pressure.

The same may be true of a purely physical illness, of course; inva-
lids, too, are hospitalized for the convenience of those who would
otherwise be burdened with their care, as are patients whose symptoms are foul or offensive to others, or who suffer from a contagious
disease. None of these categories, moreover, is wholly medical; all
have social components. A cardiac patient whose illness is too much
for a family of poor tenement dwellers to bear might be happily
ambulatory in an air-conditioned one-story cottage with built-in
chest-level appliances in a retirement community; while a scabrous
leper might be the hope and joy of a village that perceived him as a
holy man. Nevertheless, both would be perceived as suffering from a
dysfunction quite apart from any social demands that might be made
on them, though not necessarily a disabling one.

The plight of the mentally ill, however, is in most cases wholly a
matter of social definition, at least initially, before confinement and
dehumanization have taken their physical toll. And this is a definition
in which the patient need not, and often does not, concur. His objections, expressed or implied, do not matter: he is now a Ping-pong
ball, or ding-a-ling, perhaps for life. On such impotent and inartic-
ulate people, thousands of physicians, clinicians, technicians, and attendants depend for their livelihood and their social identity.

Considering the large number of people in modern industrial societies who find themselves used as Ping-pong balls in games social
agencies play, and the battering they take in the process, it must seem
strange that I consider institutional symbiosis the less important of
the two social consequences of reification of clienteles that I wish to

consider. But I believe it has less pervasive social consequences than the process I am about to discuss. As the economy becomes dominated increasingly by personnel and institutions devoted to servicing reified clienteles, people in the society lose the capacity to think of themselves as consumers or even citizens, much less as potential craftsmen serving real clients. They come to feel that they really ought to serve as Ping-pong balls in other people's games for the sake—or in the hope—of greater tolerance of their own little games. And in a society that continues to identify people primarily in terms of their job (or, as we say, their "position" and, increasingly, their "posture") there is a further decrease in the level of responsibility people feel for one another. It is bad enough that, as society has become more and more impersonal and bureaucratized, more *gesellschaftlich,* less *gemeinschaftlich,* the social connections that give people a sense of community have rotted away, so that only the economic bonds remain strong and intact. These might suffice to keep things from falling apart until new ways of institutionalizing the expression of feeling and obligation, appropriate to the consciousness of the age, have developed—provided the economic bonds were sufficiently genuine to respond to real human desires and perceptions of reality, and even occasionally to real human-felt need. But now, even this is lost, and the economic connections link only operators, who operate on their clients in their own mutual interests rather than those of the client.

Even a call-girl, justly angry and degraded as she must often feel at being exploited as if she had no personality of her own, must also feel an occasional sense of real professional pride at being in fact so much in command of herself that she can use her professional skill to give her clients the sense of having made it that is so pathetically important to them. As Genet demonstrated in *The Balcony,* and Buñuel in *Belle du jour,* prostitution is an exacting talent, though not an art since it requires falsification rather than disciplined expression of feeling; and it has a genuine and even a discriminating clientele. This is far more than can be claimed—in fact, it is the contrary of what is claimed—for a schoolteacher who, having agreed to participate in a behavior-modification program designed to "extinguish behavior" in a child deemed undesirable by others, does not respond to him at all, only to the "behavior" to be "extinguished." In all fairness it must be granted that in the less elegant houses the responses of prostitutes, too, tends to become stereotyped, under the demands of excessively heavy case loads.

Since many people who make their living servicing a reified clientele find it intolerably dehumanizing to treat people as if they were objects, they do develop ways of trying to meet their clients' real needs within the limits of their work situation; they buck the system with great personal expense and energy, or at least make the most of the opportunities for genuine human response and service that can still be found in its interstices. James Herndon, in *How to Survive in Your Native Land,* provides the best possible account of how this is done in the teaching profession. However, he also reminds his readers, especially in the sections called "Explanatory Notes,"[15] how limited and circumscribed such opportunities may be, and that the system remains essentially unchangeable by them. Most teachers continue to be stultified on the job even as they show the usual human capacities for creativity off it. For them, as for all of us who accept the self-delusion and bad faith implicit in trying to support one's sense of worth on crumbs of reality that have eluded the administrative process, working life becomes precisely a form of neurosis. People are defined as neurotic, after all, in terms of the degree to which their energy and creative potential are wasted trying to live on satisfactions they regard as illicitly obtained while playing dignified but empty roles in which no satisfaction is possible.

Contrary to what most people see as the source of alienation in modern life, none of this difficulty is attributable simply to bureaucratization and specialization of function. A bureaucracy need not be a vast, impersonal organization. A classic French restaurant, with its hierarchical organization, strictly defined jobs and precisely delimited territory, is an ideal-type of bureaucracy, but it does respond precisely to guests who know good cuisine and demand it. If it is organized so as to pinpoint responsibility for different aspects of the process of dealing with and responding to clients, a bureaucracy can bring far more resources to bear on its response than an individual could. In terms of its organization chart, the Hotel Pierre is probably even more bureaucratic than the New York City House of Detention. This is one reason—though probably not the most important one— that it is more responsive to the wishes and needs of its inmates. But its inmates remain a genuine, not a reified, clientele. The clientele of New York's classic French restaurants, however, have become less genuine as these have come to be supported by people brought there as a result of a decision that business was to be transacted, people who could not have stayed home if they were not hungry or gone to

Horn and Hardart if they were; and whose needs and interests bore no relationship to what might in fact have been offered them by a bureaucracy like that of Pavillon.

In an economy, and an age, increasingly devoted to the servicing of reified and otherwise packaged clienteles, price is notoriously no guarantee of personal, as distinct from personalized, service. Though hour-for-hour, first-class air travel is as costly as psychoanalysis, and some airlines still make use of gimmicks like having match folders imprinted with the passenger's name at his seat when he boards, in-flight personnel do not simply attend to his needs and wishes as a steward on an ocean liner or a pullman porter of fifty years ago would have done. Few of the services airline stewardesses provide are rendered at the passenger's request. Instead, they are programmed to perform routines of varying degrees of complexity depending on the class of service rather than the wish of the client, who may decline the drinks or hot towel offered in First Class, but usually cannot obtain anything, however reasonable, unless it has been programmed to be served at that time. Just try to get a snack when none is listed in the timetable, or a drink of water when the seat belt sign is on and the passenger is not free to seek it for himself, if the movie—though this is projected automatically—is being shown. Patients in $200-a-day private hospital rooms, if they do not have private nurses, have just as much trouble getting that drink of water, or bedpan.

When service to reified clienteles has become the norm, few people even complain about bad service, shoddy workmanship, product misrepresentation or even fraud. They appear, in fact, more concerned that the elimination of these practices may cool out their chances to make their fortune in an economy whose dynamism heavily depends on the prevalence of such abuses. This, I believe, is why consumer movements in America so often fail. What happens to Americans as consumers just isn't as important to them as their growing sense that they are more secure as employees or entrepreneurs in an economy in which the client has no opportunity to talk back or withhold his custom. The Indochina war that served the United States in this respect for more than a decade has been the perfect shtick; and as such, it never lost the lethally expressed devotion of the American working class, even though its sons were almost the only Americans who were getting killed in it. That is, I think, a dreadful moral datum. Though the best of men occasionally transcend their class interests, no man may be reproached for defending them. But he may surely be judged by what he conceives those class interests to be.

In this connection, it must be noted that the increased power of labor unions has, rather paradoxically, contributed to the influence of reified clienteles on the economy. By increasing the purchasing power of vast numbers of people who found themselves in a position to demand decent wages for the first time, unionization was expected indirectly to benefit the consumer and enhance his power in the market place. It has certainly increased the purchasing power of organized labor; but it has decreased the influence of consumers as a group. The era of industrial peace that America has recently enjoyed has been made possible by the development of a mutual awareness between industrial and union leaders that strife is often unnecessary and self-defeating, since the costs of concessions to union demands may be passed to the consumer. This is especially advantageous if one can arrange to deal increasingly with a reified clientele, which cannot buy less because prices rise, but which will have still less disposable income with which to express its real wants.

Most of the costs of servicing a reified clientele are paid through taxation, which makes voluntary refusal difficult if not impossible for the purchaser as well as for the client. The taxpayer, or his child, may of course be both the reified client and the purchaser, but under circumstances that deny him choice in either role. Significantly, public school administrators, faced with a mounting barrage of criticism about what actually happens to their reified clientele in school, have hardly responded at all to the bitterest and most concrete indictments, dismissing them as "romantic" and "theoretical."

The recent increase in power of the American Federation of Teachers, which has become more effective in attracting members and building new chapters as it has become more aggressive economically, has also been used primarily to support the schools in their resistance to innovations that might alter the present balance of power between teachers and administrators; both unite, even more strongly than before, to oppose any rise to power by the reified clientele—either parents or children. In some instances, wildcat strikes have successfully induced the board of education to withdraw the civil liberties that student groups had finally won—as in New York City, where teachers closed a high school in whose foyer students had finally been permitted to set up a table to distribute literature representing their views on student rights.

Teachers unions—and of course administrators—also strongly oppose "voucher" plans like that proposed some years ago by Christopher Jencks, which would allow parents freedom of choice as to which school their children might attend at public expense. Such plans clearly do not threaten to reduce opportunities for employment as a teacher; duplication in institutions usually implies a technically less efficient deployment of personnel with duplication of jobs, too. But they do threaten to give pupils and parents a legitimate choice of educational services, making them more nearly a real, and less a reified, clientele. This would be inconvenient, and bewildering, for teachers. Young people choosing an occupation today—whether teaching or any other—seem to be seeking a career-line rather than a service or productive function. This has nothing consistent to do with materialism. I am not suggesting, and have no reason to believe, that such choices are more crass; but that they do not at all envision or take into account the response of the client to whom the service is to be delivered; only of the employer, what he may be expected to offer and to demand. Underlying this disregard of what one will actually be doing, and to whom, in a job is the basic conviction that the work by which one earns a living is both alien to life and the core of social identity. It is a shtick; and a good shtick is hard to find.

In a society that, despite its high and increasing degree of economic centralization and bureaucratization, still depends for its driving force on the myth of widely available economic opportunity, and yet conceives of work as alien to life and self-expression, no shtick is likely to be abandoned or effectively condemned just because it is dirty. The people of modern industrial societies therefore become insensitive to waste and malfeasance even when they are the victims, identifying themselves much more easily with the purveyor than with his reified clientele. The most bizarre and striking example of this that I know is the notable failure of the United States—and its hotshot capitalist counterpart in the East, Japan—to establish proper sanitary controls over the supply of transfusable blood, as Canada, England, and the Scandinavian countries, which have notably less dynamic economies, have done. None of these utilize blood obtained from commercial blood banks, which buy it dirt-cheap from poor derelicts whose blood is usually deficient in protein and often contaminated with serum hepatitis and other infections. In the United States and Japan these remain major posttransfusion risks. The right to make a killing selling other people's blood remains in these countries, more important than surgical decency, even among people who agitate rather vigorously, if seldom effectively, for legislation to protect them from environmental pollution. The difference seems to lie in the fact that the recipient of a blood transfusion is the reified client par excellence, unlikely to be in a position to make discriminating choices at the time that he is in the market for blood. Any of us might be, of course, at any time, but we can't imagine it as readily as we can buying meat heavy with preservatives and growth-altering hormones, or breathing city air. Good liberals, in any case, are sympathetic to the plight of the small businessman, threatened by bureaucratic controls.[16]

There is, of course, one highly lucrative and widespread form of economic enterprise which is strongly condemned in most industrial countries, and certainly in the United States, through sustained campaigns of hysterical intensity. This is the sale of illicit drugs, which is pictured falsely by those most agitated about the drug problem as directed toward a reified—i.e., addicted—clientele. This apparent exception is, I believe, explicable, however, by the fact that the clientele envisioned is already the captive of other social agencies, with whose exploitation of it drug use interferes. The agitation and the Draconian punishments, that is, are directed wholly at *youth* who take drugs, as the Rolling Stones pointed out in their early song, "Mother's Little Helper," a decade ago. The low-level drug pusher, at least, is usually young himself, and a member of the pupil or street peer group from which he draws his clientele. Pushing provides a few young people with a degree of affluence and independence that their peers usually cannot hope even to approach by legitimate means; while the substances chosen as drugs by young people today are selected because they confer, or are thought to confer, a sense of detachment from and power to reject the socializing influence of straight institutions, especially the school and the family. Pushing drugs on kids in 1975 is rather like teaching blacks to read in 1855: in slaveholding jurisdictions, definitely illegal and strongly condemned. That there is a genuine and substantial risk to health involved in drug abuse is true, but beside the point. The most fervid and punitive advocates of a hard line on drug users and life sentences for vendors are hardly on record as friends of youth. Their obsessive concern with the drug menace appeals politically to the same ressentiment voters who supported the Indochina war and the Selective Service system, and who hated draft dodgers and long-haired students generally as much or more than they do drugs, as Thomas Szasz has shown in his recent book, *Ceremonial Chemistry*.[17]

It is, I believe, politically impossible for the modern, industrial democratic state to mobilize any considerable proportion of its enormous technical resources for the purpose of meeting the felt needs of its people, and certainly of its "least successful" people—much less for the purpose of making their lives gracious and agreeable, though its potential for destruction is unlimited. The reasons for this lamentable preference for the administration of pain and death are rooted, moreover, in the character of the citizen of the modern industrial state. This is not, in my judgment, a consequence of original sin but of the specific dynamics of socialization by which the modern citizen is made party to his own demoralization, and made to prefer leaders who have been similarly demoralized. It seems perfectly evident that persons like Henry Kissinger, Alexei Kosygin, and whoever may be President of the United States at the time this is read may be spoken of as *demoralized* in the same sense that a serpent in a circus act may be spoken of as defanged, though, to be sure, with rather the contrary implication as to the prospects of injury from them. At any rate, whatever may once have been there has been rendered "inoperative."

But the capacity for autonomous grace has also been largely rendered inoperative in their constituents, as a way of preparing them for life in the social order. There is really nothing more to be gained by fantasies about the innocence of the Russian people at the mercy of their cruel masters, the ignorance of the "good Germans," or the deception of the American people with reference to their government's actions in Cambodia and Chile. As an American national, I have experienced many and intense emotions as my country's policies have been revealed, or admitted, during the past twenty years or more (the overthrow of Mohammed Mossadecq in Iran with CIA-channeled funds in 1953 makes a convenient if arbitrary date). But astonishment was never one of them; what I knew, anyone could have known, except those determined to see, hear, and speak no evil. There was, clearly, no corresponding reluctance to do the unspeakable though ultimately neither inaudible nor invisible deed. 'Twas done, and often quickly; yet who would have thought our old history to have so much blood in it?

Opportunism as a Living Faith

An emphatic commitment to equality among human beings is a distinguishing characteristic of modern political philosophies. Not all societies share this commitment and none truly fulfills it in practice—though some, like those in China and Cuba, come uncomfortably close. But those which formally reject equality in principle suffer a loss of legitimacy that will probably prove fatal.

The equality of man is thus the last political principle to remain sacred in the modern world. No degree of tyranny or corruption suffices of itself to disqualify the government of a state in the eyes of either its citizens or its neighbors. Take, for example, the practice of torture. As Amnesty International has established, torture has once again become virtually a universally accepted instrument of statecraft; while UNESCO abrogated its agreement to allow that organization to use its hall in Paris for the Amnesty International conference in December 1973 when it learned that individual states, including UNESCO's most respectable members, were to be identified with the practices they had employed or condoned. But when torment or oppression is premised on a prior definition of the victim as genetically ineligible for full citizenship, and hence ineligible for such meager protection as the state affords other citizens, its authority becomes seriously suspect.

Or take discrimination. The liberal state can tolerate, with such reluctance as seems appropriate, discrimination against groups of people even on ethnic or psychological grounds, if those grounds are deemed meliorable through education, therapy, behavior modification, or other means of social intervention. But it must define its victims as *redeemable,* and attempt to remake them in the image of its modal or normal citizen—who may, in reality, have meanwhile vanished from the earth. In contrast, the state like Rhodesia or South Africa that adopts inequality as a valid legal and political principle risks definition as an outlaw among nations.

It seems unlikely that such a state can remain viable. Other predominately nonwhite nations of the world, as they gain in economic and technological strength, can hardly be dissuaded from redressing the indignities suffered by their brothers. And the inegalitarian state must, moreover, suffer from a debilitating sense of *mauvaise foi*. The hold of democratic ideology on the Western world is too fully established to be ignored. And it is too obvious that, if whites were really confident of their own superiority, they would not depend with hysterical rigidity on a vast and ruthlessly oppressive legal apparatus to crush men of other colors. The existence of such a structure, and the hypocrisy that supports it, paralyzes spontaneity in a racist society, destroys the arts, and falsifies relations among men. Life is rapidly reduced to so vulgarly exploitive a pattern that the only remaining claim to national prestige becomes the luxury that middle-class whites can continue to afford, after it has vanished from more democratic political climates.

This luxury is not to be utterly despised. A white mining engineer of limited political or intellectual interests who had a chance to be employed on the Rand rather than in Britain or Appalachia might be well advised to take it. He would find himself more comfortable and better cared for on the Blue Train to Johannesburg than in anything Amtrak has to offer—and also when he got home. The white South Africans shown surfing in the film *The Endless Summer* were, I am sure, enjoying themselves just as much as they seemed to be, though their quest for a suntan seemed a bit ironic. Their felicity does not even demonstrate clearly that they prefer material to moral well-being. An exploiter's conscience is not necessarily more destructive to his sense of moral worth than the continuous impotent rage many middle-class whites in Britain and America now suffer, despite their democratic pretensions, at what they conceive to be an unjust loss of well-earned status and dominance.

Nevertheless, the conviction that all men are equal is fundamental to the development of modern political thought. The main thrust of that thought prior to Marx was not, however, directed toward the elimination of the social class distinctions on which the bourgeoisie had itself come to depend for its growing political and economic power. Nor did it emphasize the rights of minorities as such. Early political liberalism was primarily concerned with the emancipation of society from the control of a hereditary monarchy and aristocracy. The chief threat to liberty, against which society was to guard itself by constitutional means, lay in the arbitrary assertion of privilege or authority based on rank. It was hardly to be expected that equal attention should be given to the defense of liberty against the intrusion of one's equal fellow citizens—though the First Amendment to the United States Constitution does attempt to provide just such safeguards against legislative tyranny.

Hereditary privilege was perceived as the problem; and firmly establishing the principle of equality among men was seen as the solution. Yet it seems obvious that the architects of the modern national state were concerned with something other—and morally something less admirable—than the equal dignity of all people. The rights of blacks to equal protection of American law were not formally recognized until the Republic was a century old; and at the time of this writing, the prospects of passage of the Twenty-seventh Amendment, which would complete the legal emancipation of women, seem poor. And everywhere the European went, carrying the force of a superior technology supported by a religion that sanctified individual achievement, he treated the people who were already in residence, and whom he perceived as colored, as so inferior that they could not even be said to exist. Otherwise, he could hardly have regarded himself as the "discoverer" of the lands they inhabited, thus reducing to nullity the aboriginal inhabitants of remote lands like the Americas and Australia. The people of Europe doubtless felt that they had been surprised by Attila; and again, shortly before Columbus arrived in the Caribbean, by the armies of the Ottoman Empire. But hardly that they had been discovered. Even more striking, in its way, is the fact that the inhabitants of the Americas turned out, co-operatively if confusingly, to be Indians, thus sparing Columbus, who had been funded for an expedition to India, some of the embarrassment that might otherwise have resulted from his errors in navigation.

It seems conclusively evident that what interested the early protagonists—and certainly the early practitioners—of the modern democratic state was not the moral equality of all men in the sight of God, but a much more limited commitment to equality of opportunity for mercantile and industrial development, as the basic ground rule of the liberalism of the day. The prospect that engrossed them, and that for more than a century had cast a dubious light on the monarchical and aristocratic economic system which derived class and status, and usually power, from landholdings, was increased economic productivity. As Robert K. Merton explained in a landmark paper thirty-five years ago,[1] science became a formidable social institution, rather than a conceptual and methodological toy with which a few savants amused themselves in improvised laboratories, because of its utility in improving navigation and technology. The authority of science derives from its success in making mercantilism possible. And Max Weber in *The Protestant Ethic and the Spirit of Capitalism* and the British historian R. H. Tawney in *Religion and the Rise of Capitalism* had already established that Protestantism, capitalism and the emergence of the individualism which lies at the ideological heart of modern democratic polity were so interrelated that, though none could be said to have caused the others, each was essential to the development of the modern, liberal ethos and the institutions of mercantile and, later, industrial democracy. Every man his own priest, competing with his fellows for the favor of God as revealed by worldly prosperity and piously maintained by the most effective technics empiricism could offer—this became the familiar doctrine on which distinctively modern life is based. The ultimate, indeed, in packaged, convenience-doctrines: religion, science and political economy premixed and guaranteed to rise.

But though a growing sense of individual freedom was necessary to enlist the creative energies needed for the Reformation and the development of a burgeoning, aggressive trading economy, the civil liberties which underwrote that freedom were a troublesome and easily fouled part of the social mechanism from the beginning. In the more advanced design of the twentieth-century socialist state they have been effectively eliminated. In the emerging societies of what we have come to call the age of enlightenment, individualism was restrained by administrative necessity. The new economic arrangements that were being developed required both freedom to contract and to enforce the long-term contractual agreements that make investment possible. The earliest major trading companies like East India and Hudson's Bay were already intercontinental giants requiring reliable bureaucracies and impersonal, evenhanded codes of governance. The dawning industrial age stood ready to reward, and lavishly, technical ingenuity. Then, as now, it had no use for freaks.

It is doubtful, therefore, that many of the men who saw the birth of the modern world experienced it as a resurgence of personal freedom, though the idea that it must be persisted long enough to lead even Beethoven for a time, and Stendhal—longer, and with better reason—to perceive Napoleon as a liberating force, sweeping away the debris of a dying monarchical system. By then, it was later than they thought. Charles II, the restored monarch who had experienced the thrust of modernization as acutely as any man alive, had chartered the Royal Society of London for the Advancement of Science in 1662. Retrospectively, we associate it with Newton, whose image the passage of time has transformed into that of a Founding Father of Science. However, Newton himself devoted more time and energy to the study of cabalistic mysteries than to mathematics, and seemed happiest in later life as Director of the Royal Mint. In fact, Christopher Wren preceded him as its first President, which was no paradox at that time. The great architect was as much an innovator as the mathematical physicist, and as fit to preside over the birth of what was to become the era of science; Wren was thus a remote but linear ancestor of the technology that, on December 29, 1940, destroyed most of his work.

For Charles himself, who relished the more expressive forms of freedom, the idea that he reigned over its dawn might have been appealing, but surely for what the liberal temper would regard as the least progressive of reasons. He was certainly the instrument of his subjects' liberation from the Puritan constraints of Britain's eleven-year republican interregnum. But it is Cromwell who represents the forces of progress and modernization. Earlier, Charles I had sealed his own doom by trying to use the prerogative Court of Star Chamber to protect a peasantry that was seeking to resist the efforts of a newly established wealthy gentry to enclose the common lands and deprive them of their pasturage and hence their subsistence—efforts which became totally successful with the passage of the Enclosure Acts after the final downfall of the Stuarts in the Glorious Revolution of 1688. Charles I can hardly be taken, on balance, as a consistent defender of civil liberty; his attempt to imprison without trial well-to-do subjects who refused to lend him money, which elicited the 1628 Petition of Right from an infuriated Parliament, would be enough to spoil that aspect of his record. But the policies of his administration toward the poor were genuinely if distractedly paternal. And in retrospect, his position seems to have been one of courageous though foredoomed defense of the peasants' traditional and crucial rights. Had he prevailed, the rural communities would have been preserved for a time; and the economic thrust which forced villagers into the cities to live and labor in squalor on starvation wages, till they died of disease or malnutrition, would have been forestalled.[2] So, of course, would have been the development of Britain's early woolen industry, which needed those lands for herds of sheep and those hands to work in its mills in town. It is not too much to say that, had Charles I retained his throne, England could hardly have emerged as the first great mercantile power, despite the naval superiority established under Elizabeth I. Not being Top Nation, however, is terrible only to nations that once were, as most of my fellow-residents in Canada would agree.

Within a century, however, ideological shifts had already gone a long way toward converting the memory of Charles I to that of a heartless reactionary defending antiquated privileges against insurgent and liberating forces. What liberation was to provide was wider access to economic opportunity and capital development. With subsequent industrialization and the expansion of Britain's empire— though Benjamin Disraeli, in delighting Victoria by conferring on her the title of Empress of India, was the first to call it that officially —came the need for recruitment and training of talent and skilled labor to support it. Britain was, and remains today, comparatively reluctant to commit itself formally to the doctrine of the equality of man—and has remained correspondingly inefficient in developing talent pools suited to a high rate of industrial innovation. Nor has it been greatly more imaginative or diverse in its conception of what equality might mean.

Equality, in England as in the rest of the Western world, has meant essentially "equality of economic opportunity." In the United States, it has meant the same thing only more so. In Russia and the Orient, it meant very little until, along with industrialization, the idea developed with the epidemic intensity of a virus that belatedly strikes a population previously sheltered. In the "underdeveloped world," the process continues and accelerates. But there, too, even such a new and fervent commitment to equality (which under Idi Amin seems likely to do almost as much for the people of Uganda as tuberculosis has done for the Eskimo) means primarily equality of economic opportunity and access. Not only is it true that alternative or complementary conceptions of what human equality might mean have failed to acquire compelling political force, but also even this limited though powerful idea of equality as equality of economic opportunity becomes politically effective only when it can be harnessed to the need for industrial development. In the chapel of nineteenth-century liberalism the dignity of man was wedded, in a most impressive ceremony, to industrialization. This promised to be a marriage of great convenience. Industrialization was expected to relieve men of the most mechanical and demeaning forms of labor as well as to raise the general standard of living and provide more and better rewarded opportunities for participating in the economic process—or as we now say, "provide more jobs." Despite the prescience of Marx, it took more than a century for men to recognize that machines might not only deprive them of their livelihood, but also that those who escaped that fate would probably find themselves working for machines—literally as well as figuratively—rather than the other way around.

Industrialization promised greater opportunity for all except the old privileged classes and landed gentry, and even they might expect to be let in on the ground floor as investors and ornaments for governing boards, and they might in any case gain more from technology than they lost in hegemony, so far as comfort and convenience were concerned. Victoria became one of the first mothers to give birth while anesthetized with chloroform and never became fully aware of her son Edward's existence even afterwards. If mercantile and industrial development required the forfeiture of privilege and the support of an ideology of equality, in order to induce men to enter the labor force and accept life under the conditions determined by a competitive, impersonal market place, it promised in return all that money could buy.

Even today, the universally accepted tenet that equality is the precondition of social justice remains the adjunct of economic development. Statesmen acting simply upon the conviction that all men are created equal and are endowed by their creator with certain unalienable rights might have fostered the development of a very different society if they had not been primarily concerned with the economic exploitation of the world, or in the words of the Firesign Theatre, "carving a new life out of the American Indian!" or whatever technologically deficient race might be available.

The belief that all men are to be regarded as morally of equal worth says nothing about economic productivity at all. It does not promise, or in any way refer to, a rising standard of living, though it

does surely imply that everyone should receive an equitable share of
the goods and services to be had. A commitment to the equality of
man if seriously meant should be quite independent of any obligation
to participate in the economic process, though the total value of the
product to be shared cannot be. People will receive what they need,
so far as the public treasury is able to provide it, simply by virtue of
being people—just people, not even citizens. If the productive
processes are sufficiently repulsive, dangerous, degrading or sicken-
ing, they will be undertaken only so far as is necessary to provide the
means of survival, until pleasanter if less efficient means of production are devised. Everybody will get less in order to live better.

The moral equality of men is an a priori assumption which cannot
be affected by variations in their capacity to make themselves useful
in the processes of economic production. A society truly committed
to recognizing such equality would not discriminate against the un-
employed, or unskilled, or persons deemed to have a low IQ—since
IQ is, itself, a measure of a set of attributes that derive their utility
from the demands of industrial society. But since moral equality is
not, and is not held to be, an inalterable condition, it is possible for a
society that is committed to maximum economic productivity and to
the moral equality of men to renege on its commitments by defining
the characteristics that are economically dysfunctional as vices that
diminish or cancel moral equity. In this way, the lazy, the spendthrift,
and people who are unwilling to take jobs and content to remain
"welfare bums" are held to have renounced their equity. But this argument avails only so long as the functioning of the economy is itself
accepted as moral, which accounts, I suppose, for the oppressive
moralizing of the Victorian age, intent on impressing masses of industrial workers into a new and obviously appalling industrial system
which promised them, in fact, very little.

Had the British poor and middle classes during the nineteenth century been permitted to develop and retain a capacity for independent
moral judgment with which to assess the highly ambiguous effects of
industrialization, that industrialization could hardly have taken place
as it did; it would either have been forestalled by public opposition,
or developed under socialist controls, directly in the public interest.
They were prevented from developing their moral sense by authori-
tarianism in the family and schools, and by the imposition of a code
which deliberately confused convention with morality and endowed
convention with greater authority. Sensuality and sexuality, which are

the sources of our most precise perceptions of other people and of our relationships to them and to the world—and hence the very basis of sound moral judgment—were discredited as immoral per se. This made it impossible to mount any politically effective criticism of industrialization as a social system on moral grounds. There was, of course, a great deal of criticism, much of it, like that implicit in Dickens' novels, still familiar and moving today. Some of it, like that of William Morris or those other eminent Victorians, Marx and Engels, was truly radical. But it had no ideological impact upon a populace long committed to the view that progress was a special case of virtue.

The moral ground from which the industrial system might be effectively attacked had already been occupied in a society that convinced itself that authentic and humane behavior would be a gross and intolerable impediment to that society's development, and hence, ultimately, to the well-being of all classes of society. Sexually authentic behavior could not be tolerated, since it threatened the family and hence the control and channeling of property; and because being well loved and loving heightens the individual sense of self and makes men more sensitive to the affront of industrial discipline and stronger in their refusal to submit to it. Individual violence in defense of one's rights or in seeking to meet one's needs could not be tolerated, since this threatens property and the state's monopoly on violence as a means of social control. Extravagance and financial irresponsibility could not be tolerated, while the direct appropriation of property to meet needs, however compelling, is, of course, theft.

Extramarital sex, held to be manifest in the lightest touch; misappropriation or mishandling of property; and violently expressive—even verbally violent—behavior if directed against authority rather than devoted to authority's ends: these virtually exhaust the categories of action Victorians were prepared to recognize as sinful. Miserliness and exploitiveness of and insensitivity to others might be condemned as defects of character, but they were not considered shocking. The Victorians accepted *A Christmas Carol* enthusiastically as a children's story; if Bob Cratchit had so much as said, "Fuck you!" to Scrooge, they would not have, though this would have somewhat improved the quality of the dialogue, and made the tale far more moral. Indeed Victorian morality provided no basis for a defense of individual liberty or the demands of defiant compassion,

comparable to the *carte blanche sans peur et sans reproche* it provided for the defense of property and the expansion of industry.

It does not seem to have occurred to George Eliot that Hetty Sorel
should not have been hanged for the murder of her bastard infant
and was, indeed, morally entitled to the means to provide for it; there
is no note of protest in *Adam Bede* as she wrote it, though the act of
writing it honestly and without sentimentality is perhaps the most
effective protest of all. And there is a note of—unintentionally—
comic genius for the modern reader in the means Tolstoi (as Victorian a novelist as any Englishman) chose to terminate *Anna
Karenina.* Only a locomotive engine could suffice for the self-des-
patch of a heroine who, through her own guilts and those of her
ambitious and uptight lover, had already become completely *embour-
geoisée.* By the time, a half century later, that Isadora Duncan lost
her life by strangulation when her flowing scarf got tangled in the
wheels of her sports car, one is not sure if nature is imitating art, or if
history, knowing that it must repeat itself the first time as tragedy and
the second time as farce, had decided to split the difference.

Today, certainly, industrial productivity has lost its grip on the
moral imagination. For many of us, values have moved full circle;
old, established companies are having to redesign their stock
certificates to eliminate the magnificent plumes of smoke emanating
from their factory chimneys in irrefutable evidence of their prosperity
and public worth. But this shift has been asymmetrical with respect
to social class, and now occasions some of the most rebarbative class
conflict in North American society. For many of the more affluent,
and especially the more affluent young, the processes of industrial
development have themselves become morally repugnant in the wake
of the Indochina war and its technological horrors. This response has
been deepened by a growing awareness that, not only has the war
served primarily to sustain an overexpanded American economy, but
that its major political function so far as the Indochinese victims
were concerned was to force them off the land and into the cities
where they would be compelled to serve as the proletarian base for
the economic development of their country within the American imperial infrastructure. That is what saving Indochina from Communism means. When Ronald Reagan stated in his 1966 gubernatorial
campaign that the United States should pave Vietnam over for a
parking lot and bring its boys home before Christmas, he was offer-

ing not so much a threat as a promise. The Fords for the parking lot
would follow.

The American working class, along with much of the older middle
class, rejects this position violently, not as false but as infuriatingly
inconsistent with their sense of propriety and self-interest. One might
think that the working class, on which the burden of industrialization
as well as of the war falls most heavily, would by now be aware of
and accept the indictment that stands against both. In fact, the contrary is true. Those who have suffered most—and survived—either
from the war or from the life of an industrial worker, are least likely
to find the means to condemn it; anything that has come close to
costing your life must be defended as worthwhile. Moreover, though
most of the burden of the war has fallen on the working class, most
of the working class has been unaffected, or favorably affected by the
war, whose total impact on the American people has been slight. Its
impact on the economy has been profound, but this impact tends further to divide the population ideologically along class lines. Its
effects have been of the kind that protagonists of industrial development define in advance as favorable: more jobs and greater job security, and the image of America as a giant which, if more helpless than
supposed, still commands a limitless supply of intimidating hardware
and an intelligence network as penetrating as Mr. Clean.

Those who would ask, "What kind of jobs, doing what to whom
and for whose benefit?" and who find the answers detestable are
again the more affluent. There is a fairly consistent tendency in many
societies for radical social critics to be drawn from among the
affluent, and especially the affluent youth. Disraeli's supporters in
seeking to alleviate poverty in Victorian England, who styled themselves "Young England," are a case in point; as, in their relatively
less articulate way, were Diana Oughton and Patricia Hearst in the
United States. To my recollection, the most moving examples of this
phenomenon are to be drawn from Chinese history during the 1920s,
when young upper-middle-class Chinese who opposed the growing
oppression of the Kuomintang government were hung in bamboo
cages in the city streets to die of exposure and thirst; their parents,
according to the accounts of the time, as in Nora Waln's classic
memoir, *House of Exile,* sadly but willingly accepted this treatment
of their sons and daughters as necessary to the struggle against Communism.

But the angrier and more ambitious members of the working class and the predominantly self-made men who identify with them, or whose political fortunes are closely tied to theirs—they might as well be called "hawks," in accordance with familiar usage—still regard equality of opportunity as the basic form of human equality; and they seldom raise questions about the nature of the opportunities provided, or the policies by which the state expands such opportunities. War creates jobs; it generates economic expansion that draws blacks and poor whites into areas of employment that were previously closed to them. Thus, they are introduced into the competitive race.

But once they have been, the state, in the hawkish view, has done all it should. The legitimate function of the state in ensuring equality of opportunity is limited to handicapping: that is, to compensating for or eliminating the more obvious advantages to be gained from circumstances of birth, genetic or economic. The state is expected to limit its efforts to equalize the contest to the earliest period of life and should act through the public school system, where pupils are regarded as still preparing themselves for real life. Subsequent efforts to compensate constitute unfair interventions in the competition. Such intervention is held to violate the principle of equality of opportunity, instead of advancing it; there can be no further concession to weakness or disability, once the race is deemed to have begun. Even the income tax is still regarded as "socialistic" by fully orthodox "hawks," though its effectiveness in handicapping acquisitiveness at high levels is limited.

Less hawkish citizens, more critical of industrial society altogether and more inclined to see all its parts as interrelated, reject this position. Competition cannot be accepted as the instrument for equalizing economic opportunity, since it nullifies the human qualities that commitment to the moral equality of man is intended to nurture. No part of life may be regarded as a training and tuning-up period for later, and more important, events; there is life and life only, and the earlier experiences occur, the more poignant and fundamental their consequences are likely to be. In particular, the public school system cannot function as an instrument for redressing inequality: observation of its function establishes quite clearly that it serves to identify and certify losers, rather than to redeem them.[3] Any meaningful commitment to the moral equality of men must respond to people and their present needs where it finds them, whether or not this helps them gain on competitors who earlier made their way without such assistance.

Actual social policy has evolved, as it doubtless must, as an uneasy compromise between these conflicting implications of human equality. There has been, of course, an enormous absolute rise in the level of responsibility assumed by the state for the economic welfare of its citizens. Even in the United States—long a laggard in the provision of social services—transfer payments to provide for welfare and social services have become the largest item in the public budget— larger even than military expenditures if state and municipal expenditures as well as federal are considered. But the prevalence of ressentiment and the popular conviction that, regardless of the commitment to equality, only those who contribute to economic development and production deserve security and a decent standard of living has prevented these expenditures from being recognized as something people have a right to expect and rely on. Some of the metaphysical distinctions between controversial and noncontroversial forms of government subsidy approach the scholastic in subtlety. The federal interstate highway program, which subsidizes the working and middle classes, does not become the target of ressentiment and is not thought to give anyone an unfair economic advantage, though the spread of freeways and the attendant disruption of established patterns of public transportation have made it almost impossible for poor inner-city dwellers to get to work anymore. But a guaranteed annual income, which would likewise stimulate the economy, is not seen as equally acceptable, but as giving lazy people something for nothing. Welfare recipients are required to demonstrate over and over again their willingness to accept distasteful and often unnecessary work in order to establish their eligibility for transfer payments carefully scaled down to inadequacy so as not to compete with the lowest paid and least desirable "job." Charges that able-bodied young "hippies" have adapted their life-style to subsist even on this allowance within the limits of their legally established eligibility are regarded as scandalous and met by the authorities with indignant denials or a declared determination to find some way of revising the requirements so as to shake these people from the rolls, rather than with a simple statement that they have claimed, and are receiving, the support for which they are eligible.

The precondition for indisputable moral eligibility for public subsidy is clearly that the recipient should already have involved himself sufficiently with the economic system that the subsidy will serve to bind him to it still further rather than to lessen its demands upon him. The federal highway system not only provides members of the construction or automotive industries with the funds to purchase a car, it also subsidizes all those, and only those, who have managed to become car owners, and increases their dependence on its use. Even more clearly, the bailing out of the Lockheed Corporation in 1971 in order to forestall its collapse and prevent a disastrous rise in unemployment in California, illustrates the same principle. It would obviously have been cheaper to let the company go since its contribution was evidently no longer in demand; and then directly subsidize the people who had worked for it and allow them to do whatever they enjoyed or deemed useful. But this would have been giving them something for nothing, and emancipating them dangerously from the demands of the social system. In order to shelter Jonah, the whale was preserved.

Thus the work ethic, though usually expressed in strongly egalitarian terms, conflicts fundamentally with the commitment to treat men as morally equal. Moreover, that commitment to more equality has been transformed by the dominant work ethic into something that is often either absurd or malignant, or both. One of the absurd—and in its effect on intellectual freedom, malignant—consequences of this transformation has been to make it impossible to raise serious questions about the possible existence of stable and significant differences between members of different ethnic or racial groups without being charged with racial bias, or at least with political irresponsibility or malice, for raising an issue that is likely to be used to the further disadvantage of the disadvantaged. Currently, the central defendants in such controversy have been, most notably, Arthur Jensen[4] and Richard Herrnstein[5]; but by the time this is published they will probably have been succeeded, as they have been preceded, by others. However Jensen and Herrnstein will serve as well as any possible successors to demonstrate the ramifications of an issue that cannot be resolved as long as it is—as I would argue—falsely stated.

Of the two, Jensen is clearly the most vulnerable to such criticism, since he, unlike Herrnstein, addresses himself directly to the question of comparative cognitive styles, and powers of black people in comparison to whites. Indeed, his study is open to serious criticism on technical grounds. His thesis, and his conclusion, is that within comparable populations of black people and of white the kinds of abstract cognitive abilities that are rewarded with success in school, and hence with the kinds of credentials that lead to subsequent advantage in American society, will be distributed more generously among whites than among blacks. The range, no doubt, will be equally extensive for both races, but the white population will exhibit higher modal *frequencies* of abstract cognitive achievement. None of the data on which Jensen bases his conclusions were gathered by him or by other scholars intent on testing hypotheses similar to his: he teased them out of studies conducted by other persons for other purposes. This is not necessarily bad scholarly practice—it is the only way research can be conducted in certain fields, for example, in history. But it certainly makes his conclusions less persuasive. He goes beyond his scientific mission, moreover, to recommend, on the basis of his conclusions, that black pupils be taught in school by different methods from white pupils, emphasizing rote memory rather than reasoning. This is a proposal that most black spokesmen who have responded to it find insulting, as I do.

But to condemn Jensen as a racist intent on subverting the doctrine of human equality on the basis of these publications is grossly unfair. A genuine commitment to treat men as morally equivalent in value cannot begin by ignoring the differences between them, or by insisting that those differences have no fundamental consequences. Fat people, too, are subjected to discrimination in our society,[6] though not such serious discrimination as blacks and, especially, obese blacks. Sammy Davis, Jr., who is black and has chosen to be Jewish as well, must, I would assume, remain forever vigilant against gaining weight. But it is no service to us fat folk to rail against the physicians who publish data linking obesity to heart disease and lowered life expectancy, though this probably does persuade some employers, especially if they don't like fat folks anyway, not to hire us. The data are useful; they help tell us where we stand, even though they, too, are somewhat contaminated by social bias and the implication that we are morally obliged to get thin and stay thin, as blacks are presumably obligated to learn to think as much like white people as they can.

That implication seems to me pure bullshit. I have no obligation to get thin and stay thin even if I can—and most fat people, in fact, fail to do so. And a society that really regards me as the moral equal of a handsome young athlete will certainly not insist that I act like one, which would make a fool of me if it didn't kill me. Instead, after having informed me politely but unambiguously as best it can of my condition it will try to spare me unnecessary stairs and leave me to select my own diet; and if I am poor, it will help me pay for it, without using the opportunity to institutionalize me and put me on an eight-hundred-calorie diet. What Jensen's data really imply, if they have any value at all, in the context of equality is that society should demand something different of black children than of white—while accepting and encouraging blacks who prefer to perform in the style whites have made conventional to do so—and reward their performance with as generous recognition as it accords conventional school achievement. The school, limited by its own commitment to train people for competitive achievement and the development of marketable characteristics, and the resulting narrowness of its own vision, is usually unable to do this, even and sometimes especially when it is run by black personnel, who are, after all, self-selected by their own choice and ability to make it on the terms a basically white social order has set for one of its more constricting institutions. But the fact that no other means of access to social rewards and a respected status in society is provided for those who find the schools' demands uncongenial or destructive to their being is merely further evidence that, in this society, equality of economic opportunity in a competitive industrial order is the only kind of equality taken seriously.

Liberals especially seem reluctant or unable to accept any broader or more diverse conception of equality. This accounts for their perception of Jensen as an enemy of equality and also leaves them morally in a paradoxical position. Quite aside from the question of the merit of Jensen's conclusions, a conservative would, I think, have to agree that those conclusions were pejorative to blacks, since they do indeed suggest that blacks will find themselves, because of their innate characteristics, less able than whites, on the average, to function successfully in the existing industrial system and less able to conform to its demands. Whether this is, on balance, a defect or a virtue depends, however, on whether one regards the system and its demands as morally acceptable or obnoxious. Jensen apparently accepts it, and may indeed regard his conclusions as derogatory to blacks. But radical social critics should surely find Jensen's conclusions derogatory to the *society,* which identifies promise by such narrow and impersonal criteria, rather than to those who do not meet those criteria. Only if equality means "equality of economic opportunity," and only that, do Jensen's findings provide a basis for regarding blacks as unequal to whites.

The problem with respect to Richard Herrnstein's work is more complex. And the hostility it has aroused is even harder to justify, since Herrnstein barely refers to race or ethnicity in his work, even though he is concerned about social class and even though his conclusions about the factors affecting the class membership of individuals do contradict the traditional liberal position on social policy. Herrnstein maintains that efforts to compensate for environmental deficiencies among poorer or deprived members of society must inevitably result in a greater influence of genetic or otherwise innate factors in distributing them among the various possible social levels. Hot lunches at school, remedial reading instruction, upward bound programs—all these, Herrnstein argues, will contribute to *The Rise of the Meritocracy,* as Michael Young called it in his macabre 1958 anti-utopian novel. Herrnstein does not oppose such programs which may be very useful on their own merits; but they cannot, he insists, compensate for the effects of innate deficiency on the outcome of a competitive life.

Basically, Herrnstein's argument is simply algebraic, and would apply to any system of two or more variables that affect the magnitude of another variable, in any field of investigation whatever. If E and H are unrelated variables whose variation is reflected in changes in the magnitude of another variable, I, and an experimenter intervenes to reduce the range of variation in E—say by raising the value of instances of E at the lower end of the scale—while H is left unaffected, then there will be two consequences for I—one probable, the other inevitable. The range of variation in I will also probably be reduced, though it may not be because this depends to some extent on the way in which E and H are related. But it is certain that of the remaining variation in I, more will now be attributable to variation in H, since variation in E is just not being permitted to occur as fully as it used to. If E stands for Environment, H for heredity, and I for intelligence, this argument is valid. It is equally valid if they stand for something else altogether, so long as E and H are the major causes of variation in I.

In the same way, when a population shifts from a marginal to an abundant diet, the correlation between heights of fathers and adult sons becomes higher during the next generation than it will have been in the preceding one—and especially among poorer families, if these share in the general increase of available food. Height is influenced, of course, by both genetic and environmental factors, among which abundant nutrition during the years of skeletal growth is most important. As diet becomes more nearly adequate for the entire population, it ceases to account for variation in rate of skeletal growth; the whole population grows taller than in the past, but more of the tallest people are those who have tall parents.

Herrnstein infers then that improvement in environmental quality through social policy, if effective, may well confer an absolute advantage on all members of society but *must* increase the relative advantage enjoyed by those with superior genetic endowments. Even people who find this position distasteful are unlikely to argue with it; if they do, they will lose. Some hostility to his position is expressed by people who do not believe that there are any genetic or innate factors that decisively affect human behavior, that vary in magnitude, and that cannot be changed by environmental influence. But the evidence Herrnstein cites is very convincing and is strongly supported by common sense. Undeniably, genetic variation in humans, as in other animals does occur, though usually in the form of tendencies rather than immutable characteristics. And in every society, differential social value will be attached to certain of those genetic tendencies and characteristics. Despite the imprecision of racial categories in the United States and the political abuses to which they have been subjected, it is a great deal more likely that two parents generally regarded as black people will have a black child than that two parents generally regarded as white will do so. The white parents then, are at a genetic disadvantage, if black is beautiful.

Herrnstein's critics do not direct their major thrust either against his inference that meliorist efforts to compensate for poor environment must increase rather than decrease genetic influence, or at his insistence that there are real differences in genetic endowment among human beings and that these have social consequences—though the second of these inferences is regarded as more offensive than the first. What most antagonizes his attackers is the fact that he maintains that intelligence testing, as reflected in IQ scores, measures such a genetic factor. Herrnstein does nothing so naïve, of course, as to argue that intelligence test scores are not substantially affected by environment, or that there is or could be such a thing as a culture-free intelligence test. He argues, rather, that a society that resorts to mental testing can develop tests that are valid in that culture, and that the superior performance of those who achieve it will be the consequence in part of innate differences that make them, indeed, superior—

genetically superior—in that culture's terms. His opponents—or those of them who resort to reason rather than epithet—argue that this superiority is artificial and his reasoning circular; that an individual with a high IQ is merely one who is well adapted to this society, and is not genetically superior at all.

There is a real issue dividing Herrnstein and his more responsible critics—an issue on which he is probably right—but it is not an issue suited to justify the acrimony he has aroused from the liberal intelligentsia. His critics, in effect, maintain that high performance on IQ tests is a consequence of elite socialization, and the designation of high scorers as successful therefore a prime example of self-fulfilling prophecy and self-serving maintenance of the existing status system. Herrnstein maintains that the kind of highly effective socialization that results in top performance on IQ tests is possible only to a human being with superior genetic endowments—superior, that is, by the standards of the society that is doing the testing. And, again, Herrnstein, perhaps more than Jensen, seems generally willing to accept and function within the norms of the society in which he lives.

But surely, persons who, like him, find American society, with all its defects, acceptable are entitled to incorporate its norms into their thinking to the extent of meaning what *it* means by superior, as long as that meaning is clear. And in Herrnstein's writing it certainly is. People who deny, as most of Herrnstein's critics—and I—certainly would, that the high IQ model is particularly atractive morally, have set themselves a different task than denigrating Herrnstein's quite competent analysis. What must then be done, if possible, is to define alternative qualities as equally desirable, so that Henry Kissinger and H. R. Haldeman, bright as they obviously are, would no longer loom so large as role-models. But in order to do that, since the high IQ model is, by definition and social evolution, especially good at winning competitions in contemporary society, the competitions themselves would have to be abandoned, or, as high IQ types sometimes say, phased out.

People who are committed to support the equal worth of those who are currently stigmatized as dull, low achievers, or culturally deprived—and these are, indeed, usually poor and often black—cannot do it by attacking Herrnstein's argument. They must attack, instead, the frame of mind that equates equality with equality of opportunity. They must insist that poor or dull children, as well as other people, be given what they need because they need it to grow on and be themselves, and not fiddle around trying to equalize the terms of competition; a genuine commitment to respect the needs of all people equally would find no reason to hold the competition at all. It is precisely the relatively deprived, however, who will insist most vehemently that the competition be held, since they are usually firmly convinced that their life chances depend on winning it—they, too, define equality as equality of opportunity. Blacks and working-class parents not only support the public school system ardently, but also they tend to be especially hostile to progressively oriented teachers whom they perceive as demanding too little of their children, not teaching them anything, not giving them enough discipline.

Yet, as Christopher Jencks and David Riesman long ago pointed out in *The Academic Revolution*,[7] an increased rate of success in American society depends on providing greater opportunity, not greater equality. So long as equality is taken to mean "equality of opportunity," efforts to increase equality will only increase the tension and antagonism induced by competition for the slots that exist; and if Herrnstein is right, these efforts will not even affect the outcome perceptibly. In his later, widely publicized work on *Inequality*,[8] Jencks dismisses the school system as a possible instrument for equalizing economic opportunity, though he urges that economic equality should be sought through direct social initiatives designed to reduce the spread of incomes in the country by even more progressive taxation and by cutting down the remuneration of the professional classes; in effect, by taxing their licenses. Committed as he is to economic equality, Jencks seems much more resourceful at suggesting ways of impoverishing the rich than of enriching the poor. This is, to me, the way of ressentiment and unacceptable. But he nevertheless recognizes that equality—even defined in economic terms—is not to be achieved by efforts at equalizing economic opportunity.

What our society's constant preoccupation with, guilt about, and occasional efforts to achieve equality of economic opportunity have achieved instead, however, is further dehumanization and an evidently destructive commitment to opportunism as a living faith: the only one sufficiently widely shared to have achieved the status of an established church. I do not intend to add further here to the already excessive and voluminous literature devoted to deploring the spiritual

and personal costs of Making It. But I do want to consider some of
the ways in which the official commitment of the society to equality
of opportunity, as colored by the dominant work-ethic, has contributed to its odd and oppressive moral climate.

As I write this in July 1973, the Senate Investigations of the 1972
elections are approaching their climax. The essential issues raised by
the Watergate affair, to continue to make use of this convenient
means of referring to the entire set of operations and events, have
become quite clear though its resolution has not. It is a fruitful
source of examples of the moral climate I have in mind; it *is* climate,
moreover—not just weather—as Watergate's relationship to certain
more fundamental and permanent aspects of American political life
show.

Mr. Nixon himself, and his loyal and highly disciplined subordinates, are the most revealing examples I know of devotion to equality
of economic opportunity, colored by devotion to the work-ethic,
though devoid of any sense of craftsmanship. The purity of this devotion is demonstrated by the paradox, often discussed in analyses of
Mr. Nixon's continuing attitude toward the presidency, that he has
for twenty years or more sought the office relentlessly, without ever
revealing the least indication of what he wanted to do with it. This is
political fanaticism without parallel, and without content. His fervor
is perhaps matched by his predecessors in an age of excessive political intensity: Stalin, Mao, Gandhi, Churchill, Ho. But all these
wanted power in order to *do* something, good or bad, progressive or
conservative, as the case may be. Mr. Nixon, however, conceived of
the presidency as pure opportunity; the idea of what he might do
with it had no interest for him. It is fairly easy therefore to understand why his cohorts—even those, like the former Attorney General, John Mitchell, who had sworn to execute fundamental and explicit duties under the Constitution—should have found it so easy to
place the matter of the President's re-election before any violation
that might be imposed on the fabric of society in the process. The
presidency was a prize to be won—the biggest and most vulgar prize
in the world—not a powerful, intricate, and precious instrument for
accomplishing social purposes.

The excessive purity of the Nixon administration's opportunism
has, apparently, undermined its relationship to the higher levels of
business and industrial power in the United States, despite the Pres-

ident's admiration for and identification with business leadership, and despite his administration's willingness—as in the case of IT&T—to put its "dirty tricks capabilities" (in the unfortunate language of the Watergate affair) at the disposal of especially friendly corporations. As Kirkpatrick Sale pointed out in analysis of the values and characteristics of the administration in relation to the Watergate developments,[9] the attitudes of the Nixon administration toward business, as well as its way of conducting it, are far cruder and more self-centered than prevailing practice among the dominant firms of the Eastern seaboard—Sale refers to the Nixonites as, in comparison, "Southern Cowboys." Sale surely intended and offered no defense of high level American and international business ethics, which are as ruthless and acquisitive as any in history. But they are not as ugly as those of the Nixon administration; they are governed at least by a kind of internal consistency and self-contained aesthetic that is reluctant to sacrifice the future and integrity (in the sense of functional wholeness, not moral worth) of the institutions of government and finance to the exercise of raw power and the immediate ripoff. The world of finance, apparently, was afraid of Mr. Nixon, much as the pope might be of a bishop who insisted on making him presents of carloads of confiscated condoms. How else can one explain the fact that even under his Republican administration the Indochina war became the first in American history in which increased belligerence consistently depressed the stock market while rumors of peace made it rise? The Nixon administration's favorable and even enthusiastic support of the big business community can hardly make up for the kind of fiscal malpractice which has ruined the dollar in international markets, or the embarrassing and sophomoric practice of demanding illegal campaign contributions from major corporations.

It may seem illogical, or just wrong, to consider Mr. Nixon's political approach, which has been characterized by an aloof reliance on hierarchy and executive privilege to protect the President in any course of action he chooses—even though it be patently unlawful—as reflecting a commitment to equality. Equality of economic opportunity seems, in fact, repugnant to a man whom Kurt Vonnegut, Jr., has justly described as behaving, in continued response to his own family's poverty during the Depression of the 1930s, as if the Nixons had all been locked up in a dog pound by mistake,[10] and he was determined never again to identify himself with the poor even so far as to permit the continuation of existing governmental programs devoted to their needs. But I have already pointed out that concentration on equality of economic opportunity excludes commitment to the moral equivalence of all men, including losers; and hatred and disgust rather than compassion for losers has been one of Mr. Nixon's most consistent hallmarks. Commitment to equality of opportunity in its extreme form also leads to another characteristic exhibited in Mr. Nixon's political career and (conspicuously though not more intensely than earlier) in his handling of Watergate: a conviction that whoever seizes anything is entitled to keep and exploit it, no matter how he damages it or uses it to damage others. The question of qualification for office does not arise. Whoever seizes the crown is a lawful king, and whatever he does or authorizes is a lawful action of the state. Equality of economic opportunity, in this laissez-faire sense, has been used at least since Andrew Jackson's day to license spoliation of national resources and oppression of the poor in the United States. Still, there is a difference in kind, as well as degree, resulting from Mr. Nixon's greater caprice. Other Presidents have waged undeclared war, but always for some realistic purpose of conquest or diplomatic gain, or in the grip of some ideological hysteria of which they were partly the proponent and partly the victim. Only Mr. Nixon continued a war of exceptional brutality against a defenseless people whose territory and very existence had no meaning for him at all, after he himself had scuttled the ideological basis that had provided its tenuous justification, dining in public triumph with the leaders of the two great Communist powers whose baleful influence he had decreed to be, for the people of Southeast Asia, a threat worse than death, and looking, at the dinner table, like a Verdurin who has finally wangled an invitation to the Guermantes'.

Watergate, I would suggest, reveals the ultimate implication of the dictum that any American boy can become President. It is a vision much prized in mass society. I had hoped someday to publish a book in which it would no longer be necessary to refer to the plangent definition in Ortega y Gasset's *Revolt of the Masses,* which begins by declaring: "The mass is all that which sets no value on itself, good or ill, based on specific grounds" and continues to identify the mass mind as "unqualified, unqualifiable, and by its very nature disqualified"; but the prospect of so long a life grows dim. Certainly, a basic source of Mr. Nixon's appeal to the electorate lies in the fact that no man can really believe himself the President's inferior; or believe, on the President's example, that his own character or under-

standing might impose any limits on his ambition or his right to attack or destroy others. Egalitarianism thus finally becomes absolute;
if no man is or can be better than another, there can be no need to
look elsewhere or allow freedom of choice. One of the clearest lessons of Watergate is that the President and the Committee to Re-
elect him defined his re-election as essential to national security, and
thus felt quite free to treat the Democratic Party and its candidates as
if they were Cuban spies.

The political implications of the Watergate incident and the sustained and penetrating publicity it has received are, I think, more
complex, and will probably prove more ironical, than a good libertarian would care to believe. It is now well established that the Watergate events were incidental rather than exceptional episodes in the
Administration's political practice. Not only did they merely continue, with different and somewhat less defenseless targets, practices
and evasions that Mr. Nixon had utilized since the 1950s, but also
they made use of some of the same personnel. The most prominent
protagonists of the Watergate affair had risen to their positions in the
Nixon administration through ruthless and continuous exploitation of
the issues that most sharply divide the ressentient working class and
achievement-oriented elder middle class on the one hand from the
less opportunistic on the other: student protest against the Indochina
war and actual or putative drug abuse, with the most picturesque-
sounding—though invisible—of the Watergate figures, G. Gordon
Liddy (among others), weaving an astonishing web of connections
between the two.

The repression of 1969 to 1971, directed especially against college
students and active demonstrators against the war (a war which the
voters had clearly endorsed by giving Mr. Nixon a landslide victory),
turns out to have been not only consistent with the burglaries and
buggings of Watergate, but in large measure the work of the same
persons. The Internal Security Division of the Department of Justice
co-ordinated a domestic intelligence network that planted informers
on every campus in the country, down to Moravian Theological Seminary with thirty-five students,[11] and led to the arrest of "at least
14,565 people" in the Department of Justice's fiscal year 1970–71; it
"instigated more than forty-five grand jury cases, including inquiries
into SDS and the Weathermen in Boston, Brooklyn, Chicago, Cleve-
land, Detroit, Harrisburg, Kansas City (Missouri), Los Angeles,
Manhattan, Seattle, Tucson, and Vermont"; and it also instigated

52 OPPORTUNISM AS A LIVING FAITH

numerous prosecutions for conspiracy[12] less publicized than the Chicago and Harrisburg conspiracy trials but no less effective as means of intimidation—this division had as its Director Robert Mardian, who, according to testimony given at the Senate Watergate hearings, became one of the central participants in the sustained and elaborate efforts to cover up the Watergate burglaries. One of these burglaries, at least—that of Daniel Ellsberg's psychiatrist—was undertaken in order to assist the work of the Internal Security Division in building its file on Ellsberg. G. Gordon Liddy, who planned the burglary of the Democratic National Committee Headquarters and organized this dubious service to the Committee to Re-elect the President, turns out to have been the gunslinging Assistant District Attorney in Dutchess County, New York, who harassed Timothy Leary in Millbrook for years, and who served as a liaison between the White House and the Internal Security Division during Mardian's tenure as its director. Prior to his elevation to the post of Co-ordinator of Surreptitious Entry for the Committee to Re-elect the President, Mr. Liddy had built his career as a law-enforcement official by zealous exploitation of the climate of prurient anxiety about "drug abuse" that had been developed in the United States as a part of oppression directed against longhairs and dissenters. This was anything but exceptional; narcotics agents and prosecuting attorneys all over the country were parlaying the publicity attendant on drug busts and the prosecution of student dissenters—many of whom were beaten and gassed or shot in the course of their arrests—into a common cause that promised, and usually delivered, advancement at the polls.

In and around Buffalo, New York, where I lived at the time, this process was especially conspicuous. The distinguished novelist and literary critic Leslie Fiedler and his wife were subjected to nearly three years of harassment by their neighbors as well as by law-enforcement officials between the time of their arrest on charges of allowing marijuana to be used in their house—on the evidence supplied by a teen-aged narcotics agent with bugs concealed in her undergarments—and their triumphant conviction, which was then overturned at the first level of appeal. In the process, however, the Erie County Chief of the Division of Narcotics and Intelligence—the two are grouped together in Erie County, where law-enforcement officials have been determined to stamp out both—got himself elected sheriff. Mr. Amico kept the pot boiling by other exploits as well: he created an international incident by having two busloads of people bound from Toronto to the Woodstock Summer Rock Festival stopped at the border and held, in sealed and unventilated buses, for six hours while the passengers were removed, one by one, and searched.

Mark Rudd, the militant leader of the Columbia University revolt in the spring of 1968 and as such a known and intolerant opponent of drug use, was busted in nearby Lockport, New York, by police who happened to stop his car when he was driving through and produced a bag of marijuana that had mysteriously and unaccountably appeared in it. The political use of drug busts and narcotics prosecutions along the "Niagara Frontier," as this part of the world styles itself, became so marked that the head of the LEMAR (a national organization advocating the legalization of marijuana) chapter at the State University of New York at Buffalo, Michael Aldrich, finally undertook what promises to be a definitive study of such practices including, according to a report in *Rolling Stone*,[13] information on the role played by Gordon Liddy. By this time, Liddy had no position as a law-enforcement officer, even though he persisted in pursuing the fugitive Dr. Leary over two continents and finally arranged for his abduction from Afghanistan.

The positions in which the Watergate investigation has placed Mr. Liddy, Mr. Mardian, former Attorneys General of the United States Mitchell and, in lesser degree, Kleindienst—to say nothing of the President of the United States himself—are certainly astonishing; these men were responsible for all Department of Justice policies during their stewardships. But I am not sure that the scandal will greatly affect the political fortunes of the Republican Party, over the long range. Mr. Nixon did, after all, win by a landslide in 1972, and his supporters presumably accepted his political style, to which Watergate added few new tricks or new faces. Many of his supporters undoubtedly voted for him *because* of his trickiness and his persecution of dissenters, potheads, and hippies; they may not know what art is, but they know what they like. For them, the only problem created by the President's involvement in the Watergate scandal arises from their own need to identify their attacks on others as law-and-order and therefore not violence. The greatest damage Watergate may do the Republican Party, in fact, is to delay it in the formation of a consensus that, under Mr. Nixon's aegis, might have gone far to increase its numbers and even end its status as the perpetual minority party, and the party of privilege, in the United States.

In this connection, some of the most suggestive Watergate testimony came from Senator Lowell Weicker's interrogation of former presidential aide Gordon Strachan on July 23, 1973. Strachan testified that members of the White House staff actively participating in planning the 1972 campaign had urged that funds and support be withheld from Republican congressional candidates not only if they had failed to support the President's programs, but also if they were running from constituencies in which organized labor, which was supporting the President, was also supporting a Democrat. To Senator Weicker, who alone on the investigating committee has combined a keen moral and legal judgment with a wary and detailed, if cynical, understanding of the precise dynamics of the Nixon political arena—a combination that prevents him from being dismissed as "old-fashioned" or a "nineteenth-century man" as Chairman Ervin so often is—this policy seemed self-evident betrayal of the Republican Party itself. And also, of course, of the Party's potential for a truly conservative position with respect to American liberties which Weicker, like Ervin, clearly holds.

But Nixon just as clearly believed that a genuinely conservative position has no real future in America, and would seek his fortune by opposing it if it did. He and his staff were building, I believe, a very different base, with a greater and malignant potential: a hard-hat base, so devoted to equality of opportunity that it is eager to reject the Democrats who abrogate it by their special assistance to blacks and the poor. This hard-hat base was more than ready to relax and enjoy the President's peculiar but dramatic conception of law-and-order. His 1972 victory, in fact, attests to the degree to which he had done so already; he broke the Democrats' traditional hold on labor and left them the blacks and the urban poor as, in a largely hard-hat country, a political liability. Whether this strategy will succeed in installing the Republican Party, for the foreseeable future, as the populist party of America, with Watergate seen in retrospect as no more scandalous than the beer-hall putsch for the Nazis, depends on just how thoroughly hard-hat the country really is. There are some grounds, certainly, for inferring that it may be less so than the 1972 election, interpreted darkly, might suggest—notably the change in the complexion of the Congress resulting from the 1974 election.

But it does seem that the career of President Nixon, and the means so well publicized by Watergate by which he has successfully pursued it, have shattered once and for all the image of the horny-handed son

of toil who is likewise the staunchest defender of human liberty and
the equal dignity of all men. The truly poor may be that defender; or
more precisely, the poor may, for a time at least, accept an alliance
with defenders of their dignity even though they are repelled by their
champion's hippie style. Disillusionment, when it comes, is likely to
be shocking to both sides. One of the factors that shattered Students
for a Democratic Society at its June 1969 Ninth annual convention in
Chicago was a speech by Rufus Walls, an official of the Illinois Black
Panther Party, with which the less politically doctrinaire faction of
SDS had identified to the point of hero worship. Walls extolled
"Pussy Power" and asserted that "Superman was a punk because he
never even tried to fuck Lois Lane."[14] This of course struck the majority of the SDS membership as intolerable male-chauvinism. By
August, relations between the groups had deteriorated to the extent
that the Panther national chief of staff, David Hilliard, attacked SDS
in a speech, saying:

> We'll beat those little sissies, those little schoolboys' ass if they
> don't try to straighten up their politics. So we want to make it
> known to SDS and the first mother fucker that gets out of order
> had better stand in line for some kind of disciplinary actions
> from the Black Panther Party.[15]

Not a very promising alliance for the defense of liberty; yet for a time
it did hold, and hostility between the two groups never precluded a
certain degree of warmth and ambivalence.

No such confusion softened the attitude of organized labor, or
lower-middle America generally toward the student left. In this respect, the working class, along with many a newly risen executive,
emerged as the backbone of political repression. Anticipatory socialization intensifies the repressive tendency of the working class, in its
haste to identify with what it conceives to be appropriately suburban
sentiments. And often, quite correctly. While support of libertarian
attitudes in both politics and human relations tends to be positively
associated with income, status, and education, the correlation is a lot
less than unity; with the self-made and provincial wealthy exceeding
the hard-hat in vindictive ressentiment. Upon just such meat has this,
our Caesar, fed. Nixon's permanent contribution to American politics may prove to be his success in perfecting the recipe for this lethal
blend and producing it commercially.

CHAPTER THREE

Liberty and Rancor

Liberty, though extolled in the slogans of nearly every nation, has never been a popular cause. It costs more than most people think they can afford. And since the burden of the costs is borne by people who don't enjoy much of the liberty, they may very well be right.

The Founding Fathers adopted their familiar reference to "life, liberty, and the pursuit of happiness" from John Locke's phrase "life, liberty, and property," which he recognized as the gifts protected by the social contract among men. And there could have been little doubt in the minds of the Founding Fathers that the possession of ample means made a successful pursuit of happiness far more likely. Liberty and property go well together; each enhances the value of the other.

People who are indifferent to property are, of course, the freest of all, since the controlling sanctions of modern societies usually consist of threats against the opportunity to acquire and enjoy it: threats of fine, imprisonment, or, much more pervasively and effectively, of denial of access to lucrative and respected social roles. But the precondition of indifference to property seems to be an early experience of economic security: not necessarily affluence, but at least enough that grasping for money or power does not become a focus of serious concern.

Liberty therefore has never become supremely valuable to a majority of any complex community, and has in fact been widely detested in most. While history records some states and cities, like Athens, as having been freedom-loving, at least at certain times, in doing so it usually reveals its own preoccupation with ruling elites and blindness to the needs and attitudes of ordinary people. History relies on inscriptions of one kind or another, and rarely takes either people or societies seriously unless they were literate.

The idea of individual political freedom as a universal social value did not even become embodied in persuasive social doctrine until about three centuries ago; and then for reasons which, as Marxists rightly complain, were sufficiently corrupt to soil the cause of liberty itself. The rights of man went unformulated until an advancing technology made individualism a useful ideology for promoting the exploitation of the planet and its less technical-minded inhabitants. Civil liberty, though it has privileged antecedents in the experience of aristocratic insouciance, is a bourgeois social device to which centuries of usage in the service of elites has given a patrician gloss.

But the fact that the modern concept of individual liberty is rooted in exploitation does not diminish the glory of liberty itself, though it does indeed raise some hard questions about its social value. Most of what has come to be prized in this world is produced at the expense of its less privileged inhabitants. The distinguishing characteristic of the modern age is not that this has become less true, but that it has become so prodigious a source of guilt and bad faith. If Spiro Agnew rather than Cheops had built the great pyramid it would certainly have been built faster and more cheaply, if not more economically. And it would have done more for the building trades at all levels. But one could hardly argue that Agnew was less exploitive than Cheops; only that, in the meanwhile, magistrates had become defined as public servants. Nothing could better exemplify the spirit of the modern state than the fact that the Vice-President was finally punished for breaking the fiscal rules and taking economic advantages that were not lawfully his, while his continued assaults on human diversity and freedom of expression had, far from getting him in trouble, provided the very basis for his political career.

As a monument to Richard Nixon, Watergate has proved far more costly than to Cheops. But, once accomplished, who would begrudge a penny of it? Yet, it is astonishing that the project was ever undertaken. He was elected by a majority that had accepted, often with prurient delight, the costiveness, mendacity, unctuous sentimentality and commitment to victory at any price that had distinguished his approach to politics for more than twenty years. These were what endeared him to middle America, which saw in him a man like themselves who could not afford the luxury of generosity or compassion for America's victims, foreign or domestic. Though the details have

been horribly fascinating, what could Watergate reveal that the Indochina war and the mistreatment of the antiwar movement and
especially students, the conspiracy trials—the whole bloody lot—had
not made perfectly evident to the electorate long before the 1972
election? After the candidate had mourned the fate of little Tanya in
the siege of Leningrad over planet-wide television, while his bombs
continued to rain on the children of Indochina, there was nothing
more to learn.

The American people, accustomed to mark the progress of four
years by academic formalities, faced a great test in November 1972.
Most of those who took it flunked; they blackened everything but the
one best answer. What later preserved the republic, or at least forestalled its disintegration, were the Constitution itself and the highly
unrepresentative values, ambiguous as they are, of some establishment gentlemen: a sprinkling of judges, senators, law professors,
Brahmins. I do not mean to overstate the case for gentlemen; to
suggest that they are always, or even usually, defenders of liberty
would be historically false. Nor have I forgotten that the judge who
most effectively challenged the President is the son of an immigrant
barber and a jurist whose own handling of the Watergate defendants,
and a good many others, was marked by a ruthless and coercive use
of judicial power to force them to co-operate in the prosecution of
their former colleagues: a consistently ugly aspect of the legal system. But, by and large, what finally deactivated the Nixon administration and made it inoperative was the reassertion of established and
conservative principles against an incumbent who is almost the ideal-
type-construct of the ambitious, thrusting, self-made man: the very
model, even in his contempt for the rules and his preference of power
to principle, of what a successful American is supposed to be.

The rapid decline, subsequently, of public acceptance of the President is not convincing evidence of a change of social values; and
does his former supporters little honor. They cannot suppose Mr.
Nixon to have changed as much as that in a year. In their readiness
to disapprove as the stigmata of failure appear, they reveal their like-
ness to him in which must still be buried a bitter resentment of his
humiliators, who have stripped away their triumph so cavalierly. This
suppressed rancor constitutes a political minefield of the most dangerous kind; and it also raises a moral issue that must be honestly
stated.

I have no doubt that the disgrace—if the word may be applied to people from whom grace had so obviously been withheld—of the Nixon administration has furthered the ends of human liberty and authenticity. But it also dramatizes the moral ambiguity of these precious values; and, especially, their roots in human exploitation. For what has made the political career of a Nixon possible is the justified resentment of people who have been tricked into accepting mean and constricted lives that make the spectacle of other peoples' peace or joy intolerable to them; and who had come to mistake the small—and sometimes not so small—properties their diligence may gain them for evidence that they are worthy and secure. Yet, if they had not been victimized in this way, the standard of living that we have come to regard as a precondition of liberty could not have been attained. Nor could it have been attained without the far more thorough exploitation of the truly impoverished throughout most of the world.

Yet, for people who have learned to enjoy liberty, there is really nothing to compare to it; certainly not the joys of Christian self-denial. If I am willing, in fact, to obtain the food for my table and even the gasoline for my car through the force and guile needed to wrest a lion's share of these things from a world largely deprived of them, how much more determined I must be to demand the political and economic arrangements needed to provide freedom for my soul, which has learned to operate, as it must these days, on fairly low-grade karma; it doesn't develop much power, but I don't hear it knock, either. The turn-of-the-nineteenth-century British clergyman, critic and snob, Sydney Smith, once described his image of heaven as eating *foie gras* to the sound of trumpets. While this is a rather vulgar vision of eternal bliss—the Reverend Mr. Smith was evidently a highly consumer-oriented individual—there is something to be said for the moral obtuseness that allowed him to proclaim foie gras delicious, untroubled by *mauvaise foi* or even *mauvais foie*. A society whose elites raven after foie gras is unlikely to be much troubled by geese in the forum. A society whose elites truly enjoy liberty may and probably will be inequitable and exploitive, but not suffused throughout with an evil banality; nor will it become more concerned about whether its members are being treated equally than whether they are being treated well.

It is possible to argue, and I think soundly, that the experience of individual liberty is beneficial to society as a whole, even if that experience is not widely enjoyed, since it results in the establishment of more tolerant and less rancorous norms throughout the society, including the norm of noble behavior. But this argument now seems both so presumptuous and so archaic that I should prefer not to depend on it. Let me grant, then, that to value liberty so highly selfishly dismisses as of secondary interest the experience and the destiny of the majority of mankind. Most men continue to lead lives of quiet desperation, or more accurately, perhaps, clamorous resignation; and I know of no exception to the historic rule that in any society concern for freedom arises only after minimal needs for food, clothing, shelter and political security have been met. Certainly, liberty cannot be institutionalized effectively by constitutional means before this is done; though a commitment to freedom may persist after the underlying affluence that sustained it has been lost, as it has done in Greece, despite many rude interruptions, for two millennia.

But the fact that a commitment to liberty, Western style, can be made only after food, clothing, shelter and the common defense have been fairly satisfactorily provided for does not mean that these preconditions are more valuable than liberty. It just means that liberty is more problematical than they, and they have always been problematical enough. I would argue that the ultimate—though obviously not the sole—value of abundance is the diversity of experience, life-style, social role and expression it provides. In English, we even speak of this kind of existential affluence as a *wealth* of experience or *richness* of expression, without any implication that the style thus identified is luxurious or ornate. Usually, the reference is to *emotional* range, depth and complexity, which is the greatest luxury of all.

It is not, however, what is meant by luxury in Bangladesh or Mauritania or much of Detroit. What the Western world now calls galloping inflation is largely a reflection of the rising determination of the deprived to become a little less deprived and obtain a somewhat larger share of what the media of the industrial world have persuaded them is a normal standard of living. The demand is wholly just, but it is understandable that Western elites may perceive it as also rather impractical, and will do all they can to insure that it remains so. There are profound difficulties involved in the concept of the brotherhood of man: psychological, social, economic and political difficulties. Sibling rivalry so often prevails. If the bonds of brotherhood had been stronger from the outset, we might by now have evolved a more useful conception of the cousinhood of mankind as a more workable model for a network of distant but interdependent and amicable relationships. But Abel, unfortunately, died without issue at an early age; our tradition knows only strangers and brothers. Both can be dangerous.

Jean-Paul Sartre argues convincingly, as a central issue in his *Critique de la raison dialectique,* that the concept of human brotherhood is marred from the beginning by being predicated on scarcity and alienation. Men enter upon a social compact, he maintains, as a defense against the probability of being eliminated as "one too many" by the savagery of their more powerful fellows or the niggardliness of nature herself. In the process, they forfeit not only their right to act independently—this much Hobbes had stated three centuries earlier—but their emotional and intellectual freedom as well. The essence of the *serment* or oath that binds the brotherhood is the undertaking to remain loyal under penalty of death voluntarily accepted, rather than become the means by which *serial alterity,* or fragmentation into a number of unrelated and competing individuals, is reintroduced into the group. This is not just, or even primarily a mutual defense pact, but a guarantee of ideological conformity as well, lest insights and perceptions chilling to the group's morale and commitment lead to its dissolution. In just this way did the little band of brothers who sought so diligently to re-elect the President in 1972 seek to avoid the exposure of their enterprise to the light shed upon it by a renegade John Dean, not only for fear of prosecution, but because this new way of looking at themselves candidly could only destroy the bond between them and pit them against one another, bringing disaster upon them even as it revealed their tragic humanity. One is grateful for Mr. Dean's apostasy; but even more grateful for the memory of the late James Dean—not his brother—whose peculiarly enduring place in the hearts of his fellow countrymen stems from his consistent characterization on the screen of the young stranger who refuses the *serment* and remains a rebel, even without a cause, at whatever cost to himself. Though John Dean too, for his belated rebellion, has surely been overcharged.

If Sartre's argument is to be accepted, liberty can never have been and can never become a genuinely popular cause. Nor can it really be the objective of any revolution, though it may be advanced by limited and successful revolt. Revolutions generate new brotherhoods, held together by new if not novel oaths which beget new tyrannies. This is not, of course, to argue that revolutions cannot be socially beneficial;

the new alignment of social forces that they bring about, and consequent redistribution of goods and services, may well alleviate the misery of the previously disadvantaged members of society. Since these are unlikely to have been permitted to develop much taste for liberty or opportunity to enjoy it in the old order, the revolution may bring them nothing but gain. It may be well worth all the suffering it entails, in terms of social justice, improved living conditions, and an increased sense of worth derived from pride in one's membership in the community. All these are very valuable. None of them is liberty.

A devotion to liberty is a serious political liability in the modern industrial state. Conventionally, of course, it is continuously asserted that freedom is rooted in the hearts of the people and that its defenders and proponents must turn to the people for support. But no one expects to succeed in a practical political situation by acting as if this were the case. No university president, beleaguered by reactionary alumni, has ever turned on them and said, "By God, if the people of this community heard that we were firing people for organizing political demonstrations, they'd have our balls!" No school superintendent has ever been publicly denounced by his board because school newspapers are censored and student organizations forbidden to invite radical speakers to address them.

The patrician John Lindsay, as Mayor of New York, found himself again and again attacking libertarian positions and principles with which he had been associated all his life, in order to win popular support in the party and in the meaner parts of his city. The most notorious example is his seconding of the nomination of Spiro T. Agnew as Vice-President in 1968; the most shocking, perhaps, his joining in the attack launched by the Patrolmen's Benevolent Association and the New York Daily News against Criminal Court Judge Bruce Wright, who on Christmas Eve, 1972, had released on five hundred dollars cash bail a man accused of attempted murder of a policeman. The accused, Joseph Gruttola, owned a driving school, a home, and an insurance business in the city and would hardly have been likely to flee before trial. Lindsay expressed dismay at the low bail set by Judge Wright, "Because the perpetrator was a cold-blooded gunman if ever there was one."[1] Undoubtedly, the perpetrator was; but he ought not to have been assumed to be Mr. Gruttola, who, in fact, duly appeared for his trial, at which he was acquitted of the charge of attempted homicide, though convicted of other charges arising from the same incident. Judge Wright, meanwhile, has been subjected to sufficient harassment for setting low bail in this and other cases that, on February 10, 1975, he filed suit in Manhattan Federal District Court to block his removal to the civil bench, and asking a half million dollars in damages against the Patrolmen's Benevolent Association and twelve other individuals and organizations. "The suit," according to the New York *Times,* "listed a series of incidents in which police officers allegedly showed 'contempt, hatred, hostility and disrespect' for Judge Wright."

When the judge presided at night court, the complaint said, police hostility toward him was demonstrated by "audible sneers, derisive remarks, conversation, belching aloud and other bodily noises."

Judge Wright is black.

This may be taken as a measure of the pressure to which John Lindsay yielded. My point is certainly not that he is an unprincipled opportunist—on the contrary, he does this sort of thing very badly. It is rather that as an even moderately successful politician he was obliged to try, usually unavailingly, to accommodate himself to the demands of his constituency for a punitive and constrictive approach to the problems of municipal government. On the basis of his total record I would suggest that a reluctance to keep on doing so may have played a major role in his decision not to run for re-election; one does, finally, grow weary of pretending to be a worse man than one is in order to win the approval of one's neighbors. In Canada, in the election of 1974, which the Progressive Conservative and New Democratic parties at the right and left ends of the Canadian political spectrum precipitated by jointly exploiting widespread resentment of inflation, Mr. Trudeau, the Liberal in the middle, was more successful in retaining his hold on the Canadian electorate; but only at the price of making a travesty of himself by adopting a populist style that denied the saturnine and philosophical arrogance that makes him a brilliant though dangerously autocratic statesperson.

Nevertheless, liberal causes are seldom wholly lost in the democratic process. They become familiar and conventional as they are modified to appeal to the social and economic interests of a much larger number of persons than would originally have supported them; and ultimately, in this much altered form, they prevail. Their supporters may not even recognize how much they have changed. Hubert Horatio Humphrey still thinks of himself as a fighter for freedom. In Mexico, *revolución* has become an establishment slogan;

the Revolutionary Party has been in power for nearly half a century, and under President Diaz Ordaz in the late 1960s, radical students were shot there as blithely as if the government had been a military junta. Mexican presidents are constitutionally ineligible to serve a second term, but the party was returned to power in 1970. In America, the abolition of slavery, women's suffrage, the right of labor to organize were each in their turn bitterly resisted as radical causes; all now are taken for granted as not merely established but traditional guarantees. But by the time each was accepted, the battle line had been drawn at another issue. The process repeats itself; and each increment of freedom and joy is resisted as bitterly as the first. Sometimes, as in the current letch for the restoration of capital punishment—which, in the United States, was abolished by judicial action that state legislatures, responding to heavy public demand, immediately began to circumvent—the process is retrograde.

Nevertheless, I do not intend to suggest that there is some form of government I would prefer to what we call democratic. My mind just doesn't work that way. Societies don't choose their forms of government; they evolve, determined by historical necessity and technological circumstances. Representative democracy, like the internal combustion engine, is absolutely essential to what in the twentieth century has come to be defined as the good life. It is equally true that the good life has come to be defined in this way so as to legitimate the government and maintain the demand for automobiles, both of which are necessary to keep the economy going and the status system intact. Under any social system, whatever is most useful in conserving existing institutions will come to seem not merely natural but indispensable. Nevertheless, neither automobiles nor elected legislatures are likely to be as prominent or as ardently defended in the twenty-first century if they continue to create more lethal problems than those they solve.

It is inconceivable, however, that in 1975 any government could be regarded as legitimate that did not base its authority on a putative popular mandate. There is simply no alternative source of power in the modern world. To object to the functioning of popular, egalitarian institutions is like objecting to the functioning of the alimentary canal. Evolution might conceivably have led to some more elegant means of providing nutrition and sustaining metabolism; but it did not, and to talk about alternatives to it is absurd. One can accept the necessity of digestion and even marvel at the intricacy of the process by which it is accomplished without, however, admiring its end product—though perhaps, in politics as in child-rearing, to say no to shit is to say no to life.

Governments today are expected to devote themselves more fully to the interests of social justice than of liberty; to reduce misery rather than to support elegance. While they have not done a very good job of that, either, the attempt clearly requires them to guarantee a different set of freedoms than those set forth in the Bill of Rights: freedom of access to desirable goods, services, jobs and social roles; freedom from the invidious application of the norms of high culture or even middle-class culture to those who have never had the opportunity or the inclination to accept those norms; freedom from competition with individuals to whom a better education and more privileged upbringing have secured an initial advantage. The classical conception of freedom embodied in the Bill of Rights is itself, in fact, an instrument of bourgeois privilege and class bias, derived from the ideological premises of a rising capitalist order and, in its emphasis on the rights of the individual at the expense of the collective, hostile in principle and in effect to the aspirations of an industrial proletariat.

Only a patrician class could have formulated the Bill of Rights, which conceives of liberty as freedom from, quite literally, unwarranted intrusion—a conception likely to occur to men of ample estates. It protects and benefits such men directly; poorer men find its provisions vitiated or made irrelevant by the circumstances of their lives. The Bill of Rights is useless to a man who cannot afford to pay a lawyer, or to spend time in court, especially if he must become a plaintiff, rather than a defendant, in order to protect his rights. In any case, the police and the lower courts rarely bother about its provisions in dealing with the poor. To a professional criminal, who regards apprehension and imprisonment as legitimate business risks, it has no moral significance; any set of rules would do as well; and due process may put him to needless expense. To a family that has spent its life and emotional essence working hard at disagreeable and unrespected jobs to keep itself respectable, the suggestion that it might be threatened by the police is more offensive than any police action could possibly be. The readers of the New York *Daily News* and the congregations of Billy Graham have no protection to gain from the First Amendment.

Lives circumscribed by the corner bar and the color bar are likely to find civil liberties infuriating. Civil liberties are, indeed, the fruits of privilege and more likely to appeal to the privileged palate and nourish the privileged psyche. The converse, of course, is not true; most of the privileged are not civil libertarians, as the social attitudes of university governing boards and the roster of contributors to the Committee to Re-elect the President clearly show. But this, then, is all the more reason to grant that the defense of personal freedom, especially in its more expressive forms, is and must remain a minority position.

What is wrong with that? It is certainly not inconsistent for a civil libertarian to defend a minority position. Guilt arises when that minority is a privileged minority, and its defense a defense of a superior class position. Yet even revolutionaries are committed by the very fact of being so to accept the reality of class conflict. They must concede the appropriateness, if not the virtue, of even members of a privileged class defending their class interests; and for some of the privileged, civil liberty is a paramount interest. Lovers of liberty, like lovers of members of their own sex, or members of any ethnic or political minority, may justifiably seek to defend themselves from the animosity of their neighbors, however outnumbered they may be. They are equally entitled to constitutional protection and need not claim that what is good for them is necessarily good for the commonwealth, except insofar as mutual tolerance is itself assumed to be of social value. American democracy, especially, is conceived as pluralistic. Why should it continually seek to conceal social conflict behind a façade of common values, repressing those, like elitism, that just will not fit, instead of accepting tension and friction as equally characteristic of social and physical systems—except for celestial models?

Severe conflict of values and interests is intolerable to citizens of the national state primarily, I believe, because that state—rather than social class, or estate in the old French sense—has come to be regarded as the basis for a sense of community.

People clearly need to feel themselves members of a viable community if they are not to become trolls and monsters, answerable only to themselves and maddened by the echo of their own desires. And the broader and more embracing the community of which they feel themselves to be a member, the nobler they may become. But the national state is a poor basis for such a community. It is as exclusive and exploitative of those beyond its own boundaries as any ethnic group or social interest group might be. It has the further disadvantage of being more arbitrary and more dependent on the school system and the other mass media to continually assert the fact of its existence, lest its citizens forget who they are supposed to be. The absurdity of the claim that common nationality means community was perhaps most clearly demonstrated after World War I, when the statesmen of Europe divided that continent and Africa as well into enclaves with scant regard for culture. Whether, after nationhood was finally achieved in 1960, Nigerian children were taught to chant "One nation indivisible, with liberty and justice for all" in English, (there was certainly no other single language even in official use throughout the country), I do not know; but if they did, it couldn't have done them much good. In due course, Biafra was stillborn.

People develop a sense of community by sharing a network of mutual or at least interlocking interests, and common experiences that come to be expressed in common symbols and mutual understanding. Social class, membership in the same profession, true ethnicity—that is, participation in a special common culture, as distinct from either biological race or nationality—all these offer a deeper sense of community than does citizenship in the same state. So, I suspect, do some of the newer forms of social organization like the multinational corporate giants or the Central Intelligence Agency, which is already less the agent of the United States Government, which can hardly control it, than it is an autonomous terrorist organization devoted to the maintenance of the economic interests and life-style of the ruling cadres of latter-day capitalism now centered in the United States but equally at home in Belgium or Hong Kong. To a local CIA agent or lawyer or minor executive representing IT&T in Iquitos, Peru, on the banks of the Amazon and cut off from the rest of the country except by air: or Kota Kinabalu, Malaysia, which was Jesselton, British Borneo, until 1963: the status and network of associations afforded him by his unusual position must affect his identity much more strongly than nationality does.

But the national state, because it depends for its stability on social cohesion among citizens of the most disparate backgrounds, is inherently troubled by class conflict and disposed to be hypocritical about the existence of class interests, preferring to insist on the transcending priority of the national interest. Exploitation of one social class or ethnic group by another is never faced for what it is—an epiphenomenon of real difference in power between social groups, to be eliminated only by eliminating those differences. And this is something the national state cannot do very effectively, as even so courageous and intelligent a leader as Dr. Allende must discover sooner or later. It is the creature of the power that exists and destroys those who try to turn it against the wielders of power unless it is first weakened or destroyed by severe disruption. For a genuinely radical party, victory at the polls of a vigorous democratic state is the quickest path to eradication, either by absorption or extinction.

National states therefore tend to respond to the misery and resentment engendered by exploitation in two ways, neither of which much affects the exploitation. On the other hand, the state adopts remedial programs designed to cushion the exploited against its most severe effects and forestall their conversion into a truly revolutionary element. On the other, it rationalizes the exploitation as conducive or even essential to the *national* interest rather than as beneficial merely to the dominant social classes, and hence as not really exploitation at all; as in administering a program of selective service in which nearly all the draftees are poor.

The cushioning programs must, however, be severely limited. They cannot be permitted to do more than provide a little relief for individual afflictions; if they threaten to become effective enough to give victimized groups more real power, they are emasculated or terminated. Legal aid programs for the poor or for convicts, for example, are usually expected by their parliamentary or congressional supporters to help with divorce cases or other legal problems not directly related to the client's subservient status. If, however, they attempt to represent inmates in litigation against prison officials; or farm workers against employers, their funds are withdrawn or their staffs dismissed. Since the historic United States Supreme Court decision in *Gideon* vs. *Florida,* indigent defendants are now entitled to legal representation at state expense in any felony trial. But no comparable provision has ever been established for *plaintiffs* who require legal assistance in asserting their legal rights rather than in defending themselves. In a sense, to be sure, this is exactly what the district attorney and the Department of Justice are supposed to provide; in practice, they prosecute the poor far more effectively than they protect them. Not only are most convicted criminals poor, most victims of crime, which notoriously occurs in areas the poor frequent, are too. It seems to me very difficult to argue that the underclasses derive a net benefit from law enforcement: they suffer from its ravages.

Welfare programs are similarly restricted by the prevalent conviction that sound public policy requires that benefits be kept too low to compete with the meanest wage an employer might offer, lest people prefer to "live off the government" rather than work. Economic intervention of the state on behalf of the poor is thus prevented from becoming powerful enough to provide them with any alternative to exploitation. Nothing demeans the modern state more than the preoccupation of its citizens with the possibility that the poorest of their number may be "getting something for nothing"; and no other attitude does more to keep those presently powerful in power; this is what permits them to mobilize the working classes against the poor rather than against *them*. And no other attitude is more nearly universal among modern industrial societies. Socialist states, indeed, are even more insistent than capitalist states that the national interest coincides with that of the no-longer-private citizen—and far more hostile to "parasites."

The state survives by denying the validity of class interest and the legitimacy of class conflict; and rationalizing exploitation as conducive to the *national* interest. Since it is held to benefit the entire commonwealth, it is not really exploitation at all.

Exploitation therefore assumes a peculiarly degrading quality in the modern state, for the victim must not only be used and often ill-used; he must be kept persuaded that such usage is in his best interests as a citizen—a refinement in mystification that would not have occurred to Attila the Hun. To avoid polarization of the society, the administrators of the national state justify their actions and policies in the name of *all* the people, and treat class distinctions as obnoxious and illegitimate, though they need by no means be disposed toward equality of condition among citizens, they must support equality of economic opportunity in principle. And they are haunted by the specter of revolution.

The national state is especially vulnerable to revolt because it depends for its integrity upon the assertion of a community of interests among its citizens that is largely contradicted by their experience, which is more strongly influenced by social class and social role than by nationality—though nationality, to be sure, affects the availability of social roles and social class positions. The life of an American bureaucrat resembles that of a Libyan or Brazilian bureaucrat more than it does that of an American garbage person; and in none of these countries is the work of the bureaucrat, foreign or domestic, likely to result in a net gain for the poor.

Societies can be held together—and often have been—by means that contrast quite sharply with dependence on an abstract and partly spurious sense of national identity; the division of the earth into nation-states is only two centuries old and the national boundaries imposed arbitrarily by European colonial invaders on the maps of the continents of the Southern Hemisphere came even later. In Europe itself, a feudal society bound together by mutually accepted and reciprocal though asymmetrical privileges and obligations prevailed as the conventional model for organizing social life far longer than the liberal national state has yet lasted. The stability of feudal society did not depend on a sense that what was good for the lord was good for the peasant, still less on any expectation that a peasant today might become a lord tomorrow. It derived from a shared conviction that each class contributed, indispensably though unequally, to the opportunity of the other to live its own life and fulfill its destiny. In such a society the very idea of a modern political revolution intended to wrest the apparatus of legitimate power from the hands of an established elite was unthinkable; rebellions could aim, at most, to remove and replace an unjust sovereign with, hopefully, a better one. As Barrington Moore, Jr., has observed in his *Reflections on the Causes of Human Misery,* revolution is an idea as modern as the state itself.[2]

The modern liberal state, however, depends on the promise of equality of opportunity and the spectacle of well-monitored though highly publicized social mobility to preserve its stability. Discrimination *in favor* of any social group as well as that directed against one becomes a major social grievance quite apart from the question of what, if any, degree of immiserization has thus been visited upon those whose candidacies were disallowed. The national state thus everywhere defines itself as devoted to the general welfare; and while it may nevertheless serve the cause of privilege, it cannot accord that cause any legitimacy. Alexis de Tocqueville put this matter, as he did so much else, succinctly in *Democracy in America:*

"The Americans hold that, in every state, the supreme power ought to emanate from the people, but when once that power is constituted they can conceive, as it were, no limits to it, and they are ready to admit that it has the right to do whatever it pleases. They have not the slightest notion of peculiar privileges granted to cities, families of persons; their minds appear never to have foreseen that it might be possible not to apply the same laws to every part of the state and to all its inhabitants."[3]

Modern democratic states do, of course, make substantial concessions to their richer and higher status members—notoriously in the case of the all-embracing, pardon-granted Richard Nixon, whom Henry VIII would doubtless have sent to the scaffold as he ultimately did Thomas Cromwell. But these concessions are suspect and granted, if possible, covertly or by indirection. "The Law," as Anatole France ironically concedes in a familiar enough statement, "forbids rich and poor alike to steal bread and sleep under bridges." The state is not supposed to establish recognized categories of privilege; it is, instead, seen as the deeply flawed instrument of a just and egalitarian social policy, continually in need of reform that seldom works, but nevertheless the true instrument of the commonwealth.

The ends of social justice and of liberty thus become one; and this has been an article of popular faith since the 1930s at least. Witness the joy with which liberals hailed the social legislation enacted under Franklin D. Roosevelt as a triumph not only for social justice but for liberty as well. Today, as the coercive promise of big unions and metastasizing federal bureaucracies is fulfilled, we are less certain that it was a triumph for either. Unions, as they have advanced the interests of the working class, have also helped to keep the really poor poor. In any case, they have done little for the cause of liberty, though a great deal to protect job security and encourage the development of a more affluent mass society.

In an industrially developed society with the productive capacity to provide abundance for its members, there is no economic reason why a guaranteed annual income sufficient for comfort, security, and variety in life should not be provided for everyone. The reasons why this cannot be done are political. It may, of course, be justly argued that a guaranteed annual income for people of industrial societies would actually add to total social injustice by widening even further the chasm that separates them from the poverty that stifles much of the rest of the world. But this is clearly not the reason why political leaders in the developed countries have not sought effectively to meet the needs of their own constituencies by providing such an income. Those reasons are domestic; and they are linked to the fact that, in such countries, social justice is conceived as if it meant merely equality of economic opportunity.

Where equality of economic opportunity is the device through which the ends of social justice are to be sought, it becomes politically impossible for the commonwealth to assume a paternalistic responsibility for the needs of its members. To do so violates the work ethic by giving some members of the commonwealth an unearned advantage in competition with their fellows. Note, as evidence, the literally fratricidal wrath aroused by the very modest efforts that have been made sporadically in the United States to redress some of the historical grievances of black people by "reverse discrimination"; or the unctuous and well-justified confidence with which Richard Nixon, in his uniquely successful 1972 re-election campaign, asserted that it was wrong for anyone on welfare to receive as much money as a worker.

Jealousy and envy have a real object in that the person who is jealous wants what someone else has, and at least imagines that he would be satisfied if he could get it. Ressentiment is even meaner and drearier; it envisions no satisfaction, but seeks merely to deny satisfaction to others. It goes beyond the notion of sour grapes to prohibit grapes and punish wine-lovers as drunkards. Its intensity is a measure of the degree to which life, including work and the spirit in which work is performed, has come to seem frustrating, meaningless drudgery and, worse, to involve a profound and continuous denial of one's own sense of craftsmanship. To feel a full, bitter measure of ressentiment, one must have become more than a victim; one must despise oneself for having consented to one's own victimization and established it as the pattern of one's life.

Ressentiment thus comes to be closely related to social class. It is politically significant in those social groups in which the circumstances that engender it are pervasive enough to establish rancor as a social pattern as well as a state of mind: an obligatory social pattern that imposes itself even on those who have not come to share the state of mind. But no social class is free of it; for all social classes have plenty of members who feel that life and society have seduced them into betraying themselves, and who have come to call their complicity in this transaction "self-control." It is perhaps strongest among those who have struggled successfully to become wealthy only to find that their money brought them neither honor nor power, as they had promised themselves it would: and who now sit aging in costly condominiums, protected by security guards.

One would expect ressentiment to be least prevalent in social groups whose members were most often brought up to feel that they could guide their lives in some degree by their own choices, which they were free to make in ways that expressed their growing sense of self and their awareness of their own nature. Such conditions probably occur most frequently among those who are, as we used to say, "comfortably off." The very rich seldom qualify; they are likely to use their power arbitrarily to impose their will on the world through their children and to leave them—and themselves—very little sense of freedom of choice despite the apparent array of possibilities. Much sorrow might have been spared the American, Cuban and Vietnamese peoples, as well as Joseph Kennedy and his children, if he had brought them up to feel free *not* to become President of the United States. And royalty, who by definition can afford their elder children, at least, no freedom of choice at all, have notoriously been the cruelest parents of whom a record exists—though, to be fair, we must grant that their image has suffered because a record was nearly always kept.

But simple affluence, experienced early in life and sustained through childhood, is a substantial protection against the development of ressentiment. It is this relationship which accounts for the by-now-familiar paradox that the roots of the counterculture, of the American civil rights and war protest movements, of the "permissiveness" that so infuriates the working class as to have become a prime political issue are to be found in the well-to-do professional and managerial classes. The faults of such people are numerous and familiar: faddishness, superficiality in personal and vocational commitments, and a tendency to respond to the predicaments of persons less fortunate than themselves with guilt rather than compassionate strength, which leaves them vulnerable to Mr. Sammler's pickpocket. Jules Pfeiffer, by now, has said it all. But they are relatively free from the bigotry and dog-in-the-manager attitude that characterize much of the working class and petty bureaucracy.

But how can ressentiment have become a dominant political force in mass society? Ressentiment is the state of mind of habitual losers: of those who accept lives forced upon them by others or by circumstances, then exhaust their energies trying to convince themselves that the humiliations and labor that have been imposed on them are the pathway to their chosen destiny. How could such a state of mind lead to or signify anything but defeat and impotence?

The answer lies in the peculiar device that modern societies use to legitimate exploitation and prevent the rancor it arouses from threatening the stability of the government and leading to direct revolt. That device is "the consent of the governed," the very cornerstone, moral and philosophical, of the democratic nation.

The reason for basing the legitimacy of government on the consent of the governed, formally and periodically assessed in free elections is, of course, to *reduce* exploitation by giving the people the means of opposing and controlling their oppressors. This is both a noble vision and, apparently, a reasonable idea. Who can blame the Russian people, who had suffered for centuries under the yoke of an absolutist regime so bloodthirsty that, at the turn of the century, it was executing an average of twenty persons[4] a year from rising in righteous wrath and putting an end to the rule of privilege, naming themselves the guardians of such liberties as they had learned to value? They got what they wanted; though they may not have wanted what they got.

Governments, however, almost by definition, represent primarily the class interests of dominant social groups and especially of their own bureaucratic cadres. In any society, the government will surely serve more as the instrument of exploitation than as the guardian that protects the nation's powerless, though for the sake of its own stability it must provide *some* protection. So the idea of a government that will protect the interests of the weak from the powerful is not so much wrong as absurd. Governments don't do that; they are thrown out of office if they try. The most that can be asked of them realistically is that they mediate between the conflicting interests of different social classes, helping to convince the relatively powerful that excessive greed will defeat their own interests, and establishing a level of exploitation acceptable enough to keep the social machinery from breaking down in social conflict. This does not mean, of course, that those in power are invulnerable to social change; and obviously the government is itself a most valuable prize in the struggle for power. But the reason why it *is* a valuable prize is that it works most zealously for those who possess it.

By emphasizing the consent of the governed, however, the state effectively implicates the exploited in their own exploitation, which makes them much easier to control. Coercion is much less effective in getting people to consent to violations of self-interest. It is bound to fail from time to time; and when it does, it leaves people angrier and more rebellious than ever. By basing its authority on the consent of the governed, however, the state minimizes this danger. Rebellion, if it does nevertheless occur, is doubly illegitimate. It is perceived as directed not only against the sovereign but against the people themselves, who proceed at once to straighten the miscreants out, whether through the vigilance of enraged hard-hats or the costive banalities of block committees and people's courts.

But the cost is great. Reliance on the consent of the governed to discount the legitimacy of protest in advance requires the development of a variety of highly effective procedures for mystifying the public and manipulating its attitudes and understanding of events. When the citizen is not only free to use the apparatus of the state to advance his interests but has been taught that he is obligated to do so, the government faces serious problems in keeping him in line. *The basic flaw in the democratic process is not that the average man is incapable of intelligent participation in the affairs of state. It is that he must be rendered incapable of doing so in order to prevent him from using his formal political powers to challenge the existing distributions of wealth and power.* If the government does not succeed in neutralizing his efforts to actually use the powers formally his under a democratic system, it will lose the support of the persons and corporations who currently possess power, which means loss of funding, continuous adverse publicity, obstruction of its program and probably loss of office. But it will also be thrown out of office if it does not flatteringly reassure the voter that he is sovereign, and seek to make his tastes, now corrupted by commercial exploitation, or bureaucratic necessity, the law of the land. In a trade-off for the political power nominally assigned them by a democratic constitution, the masses—now seething with resentment at the unfulfilled promise of their lives—are allowed to impose on a nation a constricted and punitive morality and an aesthetic so alienated that it calls violence sensation and sensation pornography. Life is X-rated, and the young restricted to high school and Disney World.

In a modern industrial democracy, a majority of the voters must, except under circumstances so rare as to be almost unimaginable, be persons who have been induced to convince themselves that their misuse by others is in fact in their own interests, and that they have chosen to permit this and indeed to establish and defend the institutions by which it occurs. The development of feelings of ressentiment is the best evidence that self-awareness has been greatly diminished or destroyed and with it the power of choosing to be active in ways that are personally satisfying, expressive, and effective in maintaining the rhythms of one's life in society. But it is also the best evidence that the *ressentient* individual is now ready to allow himself to be used by others—even eagerly, insatiably, since the more alienated he has become, the more dependent he is on other people's recognition to maintain his self-esteem. I have discussed very fully elsewhere the way in which the institutions that socialize the young, especially the school system, accustom them to a climate of ressentiment until they come to accept this as an essential characteristic of serious, adult life and, becoming *ressentient* themselves, they mistake this for the process of growing up.[5] Here, I wish merely to stress that this process does not only fit them for the world of work, it fixes in the minds and character of most, apparently irrevocably, a conception of work as something that is done to meet the demands of other persons for pay. And that it is usually disagreeable in itself. All societies must require their members to do dangerous, tedious, and disagreeable tasks; but folk societies without much technology or role-differentiation do not teach their members to think of this as we think of work: as, paradoxically, both the core of our social identity, yet so alien to our life that we would not naturally do it unless we were hired to, to fulfill somebody else's purpose.

In a society which conceives of work with such bitter ambivalence, few will be able to imagine that essential work would be done if people could live, comfortably and without guilt, even if they neglected or refuse to do it. And they certainly would neglect or refuse to do it if they were not socialized early into regarding it as their duty and pleasure to make themselves useful to their boss and demanding of their subordinates; Nietzsche referred to ressentiment as slave mentality, though slaves are perhaps less likely to suffer from it than wage slaves, since they are not required to view their enslavement as the consequence of their own choices. But it is hard to conceive that the planet could have been developed to provide so many people with— at this point—enriched bread and televised circuses without the very widespread inculcation of ressentiment as a basic social attitude. It is equally inconceivable that a populace free of ressentiment would bake or eat such bread, or find such circuses diverting.

That populace, however, may be unable to bring itself to provide all its members with anything of greater value. My argument so far implies that every highly developed industrial society that depends on the consent of the governed for legitimation of political power will

find it difficult if not impossible to adopt generous measure for
providing for its weaker members, whether these be poor, deviant, or
just too young, or too old. Their neediness will itself constitute a
stigma; and a more serious stigma if they appear to be unabashed by
their state and joyful in their approach to life. A society in which
measures must be submitted, measure by measure, to some form of
popular ratification in order to become public policy can hardly
become more generous than the prevailing mood of its people; and
conditions of modern industrial life virtually insure that this mood
will be sour and rancorous, with most city dwellers clamoring for
protection from the demands of the neediest among them; and most
rural dwellers bitterly resenting the sophistication and political agility
they attribute to urbanites. And since industrial societies keep their
members motivated by establishing a rising level of expectation that
only industrial societies can maintain, a stalemate is established. The
very dynamism that makes the promise of plenty possible technologically precludes its fulfillment by making it psychologically
impossible for the members of the society to elect to eliminate the
burden of wretched poverty and degrading labor from those deemed
indolent or unworthy.

That dynamism also makes it difficult, and occasionally impossible,
for any joyful or spontaneous activity to develop, unlicensed, in the
land. The almost simultaneous suppression throughout North America and Britain of Dionysian rock-festivals in the early 1970s, while
regimented and competitive sports events that attracted equally large
and often more disorderly—and certainly more violent—crowds continued to enjoy public approval, is a striking case in point. What is
especially noticeable about this development is its reversal of the expected status patterns. Rock music, though attractive to a mass audience, expressed an essentially affluent, middle-class urban set of social
values; it was precisely this which so infuriated and scandalized
essentially working-class police and the shabby-genteel residents
stranded in the small towns near which festivals requiring open country must be held. Far more seriously, the police riots that occurred,
usually with approval amounting to endorsement in the local press, in
major cities and on the more distinguished college campuses through
the last half of the sixties and the very early seventies can best be understood as outbreaks of previously repressed ressentiment against the
new and unholy alliance between militant blacks and flauntingly free-
living middle-class, college youth, which these police forces, drawn

largely from working-class ethnic groups and self-selectively from the more authoritarian members of these, found absolutely intolerable. That the predominantly working class and often equally *ressentient* black militants also found their self-appointed allies intolerable adds irony to the tragedy.

The period of American history from 1965 to 1970 is notable for the frequency and intensity of ressentiment-laden revolt against the hegemony of upper-middle-class values. The most widely publicized of these were the Spock and Chicago Conspiracy trials; the Kent State slayings, and the crushing of the Attica penitentiary revolt by guards and state police all the more outraged by the intervention of civil rights lawyers and distinguished liberal journalists like Tom Wicker, who were beginning to affect the thinking and policies of the central prison administration in Albany. Everyone who lived through this period in America will have his or her own memories of local incidents of equal significance and poignancy that never became familiar to the nation. The unusual and often lethal irascibility of the working class during this time may be attributed to the fact that, though exploited as usual to meet the military demands of the Indochina war, for which they bore most of the risks, hardships and casualties sustained by Americans, they were denied the customary solace of a sense of moral superiority for their pains. Middle-class youth who opposed the war and refused or evaded participation in it had not only higher status and a safer and more privileged position in life, but a morally superior position as well.

Yet, the working-class supporters of the war had a legitimate grievance, and a very serious one, though not the one they voiced against hated peace-freaks and draft dodgers who were, in truth, more innocent than they. Their grievance, of which few ever became aware, consisted in the fact that their socialization which had prepared them for exploitation in the war and the labor markets it stimulated had indeed rendered them incapable of resistance or independent moral judgment—a capacity that many recovered at great personal cost when they finally found themselves in Vietnam and rendered the American Army (though not its elite air force) ineffective through wholesale desertions and salutary neglect of duty. Greater moral sensitivity, leading to earlier war-refusal, would have been more effective and saved hundreds of thousands of Asiatic and American lives and incalculable suffering. But this kind of sensitivity is exactly what ressentiment deprives people of; it is the principal casualty of exploitation.

Uncongenial as the idea will be to democratic ideologues, it seems to me incontestable that what has shielded at least some of the people some of the time from the ressentiment of their fellow citizens, and thus kept a relatively humane and creative spirit alive in them, is social stratification; which, of course, is also the structural device that makes oppression and exploitation possible. For social stratification diminishes the political influence of individuals and groups as it adds to their grievances and to the probability that they will have cause for ressentiment. This is totally unjust, but in some ways extremely convenient. The political influence of the mentality which hobbles the working class remains limited. The work of the society gets done; but the values and world view of the worker do not come to pervade the entire society, and do not so completely mold politics. The result, at best, is an uneasy compromise in which the working class gains a spurious sense of rectitude and a share in the technically ingenious devices and divertissements valued in the society, while relinquishing any opportunity to understand clearly or influence effectively its own place in the political and moral scheme of things. The executive and professional classes above them gain a disproportionate share of goods and services and an exaggerated sense of their own importance. But they relinquish any chance to free themselves from the constraints and strictures of working-class tastes, values and anxieties. These continue to be imposed by law and custom; and by the molding of the mass market from which highly distinctive items of limited appeal are rapidly eliminated.

Life in an industrial democracy possesses some of the characteristics one might expect of an equestrian society in which horses could vote; and it is not as pleasant as Jonathan Swift, who liked his Houyhnhnms, seemed to think. "Get off my back" did not become a popular idiom for nothing. For most people—in some measure, no doubt for all—socialization resembles horse-training. Indeed, horse-training is, precisely, socialization: socialization of horses to regard themselves as members of human society, so that they use their strengths, which would be sufficient to kill a man if they would attack, as lions and tigers do when threatened, to serve men and meet their ends instead. The analogy can be made even more precise. Most horse trainers, it seems, are convinced that they love horses, and that they could not train them successfully if they did not, though they are also convinced of the utility of brief, metallic discipline when needed. Schoolteachers, especially in well-stratified societies, think of themselves in relation to their charges in the same way; and this *does* make their job easier because it confuses their victims, who need sympathy in their hurt and frustration and turn to their tormentors in search of it. One can even argue that horse-training actually serves the interests of the horse, since it prepares him for employment, fits him for a role in society and raises his standard of living; animals too savage to be trained are killed off by hunters or die out as their lands are alienated. Being born free doesn't help much if you have no civil rights.

Horse-training has always seemed to me an immoral business, and I have never found an adult horse to be really friendly; just docile, in a hooded way, like an old black servant with nothing more to learn about human iniquity. It is easier to admire those who retain some power to be treacherous, and difficult to absolve so large and intelligent an animal of its guilt for failing to develop its revolutionary potential. But riders, too, must accept discipline, and learn to respect the needs and the nature of the beasts that bear them. Unlike horses, however, they are allowed to set their own goals and pursue their own interests; or, at least, socialized in a way that encourages them to believe that their goals and interests correspond with those of the society as a whole, which can only be done by according them a relatively desirable place in it. In an equestrian society, therefore, it is probably better to be a rider than a pedestrian; and certainly better to be a rider than a horse.

The problems, and the conflicts, of equestrian society would however become much more complex and severe if horses were led to accept their position by being encouraged to believe that hard work and docile service would permit them to become riders, rather than by coercive training. Their failure to make it would then become a taunting sign of personal inadequacy; and their anger and resentment inexhaustible. And no matter how much they may value horse sense, equestrian societies do not enfranchise the horse. If they did, they might still manage to remain equestrian, but at a rather embarrassing cost. Politicians would feel obliged to pretend to share the tastes and to some degree the life-style that had been imposed on horses, and would present themselves at race tracks and on television munching oats from feed bags with grimaces of delight. The design of the race track itself would be condemned as racist, in view of its total segregation of horses and spectators. The epithets "horse's ass" and "horse shit" as applied to statesmen and to their public statements would be denounced as not merely vulgar, as at present, but as bigoted and offensive under exiting civil rights legislation; and would be dropped from popular expression.

To any reader who may feel my analogy to be insulting to the social groups who under the arrangements that now exist are forced to bear most of the world's burdens in return for a very small share of its resources, I would merely point out as Peter Singer did in his review of *Animals, Men and Morals* in the *New York Review* of April 5, 1973, that there is no moral reason whatever to justify the exploitation of any feeling creature—including other men—by man; and that the reasons for not doing so apply with equal force to all sensate beings. The only possible justification for treating animals worse than men is to argue that their difference from men makes them inferior to men and hence less worthy. But once this argument is admitted in principle, it becomes applicable to differences between men of different kinds. The argument that the differences between men and animals are innate while the differences between different races of men or ethnic groups are themselves generated by injustice and exploitation is irrelevant, though appealing to Arthur Jensen's more severe critics. Horses, too, like the children of the poor, are, as I have pointed out, cowed and stupefied by their training, regardless of their initial capacities, and forced to develop in ways that make them useful to others rather than themselves. Finally, the argument that horses are less intelligent than men initially depends, precisely as such arguments about the relative merits of different races do, on the value assigned to particular skills in particular societies and is both anthropocentric and self-fulfilling. Every horse that has read these comments has indicated its complete agreement.

In a society that did not depend on exploitation to get its dirty work done—and in such societies, literate horses doubtless abound—my comments would be totally irrelevant. But if the society does so depend, probably the less guilty its dominant social groups feel about it, and the less they depend on manipulation and mystification to achieve that subordination, the better. The dignity of the exploited may be protected to some degree if the victor does not play games with them and induce them to *consent* to their degradation. Seduction is in some respects even more insufferable than rape. The rapist at least does not expect to stay for breakfast, and does not pretend to admire his victim's cooking.

Moreover, there is certainly nothing to be gained by ripping the poor off and forcing them to bear your share of life's common burden unless by doing so you really do make yourself and your friends richer and reduce the load you carry; and it certainly seems silly to do that if you are obliged to place yourself in your victim's hands politically and live your life as he might have liked to live his, in order to salve your conscience and keep the nation from becoming polarized. But it is questionable, in any case, whether a man can free himself by shifting his burdens to others and adding his chains to theirs. The spiritual losses may offset the material gain. Ironically or not, however, they do not seem to. "As I would not be a slave, so I would not be a slaveowner," Abraham Lincoln said; he was born too late to have said it to Thomas Jefferson, who was, and whose contribution to and appreciation of liberty fully matched Lincoln's own and was far more amply expressed. That being a slaveowner flawed his vision of liberty we cannot doubt; whether it damaged his spirit more than the leisure his slaves afforded him sustained it, or more than a sense of poverty among his peers would have, I do not know. It is even possible that our conception of liberty in its highest forms, being derived from ancient Greek and therefore slave-owning sources, is intolerably tainted to begin with. It is certainly elitist. But I find it hard to imagine that Socrates was greatly confused about the nature of liberty; or that Pericles would have welcomed his execution as—thirty years after Pericles' death and in an Athens grown far more populist—the Oligarchy so enthusiastically did. Slavery is not the ideal social foundation for a noble conception of human liberty. But it has, on occasion, been made to serve.

CHAPTER FOUR

Class Conflict and Moral Indignation

One of the more perplexing difficulties in discussing social conflict in terms that go beyond the purely descriptive and attempt to make some value judgment about what is taking place is how to evaluate the role of the victim. Apologists for established social systems usually blame the victim for what happens to him. People on welfare should have been thriftier and worked harder; juveniles ought not to have antagonized the police or school authorities; people who get busted didn't have to use drugs or keep bad company in the first place, and so on. An especially disturbing way of putting the blame on the victim—discounting his rights in advance—is by what civil-rights lawyers call "the heckler's veto." Boys can't wear their hair long in school, or pupils can't wear pro-Arab buttons or peace buttons or whatever the majority feels strongly against, because other students would beat them up; if someone does and they do, the victim is punished for incitement. For years a "heckler's veto" argument was effectively used to maintain racial discrimination in employment: "We'd love to hire them, but the other men wouldn't work with them."

Critics of society, correspondingly, are likely to see the victim of social forces as innocent or at least passive and helpless, and concentrate their derogation on the institutions that victimize him. Even this approach may result, though more subtly, in putting the blame on the victim; because it defines his deviance as the problem, even though it attributes his difficulties to the social response he evokes rather than to his innate deficiencies. The most sympathetic study of homosexuality or of the black community still acquiesces by its choice of topic to the dominant view which holds that these constitute deviance; such studies seldom take account of the social dynamics and distribution of power that cause these groups to be stigmatized initially.[1]

Generally speaking, the more radically critical of society an analysis is, the less it will blame the victims of social forces for their plight and the more it will blame society's more powerful members and institutions and vested interests. To many readers, therefore, this book must seem an exception and a disagreeable one. I have been radically critical and indeed contemptuous of the institutions of industrial society. Yet, I have been, on the whole, considerably more hostile to the values, folkways, and political roles of the mass of that society's members than I have toward its elites who are held to be much more powerful and presumably bear much more responsibility for the abuses and barbarities I condemn.

There are several reasons for my attitude of which I am conscious, as well as others, no doubt, of which I am not conscious and will therefore omit from this discussion. The first reason is purely structural. Most of the systematic oppression directed against what people of my generation, race and class conceive of as individual liberty has been imposed by governments that were formally democratic and regimes that were incontestably popular. The Soviet Union *requires* its citizens to vote in elections. Hitler came into office by constitutional means and would apparently have been returned to power by any plebiscite that might have been held in Germany until his military defeat. And in the great functioning democracies, as I have argued, already candidates consistently seek and *achieve* office by appealing to the most mean-spirited and punitive motives of men. Open, generous and expressive candidates are defeated, if their party caucuses are careless enough to let them get on the ballot. Indeed, they rarely do.

The usual explanation for this continuing state of affairs is, of course, that the people are misled by propaganda, driven or manipulated by need and insecurity, given no true options at the polls, faced with issues too complex for anyone but a specialist to understand, and so on. And all this is true. But the fact that it is true cannot be used to absolve the people from responsibility for what happens when they are the source of authority in the state. It can be used as an argument against continuing to allow them to have that authority, and this is the argument used to justify *coups d'état* by dictators and military juntas who, ironically, find nevertheless that popularity comes easily in the wake of success; elections are the least of their problems. But if one rejects coups d'état and absolutism in favor of democratic government, then the people are responsible, whether or not they are competent to exercise that responsibility. And, being responsible, they may be judged, along with the rulers they suffer to abuse them and empower to abuse others. However pitiable their own lots may be, the poor whites of Texas and the blue collar workers of Detroit must be held responsible, by anyone who defends the democratic state in principle, for what was done to the peasants of Indochina. To refuse to hold them responsible for what they have endorsed is to deny them exactly the dignity as persons that citizenship in a democracy is supposed to confer.

This does not mean that they must or should be punished for what the state has done; the state and its people are far too much absorbed in punishment and mutual recrimination already. But it does mean that they suffer a certain moral diminution compared to those they permitted to be victimized and even as compared to their fellow citizens who attempted to resist the predacity of the state. To their destiny, less attention need be paid. This may seem an inexcusably smug thing to say about one's fellow-Americans, but it would probably seem fair enough to say that Alexandr Solzhenitsyn is worth more than all the members of the bureaucratic apparatus that persecuted him. The issue is the same, except that the Soviet conservative assisting his government to torment those it defined as its adversaries had, indeed, a great deal to fear had he dissented. The sharpshooters of the Ohio National Guard had very little to fear. Leave them to heaven; but mark them lower than any chariot can swing.

The conception of liberty as rooted in the will of the people has lost, it seems to me, whatever historical relevance it once had. It is no longer even the stuff of myth, effectively reminding those who share a culture of its worthier aspirations. The idea that it could be is simply a political error. The association between liberty and democracy arose, I have argued earlier, because the bourgeois freedoms were conducive to technological development and expanded economic opportunity. And at this point in time, as the idiom of the new men puts it, authoritarian governments foster economic development precisely because the cards are stacked in their favor. It is easier for them to deal with America, or IT&T, or the Politburo, or whatever one chooses to call it, for deciding which is which has gotten to be like trying to decide whether one of those "ambiguous" pictures in a first-year psychology textbook is a vase, or two people kissing. Henry Kissinger, it is widely reported, prefers to deal with authoritarian governments, and is most reluctant to lose the convenience they afford him "just because the people of Chile are irresponsible." It is easier partly because authoritarian governments are now headed by people who find what we may roughly—though not, of course, violently—call "the American way" congenial, and who have, in most cases, been helped to power because their affinity for it was recognized. Those in whom no such affinity was recognized, like Mohammed Mossadecq or George McGovern, are judged too unstable to be trusted in high office and are cut down to size by the forces at hand. What these forces are is comparatively unimportant: it may be direct or covert intervention by the CIA or the "plumbers"; it may be bad media coverage and the withholding of funds supplied to opponents; it undoubtedly includes a natural though self-destructive revulsion on the part of a constituency which is already committed at heart to expanded economic opportunity at whatever cost in exploitation of their country's expendable resources. It does not even matter whether the candidate is in fact good enough to merit widespread distrust. George McGovern, after all, had done what was necessary to maintain a successful political career for many years, during which he had often proved no friend to liberty. But, by comparison, he surely looked like one.

It cannot be denied, however, that the net effect is to associate authoritarian take-over with the burgeoning of a consumer-oriented middle class—and, in the 1970s, a middle class of consummate and intemperate vulgarity, hostile to liberty rather than in certain respects devoted to it. Chile and Brazil now look more prosperous than ever before, to people accustomed to modern modes of prosperity. In Chile, the middle class now has access to consumer goods, and breathes easily again. Among the poor and former intellectuals, breathing has become less common.

This net result has been a twofold bind on liberty in states of the capitalist order. The kinds of men who come to power in such states are perhaps less likely than ever before in history to have any taste or even tolerance for freedom. And their supporting cadres in the rising middle-class and expanding bureaucracies associate governmental coercion with economic opportunity, which they greatly prefer to liberty. The classic bourgeoisie, though equally avaricious, thought liberty and economic expansion complemented each other. Hence the pathetic and irritating absurdity of that transitional figure, the conservative American farmer, fancying himself a fanatical devotee of free enterprise and an enemy of collectivism, while insisting on government price supports and protective tariffs. His successors in later generations, dealing directly with or finding themselves a part of the government bureaucracy, are unlikely to persist in this inconsistency. Nor are the physicians of twenty years hence, lucratively ensconced in a greatly expanded public health organization, likely to persist in their resistance to the government funding which protects them from the buffets of fortune. They will not define this as "socialized medicine." Freedom for them will be a dirty word for what consumers used to use to get at them.

In the socialist countries and the third world, the idea that the state must provide its citizens with structural protection against the state itself—or the will of the majority which it mobilizes—does not even arise.

Yet one is left with a political heritage, embodied in representative institutions, which continually compels one to behave as if the people were indeed the guardians of liberty, and of their own interests. They guard neither. On the other hand, the elites, at their worst, have at least the virtue of acting in their own interests. They are usually ruthless and often vicious, but rarely punitive and spiteful—certainly, not to the point of ruining their own chances in order to keep somebody else down. Major corporations thus avoid price wars; even competition has been "phased out" of the economy so far as corporate tactics make this possible, in the interest of optimum exploitation of whatever—or whomever—there is to exploit. "Spite," Paul Goodman once observed, "is the vitality of the powerless." The mortality, too. The powerful can afford civility.

There remain, to be sure, the most culpable of all, men who already possess ample means and power but who seek to obtain even more by encouraging the ressentiment of the masses and offering it legitimacy. Whatever harm may have been done by the Chase Manhattan Bank and associated Rockefeller interests in supporting counterinsurgency in underdeveloped countries and ripping off resources that might otherwise have been reserved for public development, it seems to me that a moral abyss separates David Rockefeller from his brother Nelson. A business man who deploys his power and wealth so as to continually increase both, and who defines the effects of his policies on the society and environment he exploits as progress, may do great harm. But not, it seems to me, evil. His actions are thoroughly consistent ethically and ideologically with his actual relationship to the means of production; Marx himself couldn't ask more than that. However, a man who seeks political power at the polls by offering his constituents the pleasure of having young people sentenced to life imprisonment for "drug abuse" and who, as governor, maintained his law-'n'-order image and his political appeal by refusing to intervene in the massacre perpetrated by the armed force he had sent to Attica State Prison—and who subsequently refused to help the families of the victims obtain the measure of justice that still eludes them—such a man is really something else.

The one advantage, among many obvious dangers, of having as head of state a person who is independently very rich and powerful is that he will presumably be less easily moved by base attempts to influence him. Though he may be a tyrant himself, he will less easily serve as a conduit for the tyranny of others. Yet, during the congressional hearings which led to Mr. Rockefeller's confirmation as Vice-President, he mentioned—apparently somewhat testily, as if any reasonably sophisticated politician should have seen this for himself—that he couldn't afford to come to Attica if that meant the distinct probability of being seen on national TV looking ineffective in a situation that was out of control. Thus he offered no opposition to the violence of the prison personnel, which he appeared to endorse, or the vicious hostility of the townspeople of Attica toward the wretched prisoners who provide the community with virtually its sole *raison d'être*. No party hack who had clawed his way to the governor's mansion as the penultimate goal of his ambition could have attached more importance to protecting his image. Nelson Rockefeller may be well suited to become the ultimate President of the United States.

One cannot be elected to office except by offering the people what at least a plurality of them want. Success at the polls depends on—among other things—the candidate's ability to present to the voters an image of social and political reality that they find acceptable, and an undertaking to deal with that reality in ways that they find appealing. Whether reality is in fact anything like what the candidate says it is may be quite unimportant, although the question is not negligible. Campaigning for national office in a democratic mass society involves hazards not unlike those encountered in trying to write a best-selling novel. The author who *believes* the picture he is trying to popularize is likely to lose his readers through bathos and sentimentality; the writer who attempts to patronize them by telling tales he is too clever to believe himself is even more likely to antagonize them. Success requires a special quality of mind, not the highest.

The themes that best-selling novels—or even better, since representative of a far more inclusive public and a larger capital investment, popular television shows—present do certainly reveal a lot about the prevailing moral climate, the anxieties, and the kinds of satisfaction sought by the people in a society. The winter 1973–74 television season was impacted with police dramas, most of which took the view that what policemen did was in defense of law-'n'-order, even—indeed, especially—when it violated the laws which protect the rights of accused persons—particularly drug offenders. A spate of similar films was also notable. One, *Serpico,* the most ambitious of all, dealt with police corruption tellingly but in a way that suggested that the honest cop-hero was a fool to have expected anything else, and knew it. A detective story classic, Raymond Chandler's *The Long Goodbye,* was readapted for 1973 to make the same point and in the 1973 version the honest cop was deprived of the heroic if quixotic status Chandler had given him. The cynicism of the fucked is likewise the political defense mechanism by which the American people protect themselves from having to do anything about Watergate; ultimately, it's the Ellsbergs and the Weickers who are made to look like oddballs, even when they win.[2]

This is an important point, because it contradicts a premise that is basic to the democratic process and that, indeed, appears to have been true of democratic polity until quite recently: the premise that abuses of public power or public trust were likely to be sharply corrected once revealed. The value imputed to a free press is largely inferred from this premise, and if the premise has become false, the fundamental servomechanism on which democratic societies depend for self-correction has become dysfunctional. In the late summer of 1973, when the Senate Watergate Committee was the most publicized—though not necessarily the most popular—daytime show on TV, news stories about public reaction often suggested that the public was responding with shock and depression, even with anger. There were solemn questions about whether either the presidency or the President could be saved. Now Mr. Ford has replaced Mr. Nixon, and the risk does not appear to be quite what it was thought to have been, though President Ford's speed in pardoning Mr. Nixon ended the euphoria his installation ought never to have aroused. Among the educated, urban middle class, there was no "firestorm" this time. As any fool can plainly see, the system sure works.

But there are spectacles—live, staged or taped—that the public does respond to and endorse. Political success is much facilitated by identifying one of these public cravings and developing and exploiting the underlying anxieties and the prevailing definitions of the social problem, so that one may cast oneself as the mythic hero who promises to resolve them. Public figures in quest of power have always found it useful to exploit prevailing myths, for it is the nature of myths both to dramatize conflict—psychic or social—and to conceal that conflict's real dynamism, thus insuring that policies based on myth will not actually remedy the situation they dramatize. The day the boulder stays at the top of the hill, Sisyphus is out of office.

Despite their apparent rationalism, modern liberal societies provide an especially fertile field for the cultivation of political prominence by epic struggle against circumstances perceived as threatening to the public welfare, because such societies define their difficulties as problems to be solved. This deprives their myths of tragic dignity and reduces Sisyphus to the stature of Dean Acheson, doomed perpetually to lose China to, as it was then thought, the Russians. But defining the tragic circumstances of life as problems to be solved does make it possible for astute politicians to make careers out of trying to solve them. Some of these seem to provide endless opportunity: who could have thought that the menace of world Communism would end with the American and Soviet leaders sympathetically recognizing one another as burdened with the common maladies of senescent authority; and that the people of both countries would abandon their accustomed hostilities in favor of détente without any embarrassment at the mischief they had supported through thirty years of red-baiting and revisionist-hunting, as the case might be? Who could have thought John Edgar Hoover a mortal man? Other hardy perennials among social problems include crime-in-the-streets and drug abuse; still others are more protean. Juvenile delinquency is perceived as peculiarly malignant when it takes a politically active form; but the young, like the poor, are always with us, and almost always despised.

There is not the slightest chance that any of these "problems" will ever be solved by the measures for dealing with them that are politically expedient; for they are merely epiphenomena of more fundamental social conflicts. And they cannot be redefined and discussed by major political candidates in terms that would reveal where the real difficulties lie, for this would require a more radical critique of the society than any large segment of the electorate would support—or than the candidate could get campaign funds or party support to pursue. The very fact that politicians must accept and promote a formulation of social problems that so distorts the underlying dynamics as to make any real assessment of it impossible simply means that the popular conception itself becomes the problem, and usually a more serious problem than the one to which it refers. Communism has never been of any importance in the United States either as a problem or as a possible solution; but the destructive efforts of American leaders and its people to root out Communism damaged the nation in ways from which it will probably never recover.

Meanwhile, the threat of Communism vanished with its political utility, though no fundamental change in the Soviet system has occurred to make it more attractive.

The widespread use of marijuana and psychedelic drugs should be defined as a problem if—and only if—one assumes that keeping people socialized to a life of guilty and effortful striving is essential to the welfare of America. It is also a problem if you are an official charged with the responsibility for that socialization—as schoolkeepers are. If you are a law-enforcement official ever vigilant for newly reified clienteles, it is an opportunity.

The fuel shortage certainly constitutes a problem of some kind, and a serious one. But what is its nature? The shortage appears to be due primarily to the greed and power of large oil companies. These companies also control both the development of alternative energy sources and the government agencies designed to control *them;* and these companies planned production and development in such a way as to maximize short-term profits without serious regard to community needs. It is possible that Nelson Rockefeller or some other Republican candidate will, accordingly, develop a campaign emphasizing the need for public control of these corporations; but it is not likely. This, of course, leaves the field wide open for the Democrats. The American people might, conceivably, accept this formulation enthusiastically, which is one reason no major party is likely to risk proffering it. On the whole, however, I doubt that public control of oil companies could be made the basis of a successful political appeal in the United States, as it doubtless could in England. As I have previously argued, most Americans are socialized to regard any enterprise as a source of economic opportunity rather than as a way of meeting a human need; like blood, oil is a *shtick,* and the American dream is of striking it, striking it rich. The rich are envied, but the opportunity to get rich—easily if possible—is sacred.

On the other hand, an even more fundamental interpretation of the fuel crisis is the one that is basic to the environmentalist position: that the society has evolved in ways that make it insupportably dependent on the internal combustion engine and on private transportation and that the most effective and lasting attack on the problem would be to phase out the private automobile. The validity of this argument seems self-evident, especially in Chinese; and it is, of course, possible to be elected President without carrying either Michigan or California. Its adoption as a plank in the platform of either major party in the 1976 elections would, however, astonish me.

I have cited these capsule formulations of the fuel shortage as elementary illustrations of the way explanations of a social problem and proposals for attacking it may be influenced by purely political factors without regard for the more complex realities that are usually involved. As in psychological explanations of human behavior, what is repressed or distorted is almost certain to be far more significant than what is publicly avowed. The fuel shortage, however, has not as yet evoked such deeply and systematically irrational public responses as certain other familiar putative social crises have. It is these irrational—or in a social as well as psychological sense *unbalanced*—responses that become institutionalized in forms like the FBI and its attendant apparatus of surveillance which paralyzed the entire left side of the American body politic in a series of grievously insulting strokes. And it is precisely their irrationality that most fully reveals the social conflicts that underlie them.

I wish now to examine the peculiar ways in which certain very disturbing social conditions have recently become defined and institutionalized as official social problems. Each of these conditions is truly distressing; but the institutions that deal with them lie about what is really happening. They mislead by their very existence. Indeed, it is their social *function* to mislead, just as a neurotic ritual serves to spare an individual unbearable insights even as it reveals what is going on to an observer with a less vested interest in misunderstanding it. Societies are even less tolerant than individuals of divergent interpretations of the reasons for their bizarre behavior. Such interpretations evoke furious hostility without modifying the behavior. Like neurotic individuals, social institutions repeat their ritualized responses over and over, with minor variations. Behavior that expresses a continuing conflict in the social or human organism is not abandoned because it does not work; but it vanishes quite mysteriously when, as a result of changes elsewhere in the system, the conflict is abolished, as by détente.

While institutionalized denials of reality may be successful in suppressing some of the more disturbing symptoms that would otherwise occur, the result is always to make the society more rigid and uptight, and less effective in responding to its genuine difficulties. But there are always secondary gains to the repressive institutions themselves, which provide an enormous number of people with a *raison d'être* which would otherwise be far from obvious, as well as opportunities on the side. During the Indochina war—an irrational ritual if ever there was one—these secondary gains accrued to the entire American economy, which managed for years to export the fiscal burden to the rest of the world in the form of inflation. And police forces, with their apparatus of payoffs and licensed informers, may breed more crime than they suppress and certainly determine whether a particular, possibly unlawful, act ends up counting as a crime at all.

In the long run, it is usually impossible even to say that these conflict-repressive institutions don't work—any more than one can say that neurotic mechanisms don't work. They don't solve the problem they are manifestly intended to solve—that's for sure—but they do help make the society what it is today. And who is to say that this is not what most of the people in the society wanted all along?

The inner conflict expressed by neurotic behavior is always composed of elements which reaffirm adherence to a publicly accepted principle, in opposition to other elements that continuously deny and attack that adherence. The behavior that results remains within the limits of public acceptability, though perhaps by a narrow margin. If it does not, the neurotic defenses are deemed to have failed and the person who displays it is redefined as a patient or offender and sequestered. This sometimes—but very rarely—happens to social agencies that violate their victim's civil rights too egregiously, as when police execute an especially brutal bust on the wrong people.

But, even exceptionally annoying and destructive behavior goes un-challenged when it is accepted as demonstrating devotion to law-'n'-order.

Social crises become institutionalized expressions of social conflict; they assume bizarre, repetitious, and self-destructive character when powerful elements of that social conflict are taboo. In democratic mass societies, severe social conflict is usually a form of class conflict. In such societies, however, the expression of class feeling is taboo. The expression of upper-class feelings is especially forbidden. Hostile and exclusionary attitudes may be freely expressed by poor blacks, and are regarded as in humorous bad taste but all in the family if ex-pressed by poor whites. If expressed by well-to-do and well-educated whites, these attitudes are intolerably racist, and probably unlawful. Oscar Wilde, André Gide, and Norman Douglas, if they were alive today, would find that social tolerance had taken a paradoxical turn. Their life-styles would still be greeted with stony disapproval; they would be ostracized, but no longer for quite the same reasons. Peder-asty might be tolerated; slumming definitely no longer is, or searching for well-developed lads in underdeveloped countries. The Algerian government won't even let you blow pot.

The fuel crisis could very well become institutionalized in the manner suggested by this analogy. If it did, its most probable form would be a struggle in which ecologists, after some initial success in linking environmental preservation to the need to reduce sharply in-dustrial activity and especially the use of the internal combustion en-gine, were neutralized by sustained counterattack. This would seek to define them as lazy, self-indulgent hippies who were attempting to destroy local initiatives toward economic growth and opportunities for employment in order to retain recreational areas for the use of a leisure class and as sites for their lascivious communes. Demoralized by the charge of elitism, the environmentalists, if they may be judged by past performance, would probably retreat in disarray, vainly and unconvincingly asserting that a habitable environment is necessary to *everyone's* survival, which is true but not relevant. A forthright admission of elitism, and an effort to enlist the forces of reac-tion—some of them quite wealthy and powerful—on the side of eco-nomic forbearance might prove more effective than flailing about with the Club of Rome.

Just this sort of conflict continues, sporadically but with malice unabating, in areas like northern New Mexico. There, a magnificent and relatively unspoiled countryside has attracted throngs of people from "the counterculture" who arouse the occasionally lethal hatred of the local Hispano-American populace. *La Raza,* at least, doesn't mind being racist.

But for the present, in North America, clearer and less complex examples may be drawn from two other instances in which social conflict has already assumed well-established and persistent institutional form. Both these are characterized by public postures of self-righteous concern that becomes intermittently hysterically punitive. Neither attempts to deal with the underlying sources of conflict. Both have the perfectly predictable side effect of reversing usual social class roles by legitimating attacks of lower-status cadres on higher-status victims, in the name of the public interest. I refer to (1) airport security programs and (2) narcotics laws and their enforcement.

The public principle which the airport security program affirms is manifestly unarguable. Hijacking is wrong, especially if, as often happens, passengers or crew are killed in the process. But there is a hidden agenda concealed in the security program, which cannot be openly asserted and which distorts its operation. In consequence it can never be abandoned until there is a sharp shift in political climate, both domestic and international. Whether effective or not, it is certainly useful to many people.

What may not be asserted is that the airport security program has a basically political function. The reason this cannot be discussed is not that its political objectives are illegitimate—they are wholly legitimate—but that within American's prevailing ideology they cannot be identified as political. Doing so would legitimate the opposition; and it has long been American policy not merely to oppose political insurgency but to dismiss it as criminal.

Concretely, burning peaceable civilians to death with incendiary bombs as they attempt to go about the business of their lives is an intolerable outrage. It is an outrage if it occurs in the cabin of an airliner on the airfield in Rome. It is equally an outrage if it occurs in an Indochinese village. The former outrage is defined by Americans as criminal terrorism; the latter, of course, as an act of war, even though none has been declared. But the terrorists, too, have a serious political purpose; and the architects of the Indochina war are not highly qualified to judge either its morality or its futility.

The illegitimacy of the terrorists is further dramatized by picturing the commercial airline as an innocent, or at least private, enterprise operating miles above politics. This picture is, unfortunately, false. Terrorism is outrageous by definition; but airlines are not politically neutral. They have served for many years as paramilitary arms of the governments that license or operate them, available, when needed, for "dirty tricks." The violent and unlawful use of commercial aviation for political purposes became a matter of public record in 1960 with the abduction of a drugged Adolf Eichmann aboard an El Al Israel flight from Buenos Aires to Tel Aviv. There is a certain irony in the fact that the Government of Israel and its official airline were, within the decade, to become most intimately involved in terrorism through civil aviation, both as victim and attacker. Pan American World Airways, nominally a private corporation, has perhaps performed fewer in-flight services for the United States Government, but it has rather routinely provided cover for CIA operatives serving ostensibly as members of the airline's office staffs in foreign cities.

It is true that the wave of aircraft hijackings in North America that finally led to the establishment of the airport security program were, in a narrow sense, apolitical; they were certainly not the expression of larger world conflict. Political terrorists directly disrupted civil aviation in North America only by setting an example that free enterprise could not resist—an outcome that must have amused them. North American hijackers most often operated in the honored tradition of Bonnie and Clyde, demanding ransom; if they headed for Cuba it was in the hope of finding asylum as fellow-outlaws in the eyes of the United States, not through political sympathy. And this kind of hijacking has, in fact, yielded to the airport security program; its perpetrators have neither the organization, the militancy, nor the sympathetic refuge awaiting them that such operations require.

The airlines cannot, in any case, tolerate hijacking. But by refusing to acknowledge it as a politically serious revolutionary act when it is that, by treating it instead as wanton violence, they have invested the security program with an air of pompous moral grandeur that has made it more offensive than it need have been. Their security guards become, in effect, the only participants in the scene with an acknowledged moral purpose. This has made them agents of the social superego as well as of the ego, which leads, as in the individual psyche, to an expansion of their function beyond its rational limits.

Shortly after the airport security program became effective, security guards began busting travelers for carrying contraband—usually drugs—that was discovered when their baggage was searched. This zeal, however, placed the airline and airport companies as well as their passengers in legal jeopardy. The Fourth Amendment to the United States Constitution, which provides that "no Warrants shall issue, but upon probable cause . . . particularly describing the place to be searched, and the persons or things to be seized" appears to make such arrests unlawful. The security program itself, as the American Civil Liberties Union has pointed out, is probably unconstitutional, since the fact that a person wants to board a commercial flight does not constitute probable cause for believing that he intends to hijack the flight and is carrying a weapon for that purpose.

It would seem imperative, then, that the airlines should have made it clear to their functionaries that they are conducting a program designed to insure the safety of air transport—and only that; it is not a program of law enforcement. The airlines should have recognized from the beginning that airport checks simply must not be conducted in a way that permits their employees to dramatize themselves as assistant or associate G-men. The clarity of the U. S. Constitution in restricting unlawful searches and seizures, and the political salience of the drug-abuse issue, which makes it a temptation no ambitious or merely sadistic security guard can be expected to refuse voluntarily, made conflict and litigation inevitable.

Governments and airlines must spend billions of dollars per year, anyway, for personnel and equipment whose function is to insure the safety of air transport against the vicissitudes of climate. It is perfectly reasonable that they should extend their programs and facilities to deal with serious new hazards arising from social and political as well as meteorological tensions. This would not, of itself, constitute an aggressively counterinsurgent posture—only a praiseworthy resolution not to allow oneself to be blown up. However, the security systems that protect the passenger from storms, poor visibility and crowded airspace do not expand to fill unrelated political space.

Why, then, could not the airline companies have resolved the problem so as to protect their passengers from both hijacking and harassment, by invoking Serpico's Law: by ordering their security guards to mind their own business (which is the detection of devices that might be used in hijacking) and to ignore anything else a passenger might be carrying? The argument that an employer has no authority to demand that his employees ignore violations of the law is not sufficient to explain their failure to do so; for corporations, social institutions, like hospitals or prisons, manufacturers and businessmen who provide direct services to consumers, landlords—virtually any kind of business or bureaucracy, in fact—expect such reticence of their employees as a matter of course, and usually get it without even having to place themselves in the embarrassing position of having to ask for it. The normal conduct of business, public or private, depends—as it doubtless has always done except during those brief periods when societies find themselves in the uncomfortable grip of revolutionary, puritanical zeal—on the collusion of employees in the extralegal policies set by the policymakers of their organizations, and even on their willingness to take the rap for their superiors if detected. The universal acceptance of this arrangement as the way of the world is what has prevented the Watergate affair from having as much shock value as might have been expected, while obscuring the fundamental moral and political issues that it raised.

But the approach to the problem created by aircraft hijacking could not be limited by the usual devices of political pragmatism, because it created precisely the kind of situation that dramatizes and provides scope for intense and class-related social conflict. Most Americans have still never taken a commercial flight. Flying remains the mode of transportation primarily of the upper-middle classes. Therefore, the airport security check establishes a situation in which, generally speaking, higher-status individuals are subjected to intrusion by lower-status security personnel, reversing the usual vector of social constraint. Airline passengers going through security are a classic example of members of an elite in a situation in which democratic principles require them to submit cheerfully to an irritating intrusion. Norman Rockwell, if he were alive today, would have had a pictorial subject suited to his fancy; just imagine the picture of a portly, well-dressed first-class passenger whose briefcase yields sandwiches and underwear, to the ill-suppressed smiles and the security guard. Airline travelers, moreover, are especially vulnerable to harassment: they have to make their flight and haven't time to argue with officials; unless they are just beginning their journey they are in a strange city where they are unlikely to have easy access to a lawyer, or to funds.

For their part, security personnel have their own role and function to maximize; this is their shtick. There now exists a considerable cadre of specialists in interrogation and control, who move in and out of a succession of posts in the FBI or RCMP, insurance companies, state and municipal detective forces, private security agencies and the security divisions of private corporations. The invasion of privacy has become an established profession which, like all professions, evolves its own values and folkways, partly in response to the kind of work it does, partly reflecting the personality traits that lead people to choose such employment, partly because of the social class from which the profession predominantly recruits. To expect airline security people not to stage and execute "busts" is to ask them to violate their professional code; it deprives them of status among their peers in other law-enforcement positions that provide more opportunity for aggressive performance than the small number of airline passengers actually carrying weapons can possibly afford.

Airline companies, in any case, are unlikely to disapprove deeply of the zeal of their security agents. They partake of a far more authoritarian tradition than their carefully fostered consumer-oriented image reveals. The quasi-naval titles and uniforms assigned the captain and crew, the sexiest definition of the stewardesses' role, the ruthless campaign by which airlines in America hunted out and discharged employees suspected of homosexual tendencies after World War II, as well as their willingness, already alluded to, to help their government with its dirty tricks—all this denotes an ambience in which the law-enforcement mentality fits very neatly. Smilin' Jack is no civil libertarian, nor was Eddie Rickenbacker.

Yet, even so potent a combination of factors predisposing security guards to a broadly inquisitorial conception of their function would hardly have been effective had there not become established in America the climate of hysterical self-righteousness associated with the "drug abuse" problem. This climate promises law-enforcement officials enormous opportunities for both political rewards and vindictive satisfaction. Even if the airline companies had sought to induce their security guards not to arrest or otherwise harass passengers for violations of the law that posed no threat of hijacking, they would not in most cases have succeeded in persuading them to overlook violations of drug laws. No matter what else they may condone, twentieth-century security agents, like seventeenth-century clergymen, will not tolerate "possession," and no airline corporation would risk being publicly accused of having suggested that they should. To understand the baleful vigor of the conflict surrounding "the nonmedical use of drugs" (in the rather sly phrase of the LeDain Commission in Canada) is to understand just how oppression is rooted in the very tissue of industrial democracy.

Defining substances that alter states of consciousness as *contraband* is a twentieth-century phenomenon in America. Until the passage of the Harrison Act in 1914, there was no federal legislation forbidding the sale, use or possession of any drug; opiates could be, and were, freely available for purchase and use—laudanum, for example, was sold in saloons in New York City—without becoming popular or being perceived as serious threats to society. Five years later, the Volstead Act, which established an enforcement apparatus for the recently ratified Eighteenth Amendment, was passed over President Wilson's veto, adding ethanol to the list of contraband substances until its repeal in 1933. Marijuana, which until recently was used nearly exclusively by poor, usually black or Latin-American people among themselves, was not included among the substances whose use was regulated by the Harrison Act; it remained largely beneath the attention of the law. By 1930, however, sixteen states had passed laws regulating or forbidding its use, though it retained a limited and unimportant place in the United States Pharmacopoeia and could be lawfully prescribed by physicians as an analgesic or euphoriant. (It still can, but the harassment and legal requirements provided in the federal Marijuana Tax Act of 1937 are so entangling as to make such use impractical; pharmaceutical preparations of marijuana are no longer available in the United States.)

One of the peculiarities of federal laws concerning contraband is that they present themselves as licensing or tax laws rather than as straightforward prohibitions, as state laws do. This is necessary, because the Constitution, designed by statesmen with good reason to be fearful of centralized authority and promulgated before modern police bureaucracies were developed (they are a nineteenth-century phenomenon), does not provide for a federal enforcement apparatus. It leaves law enforcement among the powers reserved to the states. Unlike Canada, for example, the United States cannot lawfully establish a federal police force—only a Bureau of Investigation which enjoys a remarkable degree of co-operation from local authorities. It can and does maintain, however, enforcement arms within the Department of the Treasury. This is why the Secret Service, which was established in 1865 to deal with counterfeiting, became the agency responsible for the protection of the President; there was no other general federal law-enforcement agency, with an active cadre of officers, who could function without regard to state jurisdiction. When the Sixteenth Amendment, authorizing federal income taxes, was adopted in 1913, the enforcement apparatus of the Treasury Department was, of course, enormously expanded.

The Treasury Department, in any case, enjoys certain manifest advantages as the locus of enforcement agencies, since the Bill of Rights is less effective in restricting its activities than it would be against ordinary police. The provisions of the Fourth Amendment are no impediment to the Internal Revenue Service, which operates under legislation requiring the citizen to keep and produce records on demand. The Internal Revenue Service maintains its own tax courts for the adjudication of disputes involving it; a demand for such records does not require the prior establishment of probable cause to suspect tax evasion, as normal searches do. And the range of disclosure routinely required of every taxpayer permits the establishment of a permanent and expanding intelligence network involving nearly every citizen; despite his constitutional privilege against self-incrimination, he cannot lawfully withhold information from it. Much of the opposition to the Sixteenth Amendment at the time it was introduced was, in fact, directed at its potential for invasion of privacy, rather than against the absurdly small tax bite it envisaged. The evidence that emerged during the Watergate hearings, which established that investigators in various branches of the federal government are routinely granted access to income records and that Presidents have frequently sought to use the Internal Revenue Service—with varying degrees of success—to harass their adversaries, shows this concern to have been prophetic.

The 1914 Harrison Act was designed to make full use of the Treasury Department's peculiar aptitudes for law enforcement. As the distinguished sociologist and specialist in the sociology of deviant subcultures Howard S. Becker has observed:

> The Harrison Act, for instance, was so drawn as to allow medical personnel to continue using morphine and other opium derivatives for the relief of pain and such other medical purposes as seemed to them appropriate. Furthermore, the law was carefully drawn in order to avoid running afoul of the constitutional provision reserving police powers to the several states. In line

with this restriction, the Act was presented as a revenue measure, taxing unlicensed purveyors of opiate drugs at an exorbitant rate while permitting licensed purveyors (primarily physicians, dentists, veterinarians and pharmacists) to pay a nominal tax. Though it was justified constitutionally as a revenue measure, the Harrison Act was in fact a police measure, and was so interpreted by those to whom enforcement was entrusted. One consequence of the passage of the Act was the establishment of the Treasury Department of the Federal Bureau of Narcotics in 1930.[3]

Why was it not established until fifteen years after the passage of the Harrison Act—fifteen years in which there seemed little evidence that the problem of narcotics addiction was getting out of hand, even in a United States deprived of lawful access to the euphoric drug of its choice, ethanol? The word "prohibition," indeed, referred only to ethanol, and efforts to evade the prohibition and institutionalize the means of evading it became the distinguishing mark of a decade of culture. As a public problem, narcotics were nowhere in 1930. Why, then, a Federal Bureau of Narcotics?

The answer to such a question must be speculative. Nevertheless, I shall suggest one that seems to me plausible, indeed. Administration of the Volstead Act had also been vested in the Commissioner of Internal Revenue, and implemented by a large and aggressive enforcement apparatus of "revenooers" and other federal agents. And by 1930, it was apparent that the Volstead Act was doomed and, as public law, already absurd. No portentous bureaucracy could be content to rest on so shaky a foundation; and within three years the act was null and void—the Eighteenth Amendment had yielded to the Twenty-first. Yet no narcotics problem of sufficient severity to justify the maintenance of so large an enforcement apparatus had impressed itself on the public mind. No social agency allows itself to flout Parkinson's Law, or to be truncated because the problem it has been set up to solve has become unimportant. When the Federal Bureau of Investigation had harassed the American Communist Party almost out of existence, its undercover agents continued to attend meetings even if no one else did, reporting, presumably, on one another's activities and preserving the Party as well as its own red squads from desuetude.

Whatever its motives may have been, there can certainly be no doubt that the Bureau of Narcotics, once established, took the lead in dramatizing the existence of a marijuana problem. Becker, a little further on in the passage just cited, documents this fact fully, largely from the bureau's own publications. From January 1925 through June 1935, *The Readers' Guide to Periodical Literature,* which indexes standard American journals of general interest, reports *no* articles on marijuana. From July 1935 to June 1937, four articles appeared; from July 1937 to June 1939, *seventeen.* The bureau had been urging the need to control marijuana since 1932.[4] In that year it urged adoption of a uniform state law restricting traffic in marijuana; it helped to draft the law.[5] In its next annual report the bureau noted that:

> Articles were prepared in the Federal Bureau of Narcotics, at the request of a number of organizations dealing with this general subject [uniform state laws] for publication by such organizations in magazines and newspapers. An intelligent and sympathetic public interest, helpful to the administration of the narcotics laws, has been aroused and maintained.[6]

And Becker notes that, of the seventeen articles on marijuana reported in the *Readers' Guide,* "ten either explicitly acknowledged the help of the Bureau in furnishing facts and figures or gave implicit evidence of having received help by using facts and figures that had appeared earlier, either in bureau publications or in testimony before the Congress on the Marijuana Tax Act."

Not until 1937 did the Bureau of Narcotics succeed in persuading the Congress it had labored so hard to arouse to pass the Marijuana Tax Act; as late as 1936 the bureau was still deploring the absence of federal legislation:

> In the absence of Federal Legislation on the subject, the States and cities should rightfully assume the responsibility of providing vigorous measures for the extinction of this lethal weed, and it is therefore hoped that all public-spirited citizens will earnestly enlist in the movement urged by the Treasury Department to adjure intensified enforcement of the marijuana laws.[7]

But the "Marijuana Tax Act of 1937" (as the act styles itself officially in its eighteenth and final section), when finally passed, left little for the bureau to desire. It is, as its title indicates, yet another of the acts in which criminal law—in this case Draconian in character—is presented as a revenue measure, and remains today perhaps the finest flower of its kind. It is so designed as to negate the Constitutional provision against self-incrimination. Though the annual tax fees required under the act are moderate, indeed, ranging from one dollar a year for growers of marijuana through three dollars for dealers or people who give it away, to twenty-four dollars for importers, any violation of its provisions carries a fine of two thousand dollars and/or a prison term of five years. Those provisions require a record of every transaction—giving a toke to a friend is a transaction—and also a record of the amount harvested or otherwise received every three months, and other details set forth in regulations the act authorized the Commissioner of the Bureau of Narcotics to establish. The first of these regulations, promulgated with the act, covers "sixty-odd pages of administrative and enforcement procedures . . . and call for a maze of affidavits, depositions, sworn statements, and constant Treasury Department police inspection in every instance that marijuana is bought, sold, used, raised, distributed, given away, and so on. Physicians who wish to purchase the one-dollar tax stamp so that they might prescribe it for their patients are forced to report such use to the Federal Bureau of Narcotics in sworn and attested detail, revealing the name and address of the patient, the nature of his ailment, the dates and amounts prescribed, and so on. If a physician for any reason fails to do so immediately, both he and his patient are liable to imprisonment and a heavy fine."[8]

Unlike physicians, narcotics agents, whether federal, state or local, are exempted from the act by one of its own provisions; necessarily, one would assume, considering the tactics of infiltration and surreptitious purchase by which arrests are usually made. The punitive thrust of the act, indeed, is not derived from the penalties provided in it, but from its usefulness in laying anyone who attempted to comply with its provisions open to prosecution by *state* authorities. By the time the Marijuana Tax Act of 1937 was passed, forty states had enacted a standard bill prepared by the Bureau of Narcotics which, unlike the Marijuana Tax Act, did make possession or use of marijuana felonious per se. The Marijuana Tax Act is unusual, if not unique, among the provisions of American statute law in licensing activities it is really designed to render felonious. Even the Harrison Act is not intended to—and does not—hamper the medical use of narcotics, while the Volstead Act expressly provided for availability of liquor on medical prescription.

Subsequent legislation has continued to add to the federal penalties for possession or sale of marijuana, while state courts, especially in

Texas, have sentenced dealers to terms of up to a thousand years, with the intent of preventing them from becoming eligible for parole during their lifetimes, as life sentences, of course, do not. Meanwhile, the absence of evidence that the "lethal weed" has, in fact, any harmful physical effects or lasting mental ones (and neither the seven-volume *Report of the Indian Hemp Drug Commission* issued in Simna in 1894, nor the exhaustively scientific study undertaken by the New York Academy of Medicine from 1938 to 1944 at Mayor La Guardia's instance,[9] was able to find such evidence) has not deterred the Bureau of Narcotics from continuing to press successfully for ever more extensive controls and Draconian penalties. Research that does not support the bureau position is attacked as socially irresponsible and the findings of such research are ignored. The United States has continued to press through the United Nations for a highly restrictive single convention on the use of marijuana, and it lobbies successfully for the enactment of more severe marijuana laws in other countries. And, it maintains networks of informers in marijuana-producing countries—even those where marijuana is legal—to insure the apprehension of any travelers who may carry it with them. How widespread the activities of these agents may be Dr. Timothy Leary can testify.

Reports of official governmental bodies that fail to support or contravene existing punitive policies with respect to marijuana have so far been dismissed as inconsequential. President Nixon announced in advance that he would ignore the recommendations of the thirteen-member National Commission on Marijuana and Drug Abuse, nine of whose members he had appointed, if it found marijuana to be harmless and recommended its legalization. On March 22, 1972, it did; and he did. In Canada, Parliament tabled the interim report of the LeDain Commission of Inquiry into the Non-Medical Use of Drugs, which recommended that marijuana be controlled through the Food and Drugs Acts rather than the Narcotics Control Act; this would largely have decriminalized the process. It has ignored the massively researched 1971 Report of the Committee on Youth to the Secretary of State (*It's Your Turn . . .*), whose 28th Recommendation calls for the legalization of "cultivation, sale, possession and use of cannabis" under government regulation and quality control, by men and women eighteen years old and over. This recommendation was greeted with derision and hostility in the Canadian media at the time. (The American National Commission had not gone so far; like the LeDain Commission, it had recommended legalizing only private use and possession, while continuing to prosecute dealers and accept the costs and risks involved in this compromise position.)

I have made this long excursion into the development of public policy with respect to marijuana because it provides an almost perfect key by which to gain access to the tensions underlying social control and the devices that lead to its achievement. There remains, however, the question of how the targets of social control are selected; and marijuana is again an unusually revealing case in point. For, even if we come to recognize the fury and vindictiveness associated with the idea of "drug abuse" in the public mind and public policy, there remains the question of what substances, under what circumstances, will be called a drug. It is not obvious that such a category need exist at all in the legal sense, since it is not obvious that the state should assume the right to control people's selection of and access to the substances whose physiological action they deem beneficial or desirable—though quality-control legislation seems obviously necessary. And, indeed, the intent of most drug legislation—which usually concerns substances incapable of giving anybody much pleasure but believed to possess some therapeutic value—is simply to keep us from treating our own illnesses, or as its proponents would prefer to put it, to vest health care in qualified physicians rather than leaving it to the initiative of the sick. That the existing monopoly on health care by a self-limited number of highly paid licensed specialists authorized, among other things, to legitimate drugs has proved to be conducive to optimum individual health care has itself become highly debatable; and without physicians to designate the circumstances and limits of their lawful use, there could be no drugs at all in the legal sense—just physiologically active substances on whose use one might, or might not, wish to seek professional advice.

But even if one agrees for the sake of argument that there are some physiologically active substances so dangerous and so seductive that the state should limit or even forbid access to them, the question of which substances they are is a social, not a medical, one. Toxicity is no criterion. It is not necessary to control the sale of poison to potential addicts—only its surreptitious administration to the unwary. In any case, one of the physiologically active substances subject to least legal control of sale or use—nicotine—is also one of the deadliest substances known, and a true, physiologically addictive alkaloid, chemically related to morphine as the active chemicals in cannabis are not. Another substance, likewise a true, physiologically addictive alkaloid, though of low toxicity, is caffeine, and it is subject to no legal controls at all. In fact, it is the active ingredient of the special beverages American teen-agers are supposed to drink as libations celebrating their groovy status—as well, of course, as of the coffee on which Occidentals now universally depend to keep them going. Yet coffee and chocolate were both treated as dangerous intoxicants for decades after their introduction into Europe. Coffeehouses were regarded as dens of iniquity before they became perceived as *gemütlich;* and even now they enjoy a special festive status in Central Europe that Chock Full o' Nuts is unlikely to achieve, even though it may sell better coffee.

Both nicotine and especially caffeine stimulate the nervous system strongly, and are valued for that effect. Under their influence, people feel more energetic and alert, and less fatigued: concentration on demanding tasks is improved, and those that are boring become more tolerable with a coffee break or a cigarette break. Nicotine stimulates the flow of adrenaline and raises the glucose level in the blood, providing added energy temporarily, as a snack would. However, it is much too poisonous to be eaten in any form and must be administered by smoking or chewing tobacco, so that its absorption is retarded by intact mucous membranes and incipient overdose avoided by the warning signs of shock—nausea and clammy sweating—which many smokers recall from their first cigar.

Minors are still forbidden by law to purchase tobacco in most states, as the stenciled notices on cigarette machines advise prospective purchasers. No attempt to enforce this law is made, despite the existence of evidence of danger to health severe enough to require a warning message on the package—evidence of which has never been adduced with respect to marijuana. But nicotine, like caffeine, facilitates behavior that is valued in the culture; cannabis, on the other hand impairs the power, or the will, of the user to concentrate on objects or tasks designated by others and makes mental functioning more associative and less linear and businesslike. Physiologically active substances that predispose people to behave in ways that are adaptive in their cultures are not regarded as drugs at all but as ingredients of foods or ceremonial libations. Coffee, in much of the world, and beer, especially among the working classes, are regarded as both.

Marijuana, moreover, like the much more dreaded and more powerful LSD, predisposes the user to intense inner experiences and even ecstatic states, which in the case of lifelong users of massive doses of hashish and more potent cannabis preparations resemble psychotic episodes. Indeed, functionally they *are* psychotic episodes: and this, too, is a social rather than a psychological judgment. The term psychotic, as R. D. Laing has argued in much of his work and demonstrated in *The Bird of Paradise,* is used to stigmatize a mental state acutely disturbing and dysfunctional to the routine conduct of life in production-oriented societies. Whether marijuana is dangerous or not, it is demonstrably *subversive* of the states of mind and social routines accepted as normal in modern industrial communities.

Traditional societies in which the use of cannabis has become customary often prohibit the use of ethanol as a dangerous drug, as in Islam and in parts of India. As an indication of the relationships between culture and the perception of substances as dangerous drugs, such societies tend to shift their prohibition from ethanol to cannabis as they become modernized. In part this is a consequence of political pressure from the United States in its efforts to bring about "the extinction of this lethal weed"; but it also reflects local shifts in the goals, customs and anxieties associated with modernization. India provides a particularly interesting example of this transition, which is still in progress as areas subject to "prohibition" in the Western sense, centered around Bombay, shrink while restrictions are being imposed on the use of cannabis, which has customarily been taxed and sold in government-licensed shops.

Even more striking and especially pertinent to the issues under discussion here is the way different castes have viewed the use of ethanol and cannabis in sections of India where caste distinctions still strongly affected behavior and custom, and where both substances were at least tolerated. *Brahmins,* the highest if not the most politically powerful caste, drink *bhang,* or cannabis tea, while abjuring alcohol. *Rajputs,* the caste from which rulers ("rajah") are drawn and who are traditionally warriors, womanizers and seekers after wealth, feel that *bhang* weakens and confuses them and they detest its use. They are also great meat eaters—Brahmins are vegetarian —and appear to have internalized the values and self-image of leaders of Houston society. "Besides the *Rajputs,* only the *Sudras* (the artisan castes) and the Untouchables—and not all of them—are accustomed to take meat and alcohol."[10]

Devotees of alcohol, then, are likely to be hostile and contemptuous toward cannabis and its users; and vice versa. But the hostile aggressiveness of the two groups of partisans will not be equal, and neither will their social class. Both ethanol and cannabis are euphoriants; they tend to evoke a feeling of relaxation, well-being and satisfaction in the user, though they may also leave him senseless and his euphoria may be converted to a "bummer" or a "mean drunk" or "tear jag" by factors that make him miserable. Both, however, are thought of as basically festive and pleasant in their effects; they are associated with loosening up and having whatever one defines as a good time. Users of both drugs will therefore tap the vast reservoirs of hostility and punitiveness derived from the repression and self-denial that make puritanism and industrial growth possible: users of both have been defined as felons by their sober and industrious fellow-citizens, though at different times and places. But the attitude of the alcohol user, and of the society that sanctions its use, will be infinitely harsher and more punitive toward the pothead than the cannabis user, and *his* society will be toward the drunk. Alcohol, notably, and in contrast to cannabis, tends to release aggression and forestall insight, to make those under its influence erratically sensitive to what they take to be slurs and insults, whereas cannabis increases self-absorption and detachment from the situation the user is in. The ritual of alcoholic excess includes, as a set piece, remorse and rededication to renewed effort and more aggressive and industrious action. One seeks, with abject intensity, to be welcomed back into the respectable fold on the morning after. But not on the morning after being stoned out of one's mind, when reality is likely to seem more clearly trivial than ever.

The marijuana user is thus something of a triple threat to the conventional drinker. He represents irresponsible joy and festivity, as drinkers do to their abstemious fellows. But he also represents voluptuous ease, a thoughtless and relaxed disdain for the work ethic and, finally, he is perceived as a member of a superior social class who is unlikely to have earned his position by industry and self-restraint. Or who, in any case, has come to disdain these virtues. He is likely, in short, to be a Brahmin—a pejorative term in America. It is frequently pointed out that the exceptional harshness of the penalties imposed on marijuana users under American law aroused no public complaint until pot spread to the middle class, unaccustomed as it was to being searched, beaten, or jailed; and this is true enough. But it should be further noted that the laws did not even exist until marijuana *began* to be used by members of the middle class or at least by those in "bohemian" subcultures, especially those associated with music. The first victims were black jazz musicians who had become successful before America was ready to tolerate blacks with superstar status.[11] As long as cannabis use was restricted to blacks and Latin Americans who were too poor and apparently wretched to arouse envy in the heart of a 1935 five-thousand-dollar-a-year bureaucrat, there was no problem. It helped, no doubt, to keep them in their place.

At the heart of the frenzy about drug abuse are fears of subversion and, even more corrosive in its effects on social bonds, envy. These are the emotions upon which the merchants of control play—overtly upon the first, covertly upon the second—to gain mass support for programs of enforcement and make them politically advantageous. The fears of subversion are real enough, since precisely those substances are proscribed as dangerous drugs which have physiological effects antagonistic to the traits of character esteemed by the society's dominant social classes. If any society truly devoted to Dionysian ecstasy and contemplation could exist, it would certainly forbid the sale of sedatives and persecute traffickers in Thorazine. But the role of envy in fueling intervention into the private behavior of individuals is somewhat more complex.

Its target will be offenders who commit what have come to be called "crimes without victims"; actions that are defined as criminal even though they occur in private and directly involve only persons who perform them voluntarily and indeed eagerly. Besides drug offenses, the most familiar examples are sex offenses and the possession or dissemination of pornographic materials. And what is envied is, evidently, the offenders' freedom to set aside both the superego and the reality principle and luxuriate in fantasy and sensation. That this is so is inferable from the fantasies of the suppressors, who invariably and vehemently portray the illicit relationships they decry as licentious, even when what they are actually talking about is the established domestic life of a pair of middle-aged interior decorators to whom anything in bad taste is anathema.

Envy is not, of course, the only motive that leads people to intervene in the private lives of others and deprive them of their chosen satisfactions. But it is the most basic motivation. There is also the familiar, conservative argument that licentiousness leads to disorder, and is socially intolerable for that reason. But this usually turns out to be based on the principle of the heckler's veto: the disorder that is feared is not that of the licentious but of their indignant and resentful adversaries—again, the people wouldn't stand for this sort of thing. In any case, it is easy enough to forbid disorderly conduct as such, as the law indeed does, rather than go on with vicious circularity to define conduct of which people disapprove, however harmless it may be to others, as inherently disorderly.

There is also a familiar liberal argument, based essentially on the premise that experts can best determine what is likely to harm us; and their word should be made law. This is sometimes used to justify serious intrusions on personal liberty, especially of young persons or people who are odd enough to be deemed in need of restraint, in their own best interests. I find such arguments very dubious; but they need not, of course, be based on envy. But it is with envy as a primal political force that I am here concerned.

What is usually condemned because of envy is not only illicit satisfaction itself, but the capacity to enjoy it, especially if it is deep enough to be called authentic love: brothels arouse less spiteful interest and are less severely condemned than *liaisons dangereuses*. Much the same thing may be observed with reference to commodities; envy of the possessions of the rich is not regarded as a dangerously disruptive social force in a capitalist society. Indeed, it is harnessed as a motivating force, though it is ruthlessly suppressed if it manifests itself through rioting or looting, and routinely suppressed if it manifests itself as theft. But wealth itself is less freely discussed or displayed; it is protected by one of the few functioning taboos remaining effective in our society. Credit-card corporations do not feel free to demand that applicants release their income-tax returns to the company as insurance companies demand access to medical records.

The prevalence of envy also serves to reinforce the subversive effect on the body politic of forbidden fruit, which tempts not only those who might indulge in it but those who might disrupt society or certain of its functions through their intolerance and moral indignation. Sanctions against crimes without victims are not justified merely on the grounds that the forbidden actions are socially or even morally injurious. They are also justified by the argument identified at the beginning of this chapter as "the heckler's veto." Even if marijuana, uncut versions of *Last Tango in Paris,* and joyful sexual relations between members of the same sex were positively beneficial to those who enjoy them (as, indeed, they usually are, which is ultimately what makes them enviable), it would still be necessary to affirm society's judgment by prosecuting them, lest an outraged populace be led to take the law into its own hands. The plain fact that such vigilante action is itself patently unlawful, and also that the state has a prior obligation to protect the victims, seldom moves officials who find it easier and politically far more expedient to forbid a speaker to utter offensive words than to protect him in his right to do so; or to insist that lascivious behavior is not a crime but queer-bashing is. The shortest and easiest path to social unity is to make such offensive conduct unlawful and let the police do the bashing. The result of such legitimation, to be sure, is sometimes the institutionalization of excessive zeal, as the following report by Walter Rugaber, published in the New York *Times,* August 25, 1973, illustrates:

> Twelve law enforcement officials were indicted by a Federal Grand jury today in connection with a series of mistaken drug raids in southwestern Illinois last April.
> Eight Federal agents and three St. Louis policemen were accused of conspiring to search six private homes without the required warrants and of conspiring to deprive 11 residents of their constitutional rights.
> The 12th man, a member of the East St. Louis, Ill., police-force, was cited as a co-conspirator but was not indicted. He was charged elsewhere in the 17-count indictment, however, with impersonating a Federal officer and with perjury. . . . The raids which were widely publicized, brought charges from those whose homes had been entered that the agents had been misdirected, needlessly violent, and destructive.
> An investigation by The New York Times showed that the Illinois raids were not isolated incidents and that citizens around the country had been subject to dozens of mistaken and often illegal forays.
> Today's indictment charged that in connection with the Illinois raids two men had been assaulted while in handcuffs and a third had been jailed for three days with no charges filed against him. . . .
> Some of the agents illegally searched the home of Mr. and

Mrs. Herbert Giglotto of Collinsville on the same day, it [the indictment] charged, and one of them assaulted Mr. Giglotto.

The Giglottos became the best known victims of the mistaken raids. It was disclosed last month that they had fled their home because of what they called harassment and intimidation after the foray. . . .

Other counts in the indictment accused some of the agents of conspiring to obstruct the communication of information about the raids to the Federal authorities and of attempting to persuade other agents to "tone down their reports on the incidents."

Six of the twelve indicted law officers were agents of the Federal Bureau of Narcotics and Dangerous Drugs while all three of the St. Louis police indicted were attached to the Federal Office of Drug Abuse Law Enforcement. One of the other two federal agents was a member of the Internal Revenue Service, while the other was employed by the Alcohol, Tobacco and Firearms Bureau. Only the lone East St. Louis policeman seems to have represented any sort of local initiatives program. All were subsequently acquitted when the presiding judge at their trial directed the jury to convict only if they believed the defendants had knowingly attacked the wrong people. The defense, he held, had successfully established that the behavior of his clients constituted normal law-enforcement procedure under the state's "no knock" law, and could not of itself be taken as evidence that the officers had deliberately conspired to deprive the plaintiffs of their rights. Until recently, this sort of event had become commonplace only in gay bars.

One can only wonder that the Treasury Department has never—to my knowledge, at least—proposed a federal tax on homosexually oriented households, requiring that a suitably designed tax stamp be displayed in the living room and that a report be filed of the time and place of occurrence of each orgasm licensed under it. The enforcement program that would then have been needed would have required the formation of a new and seminal bureau which would have been especially attractive to highly devoted young recruits whose potentialities, especially for undercover work, are difficult though by no means impossible to bring to fruition within existing bureaus of the department. The agencies of a democratic government should always be alert to the possibility of extending their services to segments of the population who have never benefited from them, and whose special needs often go unsatisfied.

Laws defining substances as dangerous drugs and sexual practices or sexually arousing material as vicious, and prohibiting their use, serve a dual social function. It is true that the items they proscribe are injurious to the social fabric and weaken the bonds that tie its members together and keep them harnessed—which may, of course, be as beneficial to them as individuals as it is harmful to the society. But such laws also serve an unstated function in licensing certain forms of social conflict that contribute to social stability rather than lessening it. The enforcement apparatus erected and maintained by the Bureau of Narcotics and Dangerous Drugs has been one of the paramount agencies in providing an outlet for the hatred and hostilities of the most exploited—though not the most deprived—members of society. Each violent drug bust, like each attack on peaceful and private though illicit sexual conduct, serves to vent the ressentiment of the most alienated social classes, who have traded their birthright to a fully sensual life for respectability and a modicum of economic opportunity. Positively, too, the law-enforcement agency enhances that opportunity by providing a well-intrenched bureaucracy in which careers can be made.

Pot-busts, queer-bashings, and pornography-hunts will occur frequently and provide much public satisfaction in any society in which an anxious and industrious lower-middle class has achieved paramount political importance. It makes little difference whether that class has come to power by the electoral process, by a military coup which installs as chiefs of state generals with narrow, working-class backgrounds, or by the rise of a bureaucracy from which leisured and aristocratic elements have been systematically liquidated—though this is perhaps worst of all. In any case, such acts of oppression serve the leader and his constituency well. They dramatize and resolve, in favor of repression, the conflicts inherent in society—conflicts social in genesis, individual in their constructive effects. And they make it possible to get on with the future undistracted by the chimera of liberty—that mythical beast which must be slain every day, lest the people, like the wily Ulysses, escape by clinging to the fleece of its belly. They could, of course, if it were more like a sheep; and they were less.

CHAPTER FIVE

The Privilege of Violence

The prevailing public attitude toward violence in North America is paradoxical. That violence should be widely feared and publicly condemned is rational enough; one would wish, certainly, that it were even more strongly and, especially, more consistently condemned. The present era is incontestably the most violent in history, largely because technology makes greater violence possible. There have been no atrocities committed in war different in kind from those Euripides recounts in *The Trojan Women*. Sacking and burning cities, raping the survivors and carrying them enslaved into exile, murdering children for political ends—all this still pretty well exhausts the possibilities. But we do it with so much more efficiency, and on so much larger a scale, that violence must certainly be perceived as a critical social problem.

What is strange is that the public which so fears and deplores the use of violence has become, after all, its principal sponsor. Nearly all the unprecedented violence that distinguishes our time is committed by agents of the national state, covertly or overtly. The state's virtual monopoly on violence exists, and enjoys public support, at all levels of action. It is very difficult to obtain the conviction of a policeman for beating or slaying anyone, even if he is off duty; his position as a peace officer is a license to kill with little legal jeopardy. Conversely, even those states which have abolished capital punishment have been obliged by public pressure to restore it as a penalty for persons convicted of slaying a police officer or prison guard. Middle-class adults, who are what is usually meant by "public opinion," are rarely the victims of violence by the lesser minions of the law; these victims are usually poor, black, or young, in any combination. The consequence of this turn of public policy is thus to make the weakest elements of the population even more vulnerable to violence than they otherwise would be, while encouraging its use by conferring substantial legal immunity on the attackers. Public opinion, of course, perceives the poor, the black and the young as themselves the source of most violence or "crime in the streets."

At the other end of the geographical scale that runs from neighborhood to globe, since World War II there appear to have been *no* local, internalized struggles between socialist and capitalist-oriented forces in which the United States did not intervene, whether by direct military intervention (Cuba, Korea, Indochina, Lebanon, and the Dominican Republic) or by funding right-wing governments or insurgents (in the same countries previously mentioned plus Brazil, Bolivia, Guyana, Chile, Indonesia, Pakistan, the Philippines, Korea, Ethiopia, Greece, Uruguay—the catalogue runs from Angola to Zaire). One possible exception is Algeria, where the French settled their own hash before departing, leaving no pretext for intervention as they did in Indochina. And the only other exception I know of is the Soviet Union itself, where the socialists *are* the right-wing government—a fact which has confused American foreign policy for more than fifty years. Even the Soviet Government, indeed, was greatly assisted in consolidating its power by the American invasion which sought to abort the Bolshevist Revolution at the end of World War I. The consequence of each of these interventions has been to escalate limited and potentially brief conflicts into continuing holocausts leading to the torture, killing, and confinement in death camps without trial of hundreds of thousands of people in their own countries. None of these conflicts or countries constituted a threat to anything in America but its opportunities for foreign investment. This is not a pretty story, but it is hardly unique or even peculiarly discreditable. Many governments have been totally ruthless in advancing what its elites conceive to be their interests. But it does seem remarkable, in view of the record, that anyone could doubt that the state is the source of nearly all the violence in the world. Nobody else has the resources.

At the same time, persons who undertake acts of violence without at least covert authorization from the state evoke from it repressive violence on a scale totally disproportionate to their assault. This does not imply that the state will always vanquish its more primitively armed offenders. It has not succeeded in doing so in Indochina or

Ireland, while in tense urban areas in America and elsewhere totally imaginary snipers provoke fusillades in which peace officers shoot one another as well as passers-by, and fill the streets with pepper gas and Mace. But whatever the precipitating cause or the outcome may be, when the sum total of violence in the world is added up, most of it will have come from the state and its agents.

The public, however, does not regard the violence of the state as violence at all. It becomes not merely legitimate—even when, as in the Indochina war, the state abrogates its own constitutional processes for legitimating it—but largely invisible. Or, in any case, to a majority of the people, negligible. The dimensions of this neglect are staggering. It is perhaps understandable that most Americans should choose, once the United States has disengaged itself from the Indochina war, to obliterate their role in it from consciousness. But it is not at all understandable that they should, in 1974, act as if the United States had disengaged itself when it had merely withdrawn its troops and continued to subsidize the South Vietnamese military with about three billion dollars a year in aid. Consider what the public response would be if this sum were added to the domestic welfare budget!

Moreover, and more precisely, it is just that portion of the public that is most insistent upon eliminating violence from society and re-storing law-'n'-order which is also least willing or able to acknowledge that the state is itself the source of violence in the world. It is they who are most eager, as the experience of the war resistance move-ment in the United States has shown, to unleash the violence of the state on those who are clearly trying to limit that violence, but who are perceived as disorderly. Again, let us note precisely the nature of the paradox. It is not astonishing that a man who conceives himself to be a patriot should respond with anger and hatred to young men who resist the draft and impugn the nation's motives. It is not as-tonishing that, in his anger and hatred, he should become violent and advocate violence. But it *is* astonishing that he should continue to regard himself as a man dedicated to the maintenance of peace and order, at home and abroad. "Kill, kill, kill for peace!" is just as ab-surd and ugly a slogan as *The Fugs* made it sound in their song a decade ago; and middle America should have been able to perceive this, no matter how strongly it supported the war.

Some of the reasons for this disturbing inconsistency are clear enough. Much of it is surely a classic example of an ideology that justifies the actions the state would have taken anyway in support of its dominant economic interests. Some of it is characteristic of the authoritarian personality which, at all times and places, projects its own violence and destructiveness on others while seeing itself as a paragon of order. Some of it is perhaps attributable to ignorance and an utter lack of understanding of American foreign policy and its role in the world. But ignorance of things that are both vitally important and publicly reported requires explanation in itself. Unless, like "good Germans," the people are participating in the repression of what they ought to know, they should accept information about matters that may impoverish their lives and threaten their very existence, so that they can at least consider positive precautions. That, after all, is the justification given for public concern about "crime in the streets." But middle America and especially American GIs refused to raise questions about American foreign policy or the conduct of the war, and virulently attacked the peace movement that sought to spare them, as well as the Indochinese, its horrors. The bombardiers whose daily mission—missionaries bear watching—was to kill, among others, children saw Benjamin Spock, rather than themselves, as a man of violence. So, largely, did their fellow-citizens.

In seeking to understand this remarkable astigmatism, in which deeds of equal blackness appear so different and evoke such different responses, if sanctioned by the authority of the state, some of the most useful evidence is provided by Stanley Milgram's well-known study of *Obedience to Authority*.[1] What makes this investigation so pertinent is the fact that, in Milgram's procedure, the authority that his subjects so willingly chose to obey was wholly spurious and, indeed, offered no more credentials to support its demands than the familiar scientists' white coat on TV commercials. In a sense, therefore, he was studying contempt for authority rather than respect for it, just as a devotee of Ripple or Thunderbird may be said to be contemptuous of wine.

Milgram, it will be recalled, enlisted the aid of volunteers in an experiment that required them to administer apparently agonizing and dangerous shocks to a group of experimental subjects. The scientist who recruited the volunteers was quite unknown to the helpers he enlisted, and he gave them only the sketchiest explanation of what the experiment was about. They continued, nevertheless, to carry out his instructions even when informed that doing so might endanger the life of a subject. They asked only questions like, "If he dies, who will be responsible?" and accepted Milgram's assurance that *he* would be. Once he said he would take responsibility for the results, some two-thirds of his volunteers continued to participate, demanding no credentials whatever of Milgram himself.

In fact, these assistants were the real subjects of the experiment; the supposed victims were Milgram's well-rehearsed confederates; and no shocks were actually administered to anyone. The experiment was a fake. This fact has led some critics to condemn Milgram for behaving toward his actual subjects—i.e., the volunteers—as cruelly and dehumanizingly as they behaved—or were willing to behave— toward the people to whom they believed they were administering electroshock. I find this reasoning specious, since to deliberately administer to a harmless stranger a treatment that one has reason to believe is both agonizing and dangerous is quite different from leading people into a situation in which they may—or may not—reveal their own moral deficiencies and be forced to confront them. Milgram's experimental design was irritatingly godlike or at least ducal —he did to his volunteers just what the Duke did to Angelo in *Measure for Measure*. But the pain and humiliation some of them felt when they were told what, in fact, they had done was not the result of their having been treated as objects but of their realizing that they had *acted* like objects, placing themselves entirely in the scientists' hands.

Such behavior is easily condemned as fanatical respect for authority. In fact, it shows little or no such respect. Conceivably, a genuinely fanatical Christian might patronize a whorehouse, but he would not, unless exceptionally perverse, fall on his knees and worship there if he found the walls hung with Pietàs and paintings of the Annunciation. Their presence would displease him, and would hardly lead him to suppose that his hostesses were consecrated. Similarly, people who respect authority strongly may be expected to be sensitive to its abuse or impersonation. But most of Dr. Milgram's volunteers derived such substantial reassurance from feeling that their actions were *authorized* that they did not even question whether he had the power to hold them harmless from the legal—much less the moral—sanctions to which their participation in his experiment might subject them.

If Milgram's volunteers had been sadistic, or had stood to benefit in any way from their participation in the experiment, their response would not have seemed paradoxical. We are all doubtless capable of rationalizing conduct that we find advantageous if ethically dubious; and appeal to authority is one of the commonest forms of justification. But none of them were sadists; all were disinterested. They had nothing to gain in the usual sense by assisting Dr. Milgram in his human experiment. And most of them showed serious doubts and appeared to be disturbed about their task as the experiment progressed and the outcries of Milgram's confederates grew more shrill. When Milgram absented himself from the laboratory briefly, in a part of the experiment designed to see if his assistants would feel freer to refuse his directions when he was not actually present to observe their insubordination, many of them did so, "fudging" their instructions in order to spare the experimental "subjects" some of the pain they were supposedly inflicting on them.

Why, then, did not most of the people Milgram approached simply decline after raising questions about the experiment, or at least drop out of it early on, when they perceived that they were being used as torturers? How could the idea that Milgram had the authority to exonerate them from their own scruples have provided them with any solace? How could it even have appeared relevant to their concerns, when they disliked what they were doing and could expect no tangible reward for doing it? Obviously, this is a question with the broadest possible implications. It is as applicable to most of those involved in Watergate, whose interests certainly did not coincide with those of the President and who ought to have had no illusions about his willingness or power to "cover for them." And it is applicable to the participants in a psychological experiment.

One reason that this question seems puzzling is, I believe, because I may be asking it the wrong way around. I have been asking, in effect, how people can suppose that any authority can assume their burden of guilt and responsibility for actions that they themselves believe to be wrong, so that they do not, for example, even recognize their violence as violence. But this may not be the most useful question to raise. If one asks, instead, whether the sense that one is carrying out orders that one knows to be destructive can be positively exhilarating in itself, and, if so, under what circumstances—then the answer may be more informative.

The highest personal cost of being socialized to accept the prescriptions and proscriptions of other persons, whether individual or corporate, of our actions and our roles is a pervasive sense of impotence and of existential guilt. All socialization is thus alienating to some degree. But for most members of a mass society, who can survive economically only by fulfilling fragmented routines designated by others, alienation and a sense of chronic self-betrayal at having surrendered one's selfhood may be a constant dull torment. That torment is somewhat eased, however, if one feels that what one is required to do has powerful and significant consequences, even though it was not done spontaneously. A man who bombs villages, or merely helps a scientist to perform an experiment that hurts helpless subjects enough to make them cry out, can hardly be impotent. But he is subject to being rendered inoperative by the authority he serves; he need not be killed or imprisoned when his services are no longer required—he is just annulled.

Ironically, then, Dr. Milgram's volunteers learned that they had, after all, been participating in a psychological experiment so designed that it must inevitably cause pain to its subjects—themselves. When the project was subsequently explained, what humiliated them was not just the unpleasant discovery that they were capable of knowingly inflicting pain on a fellow-human who could not possibly harm them. It was the more serious revelation that their agency had been illusory; that they, indeed, were the only people in the experimental situation who had been acting without a will or purpose of their own; and that this was not a very unusual occurrence for them—they had not even noticed it at the time.

What they had gotten out of their participation, albeit fleetingly, was a sense of having been turned on: a false but comforting assurance that the scientist, by virtue of his authority, could make them somebody despite the surrender of their will—or rather because of it. This dynamic also explains, I believe, why most of the Watergate miscreants seem not to be evil men—not up to being evil men, however evil their deeds. Neither, of course, do the bombardiers of Indochina—in contrast to the North Vietnamese who tortured them when captured and who, being driven by vicious personal hatred, seem rather more human than their victims. They appear, rather, like poltergeists, malign spirits driven to create a disturbance in order to assert that they exist. This assertion is not the least of their perjuries.

To the extent that each of us has yielded, or failed to develop, his potential for self-actualization and accepted a pattern of life that makes us the instrument of circumstances or of other person's purposes while our own remain unrealized, we will yearn for authority and be uncritical of its claims. Existential self-betrayal is peculiarly debilitating because it is a cardinal sin of which it is almost impossible to repent. Those who commit it do not realize that they have unless they are apprehended for a related offense which they did not will and of which they feel innocent. Egil Krogh did not mean to commit burglary; neither Calley nor Eichmann wished to harm any man, woman or child. Their *willful* act, and hence their sin, was the abandonment of their will—and that seldom feels like a willful act. But it leaves those who commit it dependent thereafter on external sources for a *raison d'être,* and as credulous of authority as the damned would be of a rumored fountain of holy water that provided automatic absolution.

It also leaves them filled with malice and hatred toward persons less compromised than themselves. These are often identified by their spontaneity and authentic moral commitment, which, though no assurance of salvation, do establish that damnation has not yet occurred. If the authority of the state suffices to make its violence appear, paradoxically, as a simulacrum of life-giving force, the exuberance of those who retain a sense of their own moral presence must arouse the meanest sort of fear and envy. The spontaneous actions of these people must be defined as violent. The Catonsville Nine spilled blood; they brought jars of it from a slaughterhouse to the draft-board office for that purpose. What could be more violent than that?

This hatred of spontaneity is, I believe, one factor—though the seductive vagueness of the law is a more powerful one—in the eagerness of the Nixon administration to charge the peace movement with conspiracy, thereby maintaining that the actions of its members do not reflect their personal and individual views, but those of a hypothetical seducer. There has been conformity and coercion enough even in the peace movement. There has been even more conformity in its surviving fragments, which have reason to be paranoid even though the realities of government surveillance and fraud have outstripped any possible fantasy. No one, however, has protested in self-extenuation that he was just doing a job or following orders.

There is, then, built into society a profound and deeply felt conflict between those whose pride depends on their conviction that they are ethically autonomous and responsive to the presence of other persons, and those who pride themselves instead on their self-discipline and self-renunciation in doing, realistically, what their job or social role demands, however this may affect the people they act upon. It is also clear that society as it is organized requires millions of the latter and that its institutions mold them to serve, while it can barely tolerate the former; and does not when it can find grounds for isolating or repressing them. This generalization holds true, generally speaking, despite its obvious oversimplification. To be sure, the world is not divided into ethically autonomous people on the one hand and *apparatchik* on the other. And if it were, this division would not correspond to good guys and bad, or political left and right. But people do, I believe, tend to identify themselves with certain significant modalities: men and women; straights and gays; blacks and whites. We are not all simply ranged along a continuum or huddled under a bell-shaped curve. These polarities refer, rather, to bimodal distributions of human traits, usually with humps of quite unequal size and comparatively few persons rated in between. And the difference between the people in the two humps is in each case partly qualitative and not just scalar. Though the mode they establish is hardly statistical, even the rich, as Scott Fitzgerald said, are different from the rest of us.

It is always necessary and usually possible to work out a *modus vivendi* between people in different humps. But this does not imply that the conflicts between them are the result of misunderstanding or poor communication. They are real, and do not go away if ignored. Undoubtedly, the most effective mechanism for reducing social conflict is to transfer it from the external social scene to the psyches of individuals and let them take the strain off the body politic. This mechanism is what liberal democracy relies on most heavily to abort conflict between social groups and especially social classes, establishing the struggle within the self, instead. Rich and poor, black and white, old and young, men and women—each of these is left with a sense of self-denial and self-abuse, for the sake of the social order. This, precisely, *is* the political process. Conversely, even behavior as ugly and indefensible as that of the south Boston whites in their fall 1974 demonstrations against bussing must surely have made them feel less guilty rather than more. What is regrettable is the *fact* of their bigotry more than their candor in expressing it. The authorities in Boston, for their part, should have responded with a genuine sense of outrage at the contempt the whites were showing for the rights of black citizens. Instead, they sought, as usual, to defuse the issue morally by taking no position of their own, except that violence and disorder should be avoided and the law, if possible, enforced. In their fear of physical confrontation—and of defeat by a furious white majority—the politicians of the area also avoided the moral confrontation demanded by the white demonstrators' sincere advocacy of evil. Massachusetts politicians are, apparently, consistently incapable of Manichaeanism.

Today, most of us are. In order to fill successfully the roles that exist, we become, walking though uneasy compromises among irreconcilable demands, anthologies of social behavior from which, as editors, we have omitted anything personal. Especially likely to be omitted is the expression of two kinds of feeling that have proven highly maladaptive in mass, industrial society: tenderness and superiority. Feelings of tenderness are an embarrassment in most social situations. A certain place is conventionally reserved for them in relationships between lovers—though neither "swinging" nor the modest growth of the communal life-style justifies our writing *among* lovers rather than between them, as one might in a gentler society. Tenderness is precluded from most social relationships, however, by admonitions embodied in the culture's most depressing clichés: nice guys finish last; don't play favorites; howdja ever get involved with *her*—or *him?* don't be a patsy; do unto others before they do unto you. It has become a commonplace rather than a paradox of mass society that explicit sexuality gets films X-rated and bookstores raided for obscenity. Violence does not—provided the winner is a macho hero, a military man, law-enforcement officer, or superman who has allied himself with forces of law-'n'-order, rather than a criminal or revolutionary.

Censorship is intended, of course, to prevent the validation of ideas and feelings that would threaten the stability of existing social arrangements, not so much by "putting ideas into people's heads" as by confirming those that were already there to be shared visions rather than obscene fantasies. This is enough to explain, perhaps, why entrapping or beating up suspects, for example, does not count as criminal violence for purposes of rating; nor does the hanging of cattle thieves in John Wayne movies. *True Grit,* which is something of an archetype in this form, provides a wider range of satisfactions. It includes an unplayful though stimulating spanking administered by Glen Campbell, cast as a rugged and certainly durable juvenile, to the adolescent heroine for her audacity in insisting on joining the manhunt. When, thereafter, the two fall in love, Mr. Campbell is killed before he can return to the scene of his attack with a more explicitly affectionate purpose. Mr. Wayne, however, survives to reach his apotheosis as a policeman, *McQueen,* who pushes a suspect off a roof. When reproached by his bureaucratic chief, he observes roguishly and presumably inaccurately, "Well, it kept him off the streets." Mr. Wayne's movies are never X-rated.

Nor is the cop movie *Busting,* more recent and—unlike *Serpico*—vicious in its endorsement of violence against those assumed to be guilty, though untried and indeed uncharged. Like Serpico, the young vice-squadmen played by Elliott Gould and the film industry's all-purpose ethnic, Robert Blake, find themselves hampered in their investigations by their superior's shamefaced protection of the lucrative and corrupting narcotics trade. This properly infuriates them and makes them turn nasty. It does not, however, dampen their inquisitorial ardor. Compensating for their superiors' lack of zeal, they stage shoot-outs in a supermarket and a hospital, assault a suspect who attempts to assert his right to make a phone call, set fire to the automobile of the infamous narcotics chieftain and taunt him as he watches, aghast, from the terrace of his luxurious home. They break up the apartment of an accused call-girl who refuses to tell them where she keeps her appointment book. They assault suspicious-looking people encountered in the courthouse corridor and sustain beatings themselves from their enraged clients who, indeed, are shown to have no other more lawful and effective way of asserting their constitutional rights.

All such violence is privileged. It becomes so by its perpetrator's intent to protect society from the imputed permissiveness—equally contemptible whether attributed to corruption or constitutionality—of its law-enforcement procedures. The violence is, in fact, justified precisely because it is supposed to be supportive of society's real norms, and more effective at penetrating and cleansing hidden crevices than the law will permit itself to be. But its socially integrative effect is even stronger and, in some respects, more subtle.

What the heroes of such dramas seek is an assurance that their violence makes them potent, indeed dominant, factors in their situations without their having to assume moral responsibility for their purposes. Like Dr. Milgram's subjects, these police do not choose their victims actively; they are designated for them by being stigmatized as criminal and, especially, as narcotics pushers whose crimes carry an aura of black magic. Illicit drugs, as Thomas Szasz[2] has pointed out, are blasphemous as well as toxic, and threaten damnation. The police hero-victims thus even appear as apolitical: they define no values and establish no policies—they just execute them. Authority grants them the only vitality they possess; when it fails them they are as good as dead. Significantly, the vice-squadmen in *Busting* are presented as having nothing else and no purpose in life other than their attacks on their presumably criminal victims—not even a strongly felt emotional tie to each other.

The fact that a life so devoid of feeling can still be so frantic and eventful serves to confirm what these men have no reason within their own experience to believe: that there is indeed life after death, or at least after birth. *Busting,* like *Serpico,* has been received as a superior *roman policier* having social significance. Truly, it has; its significance is revealed through the audience's laughter and appreciation of the destructiveness of its heroes. Though the events of *Busting* are presented with the wealth of brutal detail that is intended to appear realistic, it is not, like *Serpico,* even a pseudo-documentary in its approach to the narrative. Its protagonists are heroes, and the audience is happy to root for them.

Heroism thus becomes a quality seen as well within the reach of the most insensitive goon. Even tragic heroism is merely the antithesis of heroin, with corrupt police sergeants in the role of Eumenides and drug pushers playing the role of Cyclops. *Busting* is sordid, but its sordidness serves a social purpose: to assure a disaffected *lumpenbourgeoisie* that its members are something more than victims—that they make things happen. No personal quality, and no political position or insight is required of the viewer; it is all included in the price of the film.

If *Busting* is devoid of tenderness, it is equally devoid of any feeling of superiority. Peter Hyams, who wrote and directed it, might have been Nietzsche's valet. Its characters are full of piss and vinegar, but these are not the ingredients of nectar. A genuine sense of superiority in the characters, based on a cool awareness of what they were really like and a realistic confidence in their own capacities, expressing real respect for themselves and other people, would be anathema to such a film and, certainly, to the people who dig it. A slightly earlier, and better, film of Elliott Gould, *The Long Goodbye,* exploited this fact ironically. Its fictional hero, Raymond Chandler's Phillip Marlowe, did possess these attributes in the original novel of some forty years ago; but the recent remake of the film version used them to convey the idea that Marlowe was now an atavism, socially obsolete and ineffectual. Times have changed in this respect, certainly. If it were possible to confront an ordinary modern audience with a faithful and well-directed film version of *Lord Jim*—to take an unpretentious but morally serious example—what on earth would they think it was about?

Alienation—in the sense that one has abdicated personal responsibility for defining one's goals or one's place in the world, and allowed oneself to become the tool of other persons or an impersonal organization—is certainly too common a condition today to be regarded as pathognomic of any social class. Nevertheless, it is undeniable that the opportunity to exercise autonomy effectively is distributed through society and even institutionalized along a status gradient. Generally speaking, the closer you get to the top the more scope for autonomy you have, and the more difficult it is to impose bureaucratic sanctions on your actions. Firing Archibald Cox from his post as Watergate prosecutor did not destroy his usefulness to the cause of human freedom; in fact it may have enhanced it by dramatizing his courage and trustworthiness and attracting attention to what he meant.

On what is still the darker side of the planet to the east of Eden, it is evident that the mere survival of such libertarian spokesmen as Solzhenitsyn and Sakharov is attributable to high status in the international roster of intellectuals. And in general, job satisfaction is everywhere highly correlated to status. A major basis of that correlation is the sense, increasingly felt by people of higher and higher occupational status, that they make the decisions that are expressed in their work.

Conversely, such studies as Ivar Berg's *Education and Jobs: The Great Training Robbery*[3] have confirmed what personnel offices have known for a long while. Education is negatively correlated with job satisfaction in routine jobs; and the requirement that applicants for routine jobs should present a diploma or a degree as evidence of qualification is, from the employer's point of view, counterproductive. Highly educated mailpersons or assembly line workers goof off more than their less educated counterparts. They quit after shorter periods of time and are less productive as well as less contented on the job. All of which is doubtless greatly to their credit. Still, it makes the persistence of employers in continually raising the ante on applications for even the least stimulating and most routinized jobs appear not only paradoxical but self-defeating.

It is not, however, inexplicable. What seems to be involved here is a partial but basic misconception of the function of the educational system. It is certainly true that the system rewards conformity and the patient mastery of trivia; and that it subjects pupils to recurrent and cumulative appraisal by a cadre of personnel who are themselves predominantly uptight, anti-intellectual, unimaginative, and both jealous of their authority and insecure in their administration of it. It is also true that teachers gossip about their pupils and schools maintain cumulative records on them which follow the pupil through the successive schools he attends; so that oddballs or troublemakers find themselves under continuous surveillance from the first manifestations of their oddity—and from the standpoint of the school creativity and originality are usually classified as unfortunate aberrations to be discouraged by disciplinary or, increasingly, clinical means.

One might reasonably expect, then, that the more years of schooling a student has completed with good grades and high recommendations, the more conformable he would be. And employers apparently do expect this, though most would doubtless prefer to express it as confidence that people with long, good, academic records are well adjusted to the demands of complex organizations and likely to have been trained to be good team-men. The problem is that success in school and protracted school attendance are also correlated to other factors which tend to cancel the schools' constrictive influence. These factors are related to socioeconomic status, which is in turn related to more open and permissive household routines and a greater prevalence in the home of the artifacts of middle-to-high culture. Higher-status parents are more adept at teaching their children to beat the school at its own games for the sake of their future chances. And the schools attended by higher-status pupils are, in fact, likely to be less oppressive than those attended by poor or working-class children: less dreary, better equipped, and with a much wider choice of possible routines and curricula. Higher-status parents are more sympathetic toward and less fearful of "open classrooms," "modular scheduling," and other innovations designed to customize instruction if not to free it. Lower-status parents are likely, instead, to see these as devices by which the school abdicates its responsibility to make their children learn. In a sense this is true, because middle-class children receive far more informal opportunities out of school to learn how to handle such situations.

" 'School' as presently understood in America was developed for the lower classes. Its infliction on the upper classes is an historic irony that proves some justice is possible in the world," George von Hilsheimer justly observes.[4] But one skill commonly shared by upper classes everywhere is the ability to mitigate the effects of justice should they begin to show themselves. They have not protected their young from debilitation and harassment by the schools; but they have succeeded in influencing the school to treat their children more favorably than other peoples'.

Such social mechanisms as these insure that as one descends the socioeconomic scale the prevalence of people who are obliged to justify their own alienation by equating obedience and conformity with maturity and what they call a sense of responsibility, will increase. So will their vehemence in denouncing as violence resistance to the state and responsiveness to one's own conscience, and in denouncing as intolerably libertine spontaneity in life-style. This relationship holds true all the way to the bottom of the socioeconomic scale. At the bottom are convicted and imprisoned felons who, of all people, have experience of the state's incomparable capacity for cruelty and violence and the strongest possible reasons to reject its value judgments about themselves, but nevertheless have long been notoriously patriotic, hostile to political prisoners and, especially, to sex offenders, and tightly conventional in their attitudes toward the society that is, as they well know, destroying them. However, this pattern of docility is changing fast. At the present historical moment, at least, there is a second variable that seems to be almost as closely related to astigmatic blindness toward the violence of the state, and to censorious hypersensitivity to autonomous and expressive gestures (whether violent or not) in private persons, as socioeconomic status. That variable is, quite simply, age.

It need not be reiterated that the civil-rights and war-resistance movements and with them, radical criticism of established social systems, have within the past fifteen years been almost entirely the prerogative of the young. The young have thereby incurred the special hatred of the older generation and especially of law-enforcement officials everywhere. The phenomenon is worldwide, and is not even limited to industrially developed society, though it appeared there earlier and perhaps more intensely. China, which is not yet perhaps in that category, has been an exception. But small and presumably tropically groovy states like Sri Lanka, in which thousands of dissident middle-class youth have been rounded up and imprisoned without trial in detention camps, have not been. The curious and incredibly heartening exception to this global slaughter of the innocents, which I note with trepidation lest I have to revise this passage before this book can be published, is Thailand, where the students in three major universities succeeded in ousting a military junta supported by massive American military and industrial investment. They even managed to elicit an apology from the American ambassador after a CIA agent who was quickly dispatched to the United States and never identified in public reports was detected attempting to sow dissension among the dissident students by means of a forged letter purporting to come from a leftist leader. This was applying the methods of American domestic politics quite as if Senators Muskie and McGovern had been Siamese twins. Thailand, moreover, has one of the most highly stratified social structures still extant and the students survived and gained their victory through the active support of the King, who in Thailand still retains some power and more influence. Ethiopia, too, was a highly stratified monarchical state supported by American assistance and riven by revolutionary ferment. The response of its venerable monarch, though his house has fallen in disarray, was marked by a forbearance that contrasts sharply with the bloodletting of populist bourgeois military juntas in Greece and Chile, and indeed, of that which overthrew Haile Selassie himself.

During the sixties, when the militance of the young was at its height, it became fashionable among older social critics to dismiss it as simply an expression of recurrent generational conflict egged on by aging, neurotic sympathizers of dubious motives. Now the campuses of the major Western countries are quiet once more, and the abuses which the students combated (including their own infiltration by government spies and provocateurs and a judicial conspiracy against the movement by the U. S. Department of Justice) have been publicly attested, and a change in public attitudes seems to be occurring. The new Attorney General, William Saxbe, has been obliged to permit a cautious inquiry by a federal grand jury into the 1970 slayings at Kent State University which led to the indictment—and subsequent acquittal—of eight Ohio National Guardsmen. Still, Mr. Saxbe was confirmed as Attorney General, though as Senator he had publicly stated that such an investigation would do more harm than good, and that, whatever had happened at Kent State, the episode had served a useful purpose in restoring tranquillity to American campuses. And he continues to be an officer of the Ohio National Guard, which did the killing. It is reasonable to doubt that his attitudes toward the civil rights of young dissenters, and especially of members of the counterculture, have changed fundamentally, in view of the events of the Tock's Island raid of February 27, 1974, of which the New York *Times,* in an editorial published March 8, stated:

Callous Eviction

The early morning raid at Shawnee, Pa., last week was carried out with the military precision of an action against a fortified enemy outpost. But the victims of the raiding party of ninety Federal marshals armed with pistols and gas canisters were not part of an enemy force; they were peaceful squatters on Federal land near the site of the proposed Tocks Island Dam on the Delaware River, where some of them had farmed the land for the past four years.

The marshals were technically within the bounds of the law in evicting the squatters. So was the Corps of Engineers which, as soon as the 65 men, women and children had been forced out, crashed into the wooded, five-mile stretch of farmland with bulldozers and smashed a score of houses in which the squatters had lived. Six days before the raid, a Federal District judge in Wilkes-Barre had denied the squatters' appeal for a stay. Attorney General William Saxbe had approved not only of the raid but of plans to carry it out without warning.

At issue is not whether the marshals were technically within the law nor whether the whole Tocks Island project is justified in the first place—or is a typical Corps of Engineers boondoggle, as a great many environmentalists believe. The pertinent question at the moment is how the Justice Department and Corps of Engineers can justify their appallingly inhumane treatment of the squatters in the course of last week's police action. Women, including a mother and her new-born baby, were chased out of their homes into sub-zero cold. Their personal belongings smashed and buried by bulldozers included, in one instance, the manuscript for a book. Protesters were herded into police vans.

The callousness of the raid is rendered particularly obnoxious by the fact that the project for which the squatters' land is to be used is still far from the construction stage. Yet even such questions of timing are far less pertinent than the sorry exhibition of arrogance and inhumanity by governmental agencies notably the Army Corps of Engineers and the Department of Justice.

Still, as Watergate opened ever more widely, the press began quoting occasional businessmen as saying things like "Gee, I guess I have to admit my long-haired kid was right." John Wayne accepts an invitation to address a Harvard audience at a meeting sponsored by the *National Lampoon* and turns up mock-heroically in an Army tank, to dismiss unanswered with rueful roguery questions about his earlier role in naming suspect colleagues to the House Un-American Affairs Committee, now treated with elegiac regret in *The Way We Were*.

Thus Mr. Nixon's "pitiful helpless giant" licks its wounds and signals to its adversaries its readiness for a truce. All this, it seems, was in another country, and, besides, the kids are dead. The national urge for reconciliation cannot be wholehearted since the underlying conflicts of value and interests continue unresolved. But it is genuine enough. Intergenerational conflict has caused a great deal of misery in the world during the past decade, not only by pitting parents against children and teachers against students, but by constituting a serious if salutary economic and political threat. The education industry will never recover its previous almost sacerdotal place in industrial society, while the political threat associated with "student unrest" continues to spread. Even as older Americans congratulate themselves uneasily on the recrudescence of high school proms and fraternities and proclaim the new quietude of campuses, broken only by the silent streaking of naked bodies, incidents of revolt and repression are reported elsewhere. They are usually initiated by "students," a word which, when applied to a variety of cultures, can refer only to the common elite status of the young people involved who, at any rate, are not proletarians.

Today's event, in which publicly protesting students were, as usual, shelled and imprisoned, occurred in the Indian state of Bihar, whose government has now been dissolved by the federal authorities. The Indian students have no Lucknow; but if they should, they may well reduce Ms. Gandhi to a state of Uttar Pradesh. Tomorrow's corresponding event may equally well occur in Portugal, or Ethiopia.

Wherever it occurs, it presents the curious spectacle of relatively privileged young people revolting against authorities who represent the interests of the social class from which the young have sprung. This is not to say that working-class or blue-collar youth show no signs of discontent. Disaffection among young workers who refuse to accept the constraints of the assembly line is widespread, and manifests itself by absenteeism, high rates of turnover, and occasionally creative acts of sabotage. (Beer cans get welded into automobile door panels.) It is not unrealistic to hope that a governor, in his official limousine, may someday be busted for possession of a highly felonious quantity of grass that will have been factory-installed along with the air-conditioning. The succession of studies of the political attitudes of youth conducted during the late 1960s and early 1970s by the Daniel Yankelovich organization—and conducted for a variety of clients including the Rockefeller Brothers' Fund and the White House—have shown a steady movement to the left of working-class respondents. The gap between them and the consistently more radical middle-class youth—Yankelovich's aptly named "fore-runner" group—remains relatively constant, though each year the working-class members of the sample evince attitudes that the middle-class young people had adopted the previous year and have since moved beyond. But working-class youth have not served as the spearhead of the youth revolt of the sixties or seventies and have often opposed it on the grounds that it interferes with their access to greater economic opportunity—as when dissident students attempt to close down university classes. Or on the grounds that it adds to their burdens, as when larger numbers of working-class young Americans are drafted to fill quotas depleted by middle-class draft resistance.

Such complaints are embarrassing to middle-class militants, who like to think of themselves as constituting a revolutionary vanguard acting on behalf, though without the authorization, of the wretched of the earth. No disclaimer by the wretched suffices to disabuse them of this notion. Their presumably more politically sophisticated elders have also usually been guided by it, and have treated their own sons and daughters as if they were indeed heralds of a new and ruthlessly egalitarian social order, as they so poignantly claim to be. Perhaps no other response could have been expected. The fact that those who revolted were themselves members of the privileged classes does not of itself make them less threatening to the constituted authorities. If anything, it makes the struggle more bitter by permitting the insurgent young to be stigmatized as traitors to their class as well as to the nation.

This source of hatred, especially, poisoned the seven-years war that broke out in Berkeley in 1964. The conservative majority of

Regents of the University of California were venomous toward the students precisely because they saw them as not merely violent revolutionaries but as ungrateful punks as well. Within the university context, militant black students were treated far more tolerantly, because they were not expected to be grateful for past favors. Meanwhile, their earlier victimization, which left them willing to come to favorable terms with any social mechanism that promised them a chance to catch up socially and economically, made them a valuable potential clientele for a system of higher education whose present customers were growing disenchanted with it.

Yet, the issues that have continually recurred in student protest until they have become identified as clichés of the—predominantly white and middle-class—student movement were not merely consistent with the students' class interest but, indeed, expressions of it. Though the student movement has been consistently and vehemently egalitarian, most of the conditions and policies it has attacked are either in fact the direct consequences of expansion of economic opportunity or are understood by their defenders to be so. The bureaucratic impersonality of the university, and its inculpation in the military enterprises of the nation, are both attributable to the rapid expansion of the university system in the economic interests not merely of the military-industrial complex but of the "new class" of academics whose careers depended on this expansion and whose students, by and large, hoped to succeed them in similarly well-financed posts. Many of these students were drawn from social classes that had never previously had access to a university; and it was precisely they who were most hostile to the movement for interrupting their education and for threatening the university's sources of support, turning away the interviewers who controlled access to the jobs they wanted whether the jobs were immoral or not, and for discounting in advance the value of the degrees they sought by sapping public confidence in the university.

The effect of the Indochina war in creating what Americans perceive as economic opportunity, even as it sapped the nation's resources, needs no further comment here. The military dictatorships in Spain, Iran, and Brazil enjoy wide popular support because they have brought about an enormous expansion of the middle class in those countries, and are perceived as sources of economic opportunity. The same thing appears to be occurring in Chile.

These nations are being, as we say, modernized; and if this process does little to reduce the number or improve the condition of the poor—it probably makes it worse—it greatly increases the chances of a lot of little men to grow bigger, socially and economically. It has also made many of the rich richer; economic opportunity in Adventureland increases rapidly as you approach the top, and you'd better not approach it if it doesn't. But through this very process the new regimes destroy the power of the old elites, as Nixon's cowboys have tried to do with the Eastern establishment in the United States. And in retrospect, those elites can be seen frequently to include, and occasionally to support, those defenders of liberty in the nation who have not become inoperative.

It is quite true that elites hardly defend liberty frequently or vigorously enough to warrant the social costs of maintaining them. It is also true that this fact justifies the distrust that the student movement has developed for the elites of its own countries. These despised elites are nevertheless potential victims of the same social forces that attack the student movement and subvert or destroy it. The experience of being threatened by the same Snopesish tendencies in modern society has been insufficient to make allies of the movement and the elites; they have remained mutually hostile.

There are ample reasons in contemporary economic realities why the student movement and the establishment should remain adversaries, and bitter ones, on current issues of policy. Still, it is astonishing and, I should say, tragic that so few members of elites have been able to perceive the movement as their potential defender, or at least as an advocate of the values they stood for, or pretended to stand for. Out of the entire anglophone world only the name of Bertrand Russell springs readily to mind. Yet, throughout this time there were voices—generally hostile, to be sure—proclaiming, justly enough, that the demands of the protesting students were romantic, reactionary, counterrevolutionary and in principle elitist. Zbigniew Brzezinski, the distinguished Sovietologist of Columbia University, was the most lucid and convincing of these,[5] but there were many others in a more popular vein.

Why, then, was there never any sympathetic response to the student movement from the Right? From the very beginning, there was plenty of hostile response from intellectuals of the old Left. SDS, which began its existence as the student division of the old League for Industrial Democracy, gained its separate identity in the summer of 1962 when the officers of the league slit the umbilical cord by locking SLID out of its offices without notice[6]—an action for which Michael Harrington, who played a major role in it, has since apologized. Years later, Steven Kelman, writing from the straight, old-Left point of view of the Young Progressive Socialist League with reference to the April 1969 occupation of University Hall at Harvard, and the bloody confrontation that followed when university authorities summoned the Cambridge police, observed:

> The hereditary radicals—the Intellectual Left extremists at Harvard—suffered a sad fate at Harvard. For they at least were good people.
> The same cannot be said for the other major social stratum which provides recruits for SDS and the backbone of the new cadres recruited into the organization between the time I arrived at Harvard and April 1969. These are WASP rebels. . . . The pale, delicate faces of the used-up aristocrat who goes into SDS reminds one of nothing so much as Spengler's *Decline of the West*. . . . It is in the guilty aristocrat that we see clearly politics not for politics' sake, but for self-expression, the possibility of recapturing a lost vitality that one feels too weak to create for oneself.[7]
> The declining aristocrats are all, *to a man,* pro-PL.[8]

Perhaps; but if so, they were wasting their affection. By the fall of 1967, as Sale fully documents, the Progressive Labor Party had opened a fissure in SDS that was to split it fatally. To this hard-lining, formally pro-Communist organization, the hairy, expressive, ego-tripping SDS, though the heart of the American student movement, was intolerably elitist. PL's view of SDS, in fact, is scarcely distinguishable from Kelman's, though its leaders' style is very different. What does not seem to be in doubt—in the eyes of all attentive observers except SDS itself and its American establishment enemies—is that SDS and with it the mainstream of the American student movement was obviously conservative. Though its own anti-intellectualism prevented it from recognizing its ancestors, they were Tocqueville and Nietzsche rather than Stalin or, except for the disciplined PL faction, Mao. Marx, too, no doubt; but Marx and his older contemporary, Tocqueville, do not differ all that much in their interpretation of what was happening in the world—only in their evaluation of it. (I have never understood, nor do I now understand, why it is assumed that a Marxist, in the sense of a person who accepts the basic premises and structure of Marx's social and economic analysis as

correct and fruitful, should be assumed to be a protagonist of proletarian revolution. Surely, this is as silly as assuming that a Freudian
must be a sexual libertine. Even more surely, one of the most striking
implications of Marx, as of Tocqueville, is that personal liberty
depends on owning the property you need to earn a living; and that it
disappears from societies in which, for technical or institutional
reasons, that is no longer possible. That Marx, himself, thought
this a temporary and therefore bearable deprivation hardly discredits
the acuity of his analysis, any more than the absurd optimism of the
medical profession about eliminating disease and keeping everybody
who can afford it alive for years after they have finally lost consciousness discredits its actual understanding of physiology and hygiene.)

Why, then, did the student movement of the sixties arouse only en-
venomed and often hysterical condemnation and lethal repression
from those Americans who regarded themselves as conservative?
And meanwhile why did liberals often seek to go along with the
movement until repelled by what they regarded as the students' moral
absolutism and rebuffed by the students for their tendency to compromise, or fink out? Why did no leading conservative speak out to
endorse or support the movement, despite the consternation this
would have caused among its members as their own endorsement
came to embarrass black militants? Why were there no influential
elders to claim the students as persons of social value whose criticism
was a useful corrective to public policy and whose program could be
accommodated within it, as the King and a substantial portion of the
Thailese elite did in 1973? Why, instead, was the students' image of
themselves as revolutionary accepted, thus permitting their rhetoric
and physical obstruction of university and military facilities to be
defined as violence—while their summary gassing and shooting (not
only and not even primarily in the United States but in industrialized
and industrializing countries over most of the world and often on a
far larger scale than in America) were enthusiastically accepted as
proper law enforcement? What moral and ideological bond linked
together the conservatives of Portage County, Ohio, and Indonesia?
And what blinded them to the moral stature of their own sons and
daughters and led them to applaud their slaughter and indict their
few defenders? Why was this action not, at least, *controversial*?

It has become commonplace in cataloguing the ravages of the Indochina war to say that it polarized public opinion and deeply

divided the American people. But this seems to do public opinion too much honor. It certainly divided the American people, but, even so, no substantial part of the protest movement ever became legitimated. The Congress, as well as the President, still regards draft refusers as criminals; it speaks of amnesty only to withhold it without responding to the draft refuser's contention—correct in my judgment—that their action deserves honor rather than pardon, much less punishment. Even late in 1973, in the trial at Gainesville, Florida of young men whose right to oppose the war had been purchased by their participation in it and in some cases having been wounded in it, the Justice Department continued its established pattern of harassment, infiltration, and false testimony. It lost the case but successfully exhausted the time and resources of the Veterans Against the War. The jury acquitted them of the charge of conspiring to disrupt the Republican Convention in Miami a year earlier. But by this point in Watergate time, it ought surely to have politely expressed its regrets, as well, at having been forced by the evidence to deny the defendants credit for an action that might have spared the nation much humiliation, had anyone in fact undertaken to commit it.

Why, even today, does "the movement," as such, still have no proud constituency and, especially, no *conservative* constituency?

A major reason for this lack is the fact that hostility toward elitism as an element of social philosophy is so pervasive that no social group can admit to an elitist position without losing both its constituency and its self-esteem. Any imputation of elitism automatically elicits the kind of embarrassed denial and insistence that one is a regular guy that used to be evoked by charges of homosexuality. Certainly, the student movement finds it easier to countenance gay tendencies among its members than elitist ones. SDS meetings and even chapters have frequently been split by charges of elitism, whereas attitudes toward sexual conduct have largely been governed by the traditional Marxian slogan: "From each according to his talents; to each according to his needs"—a fact which, as the quotation from David Hilliard given in an earlier chapter illustrates, has elicited strong hostility from the macho-ridden black-power and Chicano movements. Yet, despite its insistent quest for working-class support, the basic demands of the movement were clearly elitist both in style and content. Many critics of the movement have, for example, condemned its arrogant disrespect for legal process and its willingness to use extralegal means in opposing a war it had unilaterally declared to be illegal. Such critics pointed to past occasions in which fanatical groups, convinced of their own rightness, have committed acts judged by the rest of the world to be atrocious, as in Nazi Germany. I have little respect for the moral or political basis for such criticism. The fact that atrocities have been committed by fanatics in the past and will be again in the future does not seem to me to make all moral judgment relative or all moral positions ambiguous, even when the situation to which they are applied is complex. By the time the movement had resorted to illegal—and still remarkably nonviolent—means of opposing the war, the war had been deprived of all shadow of legality, let alone moral justification. The pretext that American intervention was undertaken at the independent behest of a lawful government, the refusal to permit the elections provided in the Geneva Accords, the lies underlaying the Tonkin Bay resolution—one could go on and on—all these had been exposed. A mind that must wait to hear the other side of Song My before arriving at a moral judgment is too heavily compromised to serve as an example of balance. There is no question here of students in the movement believing that the end justifies the means, as was charged against them—though the American government and its allies evidently believed that all means were justified even though the war served no ends that could be stated. The movement was remarkably fastidious in its choice of means.

The comparison to the Nazis is especially stupid, as well as odious, for the Nazis did not commit their atrocities through fanaticism, any more than American GIs did and bombardiers did. The Nazis committed their atrocities through banal acceptance of the roles bureaucratically assigned them. Moreover, they even took the pains to legalize their atrocities before committing them, a fact which surely adds to the honor as it did to the jeopardy of those few Germans who broke the law of the land in order to resist them. The officers who finally plotted against Hitler, the industrialist and former nobleman, von Moltke, who, like the fastidious theologian Bonhoeffer, was hanged for treason; the despairing aristocrat Reck von Maliczewen, who found the Nazis odious because of their vulgarity, which he perceived as the source of their lethalness and who opposed them until he was killed in a concentration camp, like the French industrialist Michelin—all these demonstrated their devotion to freedom and justice by their willingness to set themselves above the law which finally took their lives. No one has adduced this fact as evidence that they were either fanatics or totalitarians.

But elitist they certainly were; arrogant, too, and unwilling to be swerved from their course by either public opinion or public law. That no member of the movement in the United States met a similar fate—the Kent State victims not only were not executed by law, they were not even political activists—is, I think, a genuine and solid tribute to American institutions, though not to American leadership. Governor Reagan promised a blood bath, but lacked the judicial equipment with which to provide it. Judged by the single but vital criterion of its tolerance for dissent in wartime, the American record remains relatively good. This does not, however, imply that the war-resistance movement exaggerated the heinous character of the war. Nor that it exaggerated the repressive intent of the government against the resistance, which the Watergate revelations have thoroughly documented, or the futility of attempting to fight it by legal means. Nor was either the war or the leadership that maintained it ever repudiated at the polls; the contrary occurred, by a landslide, in 1972. There can, therefore, be no doubt that the movement placed itself and its moral judgment above the position occupied by the American people and their government. The movement was elitist. It had to be.

It was also elitist in the comparatively low value it placed on the immediate economic interests of the American working class. Disastrous as the burden of the war on the economy may have been over the long run, its current effects were certainly and consistently those that the American people have come to cherish as economic benefits. It reduced unemployment, created and maintained jobs, reduced the hazards of enterprise—for some fortunate corporations and their employees like Lockheed, whose failure was simply deemed unacceptable politically, to the vanishing point. The economic damage that it did appears principally in the form of rapid inflation, which is relatively easily borne by the well-unionized—and hence politically effective—portion of the working class which is protected by cost-of-living clauses and the opportunity to rebargain for higher wages at frequent intervals. It is, however, disastrous to economically more marginal workers and the aged. The effects of ending the war are potentially much more threatening, since capitalist economies like that of the United States respond to decreased demand by cutting production rather than prices. If the macabre *Report from Iron Mountain*[9] is to be judged critically on the correspondence of its message with the apparent economic functions of the Indochina war itself (instead of dismissed as tongue-in-cheek satire, as it usually was at the time of its publication), then the war-resistance movement appears to strike at the very heart of modern society. The report portrays modern society as dependent on war and death to maintain not only its economy—Marx said as much—but its entire legitimating system of social sanctions and hence such integrity as the society itself possesses.

> War itself is the basic social system, within which other secondary modes of social organization conflict or conspire . . . Once this is correctly understood . . . some of the puzzling superficial contradictions of modern societies can then be readily rationalized. The "unnecessary" size and power of the world war industry; the pre-eminence of the military establishment in every society, whether open or concealed; the exemption of military or paramilitary institutions from the accepted social and legal standards of behaviour required elsewhere in society; the successful operation of the armed forces and the armaments producers entirely outside the framework of each nation's economic ground rules; these and other ambiguities closely associated with the relationship of war to society are easily clarified, once the priority of war-making potential as the principal structuring force in society is accepted. Economic systems, political philosophies, and corpora jures extend the war system, not vice-versa.
>
> It must be emphasized that the precedence of a society's war making potential over its other characteristics is not the result of a "threat" presumed to exist at any one time from other societies. This is the reverse of the basic situation; "threats" against the "national interest" are usually created or accelerated to meet the needs of the war system.[10]

War, the report indicates, solves the problem of excessive inventory of people as well as goods. War alone, since it performs no useful service and produces no useful goods, can massively stimulate economic activity with no threat of glut. It most effectively provides the justification for an iron system of social controls adequate to insure social stability. No wonder the hard-hats freaked out against the peace movement, seeing it, correctly, as a threat to the very basis and meaning of their lives. No wonder that the war continued to receive massive American support or, perhaps more precisely, to provide such support to American society.

In the light of this *Report* the peace movement appears not merely elitist but presumptuous. Equally, and perhaps more evidently, elitist are several other attitudes fundamental to the student movement though tangential to its opposition to the war. Its devotion to the preservation of the environment, for example, runs directly counter to working-class interests. It hampers economic development in the interests of preserving an environment that few members of the working class get much access to. And it opposes their established interests when they do have access, discouraging hunting and fishing, and even, as Calvin Trillin has pointed out in a recent issue of *The New Yorker*,[11] such apparently innocent activities as running hand-built dune-buggies over the desert. This practice is highly but undramatically damaging to the ecosystem. Brewers, according to Trillin, at least recognize where their interests lie and publicize the contempt in which they hold environmentalists. Their loyalty to the convenient but non-biodegradable snap-top aluminum can is not without its symbolic meaning. Most fundamentally elitist and, as such, challenging to conventional working-class life-styles, of all the movement's attitudes is its hip acceptance of leisured poverty; its emphasis on being rather than doing, its disbelief in planning and progress which looks to working-class and other critics like sloth; its dislike for linear order, which looks like filthiness; its welcome acceptance of its own impotence in the face of destiny, which looks like shiftlessness, which it sometimes is (hippies, too, are imperfect). Enraged, hard-working critics of this approach to life delight in pointing out that it is parasitical, and can endure only so long as other people work hard at disagreeable tasks to provide the goods and services the counterculture needs in order to survive. This is true of students who reject the system. It is a lot truer, however, of the armed forces, whose demands tend to be less modest.

To its hostile critics, the student movement, despite its revolutionary pretensions, was recognizably and intolerably privileged in its demands and its demeanor. Indeed, it has been. The word "privilege" still retains much of its original meaning even though it has become a pejorative. What it refers to is a *private law,* anathema to a society that bases legitimacy on public law. The students demanded, in effect, a version of the Selective Service Act, of the legal code pertaining to trespass and the established right of owners and governing boards to determine how their property might be used, of the laws regulating which parts of their body might be used for what forms of communication and which chemical substances might be enjoyed for their effects on the psyche, applicable solely to themselves. They also tried to have the public law amended to provide everyone with the freedoms and safeguards they wanted for themselves. And they ascribed to the public and especially to the working class an interest corresponding to their own in having these changes made, which is what all lobbyists do in America, and what you are supposed to do. But when other special interest groups object to the way the provisions of the law affect them, they may attempt to corrupt the inspection and enforcement process and evade it (like the aircraft company which ignores the directives of the Federal Aviation Administration while certain of its planes continue to explode in mid-air; or corporate executives who make illegal campaign contributions in the usually well-justified hope of evading the controls that have been established to bear on their businesses). Or, they may try to get the law weakened or repealed. Or both. They do not, however, feel it their moral responsibility to flout it publicly, as an assertion that bad laws are not good enough for them, though they apparently are for the majority.

Even committed advocates of civil disobedience as a means of influencing public policy do not thereby claim to be privileged. They acknowledge the right of the law to punish them and indeed insist on its execution, as a means of demonstrating their basic loyalty to the community and acceptance of its authority. But the student movement did nothing of the sort; Socrates, similarly motivated, would have rejected the hemlock as an instrument of oppression—which it surely was—and as contaminated with additives and not even organic—which it may or may not have been. I wish he could have; I think it would have set all of us a far sounder moral example. But to do so is elitist, and asserts a claim to privilege. The media would then never have preserved his memory as a symbol of heroism.

But a claim to privilege need not be based on a corresponding claim to be "better than anybody else": a difficult claim, indeed, to substantiate empirically except with respect to parameters so narrowly defined as to be morally ambiguous or irrelevant. If the privileged have come to insist on their own superiority as a justification for their privilege, they must already have accepted democratic doctrine—enough of it, at least, to induce the characteristic guilt feelings. The voice of privilege makes no such claim. It merely asserts:

"I will act authentically and with regard for my needs and actual human characteristics. If, in practice, this means that I insist on being treated better than other men are, this is not because I regard myself as more valuable, or brighter, or more moral; it is because I am *me;* quite ordinary, perhaps, but fairly clear about how I mean to live. I do not demand this as a reward for merit, or recognition for distinguished services rendered. I merely intend to provide for it if I can, and to support such social arrangements as this may require."

This is as much as the movement demanded in its opposition to the war, in its establishment of communal life-styles, and in its refusal to accept legal constraints on matters it regarded as essentially private. It is enough to explain its anger and bitterness at the infiltration and surveillance techniques which the American public largely accepted until Watergate, and does not seem unduly distressed by even today, even though such surveillance destroyed not merely privacy, and hence much of the opportunity for individualized growth, but basic trust among friends as well. Despite its obviously subversive implications and its implicit rejection of public, democratic discipline, there is much in this position to appeal to the conservative mind and heart—traditionally, bastions of privilege and by no means reluctant, on the historical record, to assert their claims against the legitimate restrictions of democratic policy. Indeed, that is exactly what American foreign policy is usually thought to have done in its customary support of established right-wing governments abroad and its almost equally consistent support of insurgents against lawfully constituted socialist regimes within the American sphere of influence—usually with the enthusiastic support of conservative voices at home. How could any sane person who had endorsed the American intervention at the Bay of Pigs condemn the actions of war resisters as either unlawful, violent, romantic, or futile? Having cooked its goose, how could America have so little sauce left for the gander?

The answer is not very startling. Despite the consensus which exists among persons of quite disparate political views that the influence of American policy on the distribution of power and resources in the world has been for more than a century overwhelmingly conservative, it has not expressed a conservative pattern of values. Nor has American policy been conservative in its effects. Its intent has been purely expansionist. Where they stood in the way of American-based enterprise, an in Iran, established preindustrial elites have been liquidated by America's client governments as ruthlessly as socialist insurgents have. The occasions for this have been fewer, since in states that had already been colonialized or modernized the destruction of elites had largely been accomplished before the development of American hegemony. In those areas which have not been modernized neither the elites nor in some cases the state itself was recognized as such. Despite the claim advanced in the Marine Hymn, its tune was composed by Jacques Offenbach in the nineteenth century, a little too late for Montezuma to have had halls to call his own. And from Montezuma's point of view, Cortez was a liberal, the first he had ever seen. Colonel Qadaffi is likewise a conservative culturally as well as economically, which is one important reason why he has so little success defending the shores of Tripoli against American fiscal razzle-dazzle in the Near East.

To be a conservative or a consistent elitist in the modern world is to pit oneself against economic development as such. And also against spoliation of the environment by the extension of industrial development—and with it, a rising standard of living—to areas of the world as yet unindustrialized. And against the rise of the new middle classes like that of Brazil, which will doubtless suffocate us all when it strikes at the rain forest, which provides two-thirds of the world's oxygen and cries out for either development or the imposition of an export tax on air; against the wars that implement this expansion; against the expanding bureaucracies that attend economic development, and the security forces that keep it in line. This is so whether the institutional devices through which expansion is sought are nominally capitalist or socialist. To be an elitist or consistently conservative means, then, to opt—so far as a choice is possible—for a world in which economic opportunity is reduced, at a time when a rising level of expectations and ever-widening demand for equal access to the world's goods and services have created an inflationary spiral more revolutionary in its redistributive effects than any consciously planned revolution could be. This may prove a far more embarrassing obstacle to student movements in such countries as India, with their frail economic infrastructure, than it has in the United States.

All these implications lay—as inconspicuous and as inevitable as genetic traces—in the peace movement itself, threatening its self-esteem which was largely tied to its image of itself as a politically and economically innovative force, and insuring the implacable hostility of the entire political spectrum of the modern state, from Goldwater to Mao. Of course, the peace movement was perceived as violent even as it was denied the privilege of violence accorded others; the violence of the youth who immolates himself or casts his body in the path of the juggernaut. This does not impede the juggernaut and is not expected to; indeed, those who do it have traditionally meant it as a form of tribute. The destructive—and inevitably self-destructive—acts of the peace movement have largely shared this character; they were meant as tributes to the conscience of the American people and as assertions of faith that the democratic process might be induced to divert public policy from its appalling course by shocking the public into awareness of its own brutality.

When this proved to be futile, and it became evident that most Americans acquiesced in their sponsorship of the juggernaut and were even willing to rent advertising space on its sides—though increasingly critical, on pragmatic grounds, of its effectiveness—genuinely violent and clearly elitist and antidemocratic programs were indeed adopted by tiny but not necessarily negligible elements whose intentions were truly political rather than metaphorical. Weatherpersons, the Symbionese Liberation Army, and other anonymous groups who bomb buildings and kidnap executives and diplomats can hardly be called a part of the peace movement; but they are certainly spinoffs from it. Officially they become outlaws and fugitives, often from a capital charge. Whether they are to be regarded as terrorists —or as cadres to be accorded the "exemption of military or paramilitary institutions from the accepted social and legal standards of behavior required elsewhere in society" referred to in the *Report from Iron Mountain*—depends on one's political position as well as one's moral judgment. Those who really prefer a world free of bombings, "terminations with extreme prejudice," and politically motivated abductions might wish to strive to eliminate these atrocities from the repertory of official military, intelligence, and law-enforcement agencies, as well as of insurgent groups.

CHAPTER SIX

Populism or Polarization

Earlier in this book I asserted, referring to the moral stance involved in the defense of liberty against a hostile majority, that "it would seem fair enough to say that Alexandr Solzhenitsyn is worth more than all the members of the bureaucratic apparatus that persecuted him." While Mr. Solzhenitsyn has again become—doubtless to his great relief—a distinguished novelist rather than a celebrity, his expulsion by the Soviet authorities in 1974 raised the fundamental conflict between liberty and equality to a prominence one would hope will seldom be achieved. In this chapter, I wish to return to this episode in the history of culture, for the sake of what it revealed about that conflict.

The Soviet bureaucracy, except for brief and freakish thaws attributable to local climatic conditions, has not grown less oppressive as it has become more prosperous and better established. It has noted, correctly, that the people value the bureaucracy's services, which they have been taught are essential to their welfare, far more highly than they do liberty, which they have never enjoyed and for which they have apparently developed little taste. In an egalitarian society there comes a point at which dissent need not be represented as a "threat to national security" in order to mobilize popular support for repression. So I would infer; and so I would interpret an extraordinary article about Mr. Solzhenitsyn by the novelist Hans Koning, published on the Op-Ed page of the New York *Times* of Monday, June 10, 1974. Since Mr. Koning adopts in this article a viewpoint contrary to mine, I find the fact that we reach certain common conclusions—though evaluating them in opposing ways—quite illuminating. Mr. Koning observes:

Mr. Solzhenitsyn does not speak for 'the Russian people.' He
may speak for a small, or large, number of the Russian elite, and
it indicates a certain failure in the Soviet brand of socialism if
there is a large number of that elite in opposition. . . .

The sympathy in the United States for the dissenters is elitist
too. . . .

Our indignations are elitist indignations: We, Western liberals,
have been reared on our mothers' milk with the private tragedy
of private fates; all our arts and letters are about it; we have for
centuries cried over Young Werthers and Madame Butterflys,
and we have yawned over the starving Bengalis.

Soviet Society is at least in its rough outline a society run for
the commonweal. To conclude from its treatment of dissenters
that it would be immoral for the United States to deal with such
a society, while nearly all our allies are dictatorships or autoc-
racies run for tiny groups, is fantastic. So is the entire parallel
issue of morality versus pragmatism.

. . . .

The United States, while not taking care of its people in the
way socialist and semisocialist countries profess to try, does leave
them alone—that is, free. In the United States that is the main
gift of our government—as compared with jobs, health, education elsewhere. Thus, we are rightly anxious that they do not
take that away from us and leave us with the worst of all possible
worlds. But for a writer or artists to be left alone is not necessarily the greatest good. It is all Mr. Solzhenitsyn wanted; it is
not all Vincent van Gogh wanted. Belonging may be as important to some people as freedom is to others. The first category may be weak, the second strong, but then the weak may
be a majority on this earth.

In fairness to Mr. Koning, it should be pointed out that these ex-
cerpts constitute part of an argument which is not intended to exonerate the policy of the Soviet Union toward dissenters but merely to
establish that it would be excessively fastidious for the United States
to refuse to establish mutually advantageous economic relations with
the Soviet Union after having unilaterally supported the most oppressive dictatorships in the world for at least thirty years—a position
with which I cannot argue. Nevertheless, his empathy for Mr. Solzhenitsyn's tormentors does seem to have coarsened his moral vision.
To state that "to be left alone . . . is all Mr. Solzhenitsyn wanted" is
clearly false and gratuitously insulting. The statement that the United
States, with the highest proportion of its population in prison of any

stable democracy, leaves its people alone is perhaps excessively charitable. But, with reference to the argument that I am advancing, the crucial point is Koning's statement that "Mr. Solzhenitsyn does not speak for 'the Russian people,'" which illustrates precisely the moral weakness of the egalitarian democratic position with which I am here concerned.

Mr. Solzhenitsyn may not speak for the Russian people; he nevertheless speaks with the authority of intense experience and critical intelligence, and thus constitutes what Thoreau called "a majority of one." The problem, for a libertarian, is not that he "does not speak for 'the Russian people.'" It is that they do not speak up for him, and see no reason to. And Mr. Koning's justification for that fact unhappily coincides with my own. "The dispossessed of this world," he further concludes, "are not pining to emigrate—their governments would give them a happy good riddance, and no one would receive them—but rather, they want the right to eat, to have a school for their children and a doctor when they are sick. These are the basic rights, and they are withheld from many in the United States as in the rest of the world."

But treating Solzhenitsyn with respect and allowing him to publish freely—which would have been preferable, surely, even to allowing him to emigrate—would not impair these basic rights of the Soviet people. Mr. Koning simply implies that in a state which strictly defines the needs of all its people as of equal political importance, no championship of individual liberty will be countenanced. And that, I fear, may be true. But it does not, of itself, tell us whether freedom or equality should be chosen, if a choice must be made.

This is not at all the same issue as the question whether particular liberties should take precedence over public welfare in those situations where a genuine conflict exists, as of course it sometimes may. A government may find itself so short of the foreign exchange needed to keep its economy going that it must forbid its citizens to travel abroad on pleasure; or so in need of technically trained personnel that there is little or nothing in its education budget to support high culture. No reasonable person would call such a government oppressive for these reasons. But if it forbids foreign travel or starves or suppresses the arts because its commitment to equality has made it politically impossible to muster legitimate support for good things unequally shared; or because they would give the wrong people ideas and disrupt the political process—then that government is certainly hostile to liberty in principle. Mr. Koning is quite right in implying that it might nevertheless be preferable to one that is callous of welfare. But there is no reason to assume that it *would* be preferable. Presumably, whether or not it would be would depend on, or at least be influenced by, the class position of the person who was expressing the preference. And there is no a priori reason to declare class interests illegitimate—though they are supposed to be in an egalitarian society. Or class conflicts unreal.

Mr. Koning's argument does, surely, support rather strongly one of the more controversial positions I have maintained throughout this book. Most liberal readers would, I think, insist that the abolition of privilege in society has resulted in a *redistribution* of, rather than a net decline in, the enjoyment of liberty in society. I cannot agree. Other goods have resulted from this abolition, though just how good they are is a difficult question to answer conclusively. Ivan Illich, for example, would not agree that institutionalized schooling and professional medical care do, in fact, provide for people's needs for health care and opportunities to learn. Such institutions seem to him literally their nemesis.[1] Nor is it evident that the standard of living of the people of the Soviet Union as a whole is higher than it was before the revolution, unless one counts the presence of certain technologies as evidence per se. And it is certainly not evident that it is higher than it would have been by now had no revolution occurred, for Russia before World War I had the most rapidly developing economy in Europe. But however these questions of fact or conjecture may be answered, there seem no grounds for believing that the values promoted by so ultimate an egalitarianism include a net gain in liberty. As Mr. Koning notes, sympathy for dissenters, and not only in the United States, is elitist.

It is true, however, that liberty cannot flourish in a society so stratified or static that it can sustain neither growth nor innovation. Liberty is hardly to be found in the stagnant provincial backwaters even of a more active society. There was not enough in the town of Perm, as Chekov noted, to nourish the lives of *Three Sisters;* and there would not be in Molotov, as the town is now called. There is no need to speak further of the cultural diversity afforded by the teeming life of great cities. Or of the diversity of the frontier which, in the United States, afforded those who were misfits in the East the opportunity to escape its constraints. In Canada, where the RCMP and the Hudson's Bay Company preceded the settlers on their westward journey (protecting the Indians, though not their culture, from destruction), the association between freedom and westering is weaker. Even there the development of the west could not but provide the European with a sense of economic expansiveness even as it destroyed the lives of the native peoples. The fate of those of the Indian and Eskimo peoples who tried to retain their ways of life in the face of North American white economic expansion is evidence enough that a static society cannot effectively protect the rights or liberties of its members against the ruthless bearers of a forceful technology. That expansion enhanced the liberties of their oppressors is, however, less obvious. It certainly gave them more choices. But the ruthless and pragmatic mind-set of the Continental entrepreneur is ill suited to the enjoyment or even tolerance of cultural diversity or dissent. Nevertheless most people feel freer and livelier where "there's a scene" and "things are happening" because of rapid and vigorous economic activity. Boston or Philadelphia may be the cradle of liberty, but New York is the home office—as it is of oppression too.

Liberty, in short, is often associated with ugliness, violence, mess and exploitation. Except for the occasional Caesar who is allowed to enter the world through a special VIP gateway, *inter faeces et urinam nascitur* is still true. Yet birth, whatever one may make of it, does open up certain possibilities which could not otherwise be realized. And the variety of these possibilities is greater in an open and dynamic society—though not necessarily in an egalitarian one, especially at a time of heavy standardization of both roles and products. Economic growth and development, for those who participate in them, lead to increased freedom of choice of life-styles, occupations and activities—and this is the daily stuff of liberty, if not its noblest form.

Economic growth, finally, reduces the general level of certain kinds of social anxiety, though it raises others, and leads to a generalized boom-town euphoria which is liberating if it does not pass into a manic stage. People feel freer if jobs are easy to find; and they are more likely to be able to find a congenial place in society if a variety of jobs and roles is open to a large proportion of the population. There are, certainly, corresponding insecurities. It's even more humiliating if you don't make it, if making it has become the norm. And your particular life is more likely to be plowed under to make way for progress. The truck farmers of Santa Clara County, who grew some of the finest produce in the world, had no more chance of re-

taining their farms than the kulaks Stalin collectivized, once the area
was zoned and assessed for tax purposes as suburban housing.

But it remains true that a sense of freedom can prevail only in a
society that can provide a place for most of its members consistent
with their self-image and capable of supporting their self-esteem. In
feudal times a static, stable economy could keep such a society going.
But not in an era in which a prevalent egalitarian ideology has
inflated everybody's expectations. The greatest threats to liberty
occur during times of economic depression, not because these periods
spawn revolutions but because they induce a fearful and costive deference to authority.

A society committed to liberty must provide people with either full
and varied employment or a guaranteed and honorable place with
adequate income attached, independent of employment. But an egalitarian society commits itself to something quite different: the right to
compete for any position on equal terms. This seems a dubious asset
in the struggle for liberty, compared to a guaranteed right to enough
goods and services and access to the social roles needed to make life
meaningful on one's own terms. Concretely, and for most people,
there may be very little difference in practice between these two
rights. Discrimination against any social group must certainly deny
its members access to certain roles and certain valued goods and services that they need for their self-realization. But that, of itself, may
have nothing to do with equality. I recall, as a child growing up in
Louisiana in a family that traveled a lot, that the thing that most
impressed me as unfair about racial discrimination was the fact that
black people were not allowed to travel in pullman cars even if they
had the money or if a white person bought them a ticket. What
troubled me was not that this was *unequal* treatment but that it denied a basic human need for a bed to sleep in at night if you are
traveling. Since Negroes, as they were then called in polite discourse,
were stereotypically pictured by whites as drowsier and more somno-
lent than themselves, this seemed to me a peculiarly mean-spirited
form of discrimination. And as a youth I was delighted when, owing
to the firmness with which the Supreme Court upholds interstate
commerce, the right not to be segregated in trains that crossed state
lines was affirmed, many years before the court pulled itself together
in defense of more basic human rights, thus partially reversing its infamous 1896 decision in *Plessy* vs. *Ferguson*. But I certainly would
not then—or now—have refused a pullman berth myself, or slept

less easily in one when I had it, because it was arbitrarily denied to blacks, unless they were personal friends. If it is good to sleep at night, it is better for some to do so than for none; and the role of a Turandot proclaiming *Nessun dorma!* until my mild sense of moral outrage had been quelled did not appeal to me.

What is wrong about inequality is that it often results in denying people what they need for self-fulfillment. But when, in fact, it does not do that, its relation to liberty seems to me ambiguous. It has been demonstrated time and again, for example, that Jews are negligibly represented among America's most powerful law firms or the directorships of America's largest and most powerful corporations. If we were, things could scarcely be worse; but the fact that my country has never given me an equal—or, in fact any—chance to become a Dulles or even a Crawford Greenwalt does not seem to me a gross violation of my civil rights. Nobody really needs to be President; it may not even be good for him.

I have neglected, of course, the second and for many persons more compelling argument for equality of opportunity as a source of freedom; that it permits the commonwealth to avail itself of the best talent available, and hence improves the quality of life in the state for all. But the premises of this argument seem to me false. Equality of opportunity permits the widest range of candidates for any position to enter the field. It also for that very reason both makes it harder to identify the talented among so many strangers, and makes special recognition of their peculiar virtues illegitimate until they have defeated all their competitors, in a number of tests of doubtful relevance to those same qualities which led to their recognition in the first place. Indeed, as the tests become more relevant, they are criticized, correctly, as class-biased since, in any society, characteristics like those possessed by the ruling classes are likely to be perceived as qualities of leadership. The more egalitarian the society, then, the more abstract, meritocratic, and impersonal the procedures for advancement are likely to be made. Nobody has stated this problem more clearly than Tocqueville nearly a century and a half ago.

> In a democratic society, as well as elsewhere, there are only a certain number of great fortunes to be made; and as the paths which lead to them are indiscriminately open to all, the progress of all must necessarily be slackened. As the candidates appear to be nearly alike, and as it is difficult to make a selection without infringing the principle of equality, which is the supreme

law of democratic societies, the first idea which suggests itself is to make them all advance at the same rate and submit to the same probation. Thus in proportion as men become more alike, and the principle of equality is more peaceably and deeply infused into the institutions and manners of the country, the rules of advancement become more inflexible, advancement itself slower, the difficulty of arriving quickly at a certain height far greater. From hatred of privilege and from the embarrassment of choosing, all men are at last constrained, whatever may be their standard, to pass the same ordeal; all are indiscriminately subjected to a multitude of petty preliminary exercises, in which their youth is wasted and their imagination quenched, so that they despair of ever fully attaining what is held out to them; and when at length they are in a condition to perform any extraordinary acts, the taste for such things has forsaken them.

In China, where the equality of conditions is exceedingly great and very ancient, no man passes from one public office to another without undergoing a probationary trial. This probation occurs afresh at every stage of his career; and the notion is now so rooted in the manners of the people that I remember to have read a Chinese novel, in which the hero, after numberless crosses, succeeds at length in touching the heart of his mistress by taking honors. A lofty ambition breathes with difficulty in such an atmosphere.[2]

The force of envy is probably more effective in making excellent people unavailable, in the political sense of that term, as societies become more egalitarian. Envy may not be more prevalent; the teacher's pet and the King's favorite are hated everywhere. But such hatred is less effective in blocking his path if the society recognizes the King's right to have a favorite or the teacher a pet; and the King and the teacher are likely to have a more complete basis for judging the quality of a chosen favorite than a battery of tests can provide. Judgments from either source will be class-biased, since the norms applied, however derived, are derived from the status system of the society. Pascal's comment about the effect of Cleopatra's nose on history is imprecise in emphasizing its shortness; the point is, it was a *Roman* nose. And, in this case, indeed, Rome would have been better served if Antony had been obliged to have his choice confirmed by the advice and consent of the Senate. The democratic process in the Middle East evidently tends, however, to select women as heads of state on quite different grounds. Even the author of *The Merchant of Venice* might have had some difficulty composing *The Tragedy of Antony and Golda Meir*.

Men do not become freer as the society they live in becomes more equitable. The belief that they do is a confusion resulting from the fact that equality and social justice are such great goods in themselves that people in our century tend to assume that all other great goods must flow from them. This assumption underrates the effects of great good fortune, or excellence, or amplitude of means—social or economic—which may vary so greatly from the mean experience as to constitute something that is qualitatively different and uniquely valuable. Miniver Cheevey, child of scorn, who loved the Medici albeit he had never seen one, is an object of ridicule to the poet who created him. But he was right in recognizing that Lorenzo the Magnificent had enjoyed something of supreme value that he could never hope to find in his time and place. He did not even know what it was, though his fellow-townsman, Richard Cory, probably did.

I would suggest that a society which affords some of its members extraordinary privilege and celebrates that fact, instead of apologizing for it and validating its less privileged members in their sense of grievance, will enjoy an unparalleled sense of human possibility. But there are certain caveats that must surely be observed in making such a statement.

First: though I have made this point before, I would again state that this does not establish that such a society is superior to a more egalitarian society. It depends on who you are and what you want. But there is no reason why the preference for such a society should be ruled illegitimate per se. Most people in the world today live under governments which are committed in principle to seeking "the greatest good for the greatest number." The results, so far, do not add up to a whole lot of good per capita. Misery abounds, while joy is replaced by commercial synthetics less like it than margarine is like butter.

Second: if the acceptance of established elite positions in society is favorable to liberty, this is seldom because the elites themselves are enthusiastic defenders of freedom, especially other people's. On the contrary, they are oppressive to liberties that might threaten their pre-eminence. And they have a vested interest in the preservation of order. One of the sadder and more discouraging things about the

Portuguese coup in the late spring of 1974 has been the way the initial liberation, instigated bloodlessly by progressive younger members of the Army and ruling class, almost immediately began pulling back at signs that the people were beginning to use freedom for genuine political ends—within six weeks, they were even censoring the press again and shutting off exuberantly satirical TV shows in the middle of the broadcast. And Ophuls' remarkable film about the French occupation and resistance during World War II portrayed accurately and convincingly *le trahison des hommes de grandes affaires* as well as *des clercs*. German industrialists similarly supported the rise of Hitler. The persons who take personal risks to defend freedom are always marginal in any society; and Ophuls' film added the further terrifying intelligence that even those who do, once victory is won, are likely to brutalize indiscriminately the persons they believe to be their former oppressors, without much concern for due process. No social class places liberty, as a general principle, above its political and economic interests.

Third: There is no race, nation, or other group of people in the world whose innate characteristics qualify them to serve as an elite. There cannot be. Even to raise the question is to misconceive the fundamental issue.

An elite is not a meritocracy. If it conceives itself as more competent than its subordinates, it has already opened the way to its own decline, since, in principle, it has suggested that it might be replaced if more competent people could be found. Elites don't have to demonstrate skills. They have tenure. They may, of course, lose their position through incompetence, by bringing about their own downfall. But as incumbents, they need not present themselves to their subordinates as candidates. Their relationship, instead, resembles that of Greek gods to mortals: not omnipotent, not superior, morally or intellectually; not admirable, not invulnerable; and God knows, suffering from plenty of troubles of their own. But privileged? Yes, indeed.

The problem of recruitment of elites is surely no closer to solution now than it was in Plato's day. Philosopher-kings are as rare, as difficult to identify and install, and as subject to corruption as ever. But the beneficial consequences that elites confer on liberty depend neither on their personal superiority nor their personal commitment to freedom. They advance the cause of liberty by displaying it to advantage, and by supporting institutions favorable to it, as among their own vested interests.

In egalitarian societies, and certainly in our own, there are, of course, many people who enjoy extraordinary liberties unavailable to most of their fellow-citizens, with damaging results. President Nixon and his alleged co-conspirators, indicted and unindicted, were among them. Their actions have certainly not brought the rest of us "an unparalleled sense of human possibility" in any positive sense, though it is true that before the event it was hard to imagine that public officials could act like that. But they, precisely, do not constitute an elite in my sense of the term. They were candidates and had been since birth, lacking all established position and even a firm sense of self—conditions peculiarly prevalent in mass, industrial societies. Not all the privileged in America are so insecure. The destruction of the Nixon administration has been characterized by some interpreters of public events as the consequence, among other factors, of a backlash among members of the genuine Eastern establishment against policies that were far more populist than their own, at least in the sense of introducing into the realm of high finance the indelicacies of the used-car lot. But even if this is true, it must be granted that the wielders of immense economic power in the modern world do not seem to conceive of themselves as elites and are neither defenders nor exemplars of liberty. Their public images as well as their personal life-styles are furtive and conventional. The culture derives no increment of grandeur to compensate it for the disproportionate share of wealth they appropriate. This is really unusual historically. Even the Roman emperors, who were seldom men of acute artistic sensibility, left their people inspiring if heavy monuments. Trajan's arches convey a sense of triumph that McDonald's never will, though McDonald's empire probably has the greater assessed valuation.

But it is precisely the egalitarianism of the society that makes its top dogs often so useless an extravagance culturally. Aristocracies at least contribute the record, the example, and the paraphernalia of a distinctive life-style to their society, which suggests new possibilities for what life might be like—possibilities not merely of grandeur, but of insouciance. This is a public service. It is sad and silly to suppose that the public have been enriched when a palace or great country house is opened as a museum. On the contrary, they have lost whatever the life that once went on there, which was quite unlike their own, might have contributed to theirs in color and vividness. This is not to say that the support of the aristocracy was worth what it cost them; on this question, the judgment of history must be accepted. But old furniture and pictures on public view are worth infinitely less. In the new context they are mostly a source of bad examples.

It must be affirmed, however, on the verge of the great Bicentennial, that two centuries of popular, egalitarian government has generated new forms of freedom as it has threatened and obliterated others perhaps more precious but less widely enjoyed. The relationship of Americans to the automobile is a paradigm of their relationship to freedom, and helps greatly to show why that relationship is problematic. Americans believe, falsely, that they invented the automobile. What they have done, rather, is build their economy and hence their lives around a certain conception of it that is all most people want and more than they can manage. Designs that are both nobler and more practical exist and flourish elsewhere, but are not really suited to the American market.

Americans have pioneered in creating the cars and the freedoms that are suited to the productive processes and psychic needs of a mass industrial society. A Mercedes 280 can't really catch on in the United States. It costs as much as a Cadillac, and it still isn't top of the line. Being small and luxurious gets you nowhere. So what if it's maneuverable; in that class, the other fellow is supposed to get out of *your* way.

My analogy between cars and freedoms in America is not really close enough; it isn't an analogy but an identity. A car is the first freedom a "teen-ager" gets and it carries a heavy load of indoctrination. It is a *rite de passage,* the right graduation present for parents who can afford it to give their sons. In some states you can get a driver's license at sixteen if you take driver education in school, and pass an examination on "proper attitudes" as well as skills. Auto didacts have to wait till they're eighteen. Either way, the Bureau of Motor Vehicles reminds you that "driving is a privilege and not a right." So, increasingly, is privacy.

A car is evidence of socialization. Sons who say they don't want a car for graduation or consider it a polluter or an economic drain make their parents very nervous and hostile; but of course, they don't talk that way as much as they used to in the sixties. A car is the kind of freedom Americans understand. A gasoline shortage is a real crisis; people shoot filling station operators and truck drivers abandon their law-'n'-order stance and block the highways with their rigs. They are more patient with officials who stifle dissent, impede the flow of ideas, or just run hippies out of town, than they are with anyone who holds back gas.

The obvious answer to this comment is that the freedom the automobile both represents and embodies in American life is something that most people depend on and utilize every day to make their lives possible. If they can't drive, they may lose their jobs. The freedom embodied in civil liberty works in just the opposite way. You are likely to become involved in endless hassles, and perhaps lose your job and your status in the community, if you try to assert your supposed constitutional rights and become known as a sorehead or a shit-disturber, let alone a radical. Civil liberties are what most people know better than to exercise. Without exercise, they atrophy.

Still, it is heartening to see, in the garage of the Little White House that Franklin Roosevelt built for himself in Warm Springs, Georgia, with eight thousand dollars of his own money, the special automobile that was designed and constructed to permit him to drive, though poliomyelitis had deprived him of the use of his legs. Can one imagine that this indomitable man would have allowed public opinion to silence his at that time highly controversial political voice any more readily than he allowed disease to deprive him of his mobility? His adversaries tried; throughout most of his more than twelve years in office he was vilified as a sympathizer with Communism and, occasionally, as a sexual libertine in a manner calculated to drive him from office as similar attacks were later to drive Willy Brandt. Franklin Roosevelt, however, was brought up to transcend norms rather than to fear them, as one glance at his mother would have made clear. From his responses to the nation, as in his famous speech about his little dog, Fala—a less bathetic beast, apparently, than Mr. Nixon's Checkers—he apparently found these attacks comical.

Franklin Roosevelt was, of course, an exceptional though quintessential American, and one does not expect everyone to be like him. But that is just the point. His qualities and especially his sense of security could only have been brought into being through his patrician rearing and education. Privilege played an indispensable role in making Roosevelt himself, and Roosevelt, it is now apparent, played an indispensable role in forestalling the decline of privilege, or at least retarding the decline, even though he was denounced at the time as a traitor to his class.

In the political spectrum of the thirties, of course, Roosevelt's position was that of a populist. It is easier for a patrician to be a populist than for a self-made man, especially when the abuse of privilege has been a major factor in bringing on an apocalyptic depression. Paradoxically, the peculiar—one would hope unique—circumstances of the Depression of the thirties are what made Roosevelt's elite characteristics political assets. Psychologically, they were indispensable: the statement "the only thing we have to fear is fear itself" would, from Mr. Nixon's lips, have been enough in itself to create panic. But there are more fundamental reasons.

The Depression provided the only conceivable set of economic circumstances in which Mr. Roosevelt's populist leaning would have coincided with his class interests as correctly perceived. Members of elites seldom betray their interests and when they do they are usually swiftly forced into marginal positions within the elite, if not out of it altogether. But Roosevelt's political insight was great enough to permit him to recognize historical necessity and act on it. He was rather in the position of a first-class passenger on a teeming and endangered ship who wins a mandate from most of the passengers to seize control of the vessel and navigate it with due regard for the shoal waters into which its officers have steered it, undeterred by the outrage of the other first-class passengers who still see the officers as their kind of people. In the process, he became acquainted with the people in steerage, sympathetic to their plight and aware that their desperation contributed greatly to the instability of the ship and was hence adverse to the interests of everyone on it. He sought to ameliorate their lot and give them a new and somewhat better deal, which infuriated the other first-class passengers still more. He thus comes to be recorded in history as a great insurgent captain; but it is doubtful if, in a normal voyage, he would have found much reason to interact with the steerage passengers, or any occasion to demand their trust. If the result of his reforms was to decrease somewhat the disparity in amenities that existed between classes, he certainly did nothing to encourage the steerage to expropriate the ship and run it as a one-class vessel. And he did a great deal to prevent them from being forced into piracy by sheer want.

Genuine populism, also associated with a marked degree of political genius, was likewise to be found in the Democratic party of Roosevelt's time. Huey Long, who called his book *Every Man a King,* who abolished the poll tax and provided free textbooks for all school children and free hospitalization for the poor in Louisiana at a time when these were not even socialist visions elsewhere in the South, was much more nearly a man of the people. Roosevelt and Long loathed one another and were mortal political enemies despite their common party affiliation. Both were hated by conservatives as dangerous radicals. But their actual assailants were not deceived. Roosevelt's unsuccessful assassin was a rootless lumpenproletarian; Huey Long's successful one was a physician whose father Long had gerrymandered out of a state judgeship of long standing. Dr. Weiss, who removed from American politics the only broad-spirited populist to have become a significant national figure since La Follette's day at least, is one of very few men who may really have altered the course of history by a single act of violence. Huey Pierce Long was genuinely uppity. Had he lived, he might have cajoled the American poor into acting in their own class interests, seizing a greater measure of equality and reducing the resentment that builds up when each set of ritual promises exacted as the price of victory is betrayed as the price of power. Since this was a real possibility, however, if Dr. Weiss hadn't killed him someone else almost certainly would; and for far less human reasons.

Roosevelt and Long exemplified two quite antithetical modes of response to underclass social and economic demands in America, at a time when those demands were most desperate and authentic. My family, like most middle-class Louisianians, detested Long and all he stood for, which was a pity from my point of view since he was the only politician who had ever taken any notice of me. Once, when I was a child, he came up to me in a barbershop in Shreveport and asked me if I was going to vote for him when I grew up. As he was murdered when I was fourteen, we never found out, but I probably would not have. I was never a populist, though I certainly like the ringing affirmation of "Every Man a King" better than its latter-day equivalent, "Nobody Here but Just Us Workers."

Mr. Roosevelt's style suited me much better—in fact no other president during my lifetime has had a style that suited me at all—and his policies were more congenial to my class interests than Huey Long's were. But, in retrospect, I respect Long more for his willingness to make enemies of his opponents and hence to preserve the clarity of his position. (Harry Truman possessed a little of this quality, but he really thought he *was* a common man, while Huey knew better about himself. They were both right.) On a national scale, bourgeois interests could probably have fought Long and won an even greater victory than Roosevelt's gifts for compromise achieved. But even if we had lost we would have known better where we stood. The country would have been far abler to confront its political difficulties clearly if it had been sufficiently responsive to genuine class interests and class conflicts to permit Long a real chance to win and wield power. Whether he had won or lost, his campaign would have helped to establish that cultural conflict may express truly adverse interests which cannot all be resolved by incorporation under the presumably overarching interests of the commonwealth. Once this is recognized, the legitimacy of seeking to protect and advance those interests, not ruthlessly, but without guilt, follows. The growth of unions, for example, which the Roosevelt administration fostered as potentially beneficial to the entire country, maligning their adversaries as "economic royalists," could have been supported equally vigorously and far more honestly by claiming only that stronger unions would benefit the working class and leaving industrialists free to be less hypocritical in their opposition. Huey Long was usually far too arrogant to try to placate his enemies; he confronted them, but he did not try to cut the moral ground out from under their feet by alleging that his policies really subsumed their interests. This is not to suggest that Roosevelt's position was false; he really did save capitalism for the "economic royalists" even as he invited labor to wax great and join the feast. My point is rather that the Roosevelt style, which carried the liberal tradition of political compromise even further than it had yet been carried in America while assuming a progressive guise, further dishonored the possibility of legitimate conflict, which is now probably lost to American culture.

It has never been a prominent possibility. Despite its commitment to pluralism, the American political system is notoriously unable to accommodate the kind of confrontation that Huey Long might have established had he lived to become a national force in the Democratic party or to found the populist party the American political array so conspicuously lacks. Serious ideological conflict in the mid-nineteenth century resulted in neither assimilation nor secession, but in a destructive military paroxysm in which the North not only defeated and ruined the South but successfully reduced the South's position to a moral nullity. Therefore, the South's position could no longer be examined as an alternative, even to be dismissed.

Terrified perhaps by its own history, the nation has ever since aborted ideological conflict. And liberalism is as far as it has ever been from acknowledging that abortion is an act of extreme violence—as violent as combat. Indeed, there emerged in the late 1950s a recognized school of political thought which proclaims "the end of ideology," insisting that the introduction of ideological issues into American politics is destructive and irresponsible, since America has become what it is by pragmatic accommodation among conflicting groups and interests, regardless of doctrine. To examine the premises on which policy is based in the United States and insist on logical or moral consistency is condemned as political immaturity and adventurism—a charge continually leveled against opponents of the Indochina war; and still utilized, on various occasions, by Henry Kissinger against adversaries he perceives as moralistic.

Every society with the power to do evil has done plenty; and many have done far worse than America—often, indeed, through ideological rigidity and excess. But only in America does any recognized group of intellectuals insist, not that their nation's policies are right, but that the act of making moral judgments about them is itself disruptive and subversive. The application of moral judgment, as Mr. Nixon insisted in the hope of disarming his Watergate critics, interferes with the process of government in America and keeps it from getting its essential business done.

The fact that ideology is illegitimate per se in America goes far toward explaining why freedom of speech has fared as well in the United States as it has. The fundamental bases and purposes of policy are simply beyond the scope of effective political re-examination and assessment, though not of theoretical discussion. Americans would not and probably by now could not consider forming a political action group designed to analyze and publicly represent the interests of a social class or set of ethnic groups. This is done, instead, by licensed pressure groups, all of which claim as a matter of rhetoric to be advancing the public interest along with their special claims. Conflicts of interest are then compromised within the machinery of major parties on purely empirical grounds. American political machinery is equipped to resolve conflict about the share of goods, services, and power to which different pressure groups may be entitled, and to consider moral factors in making such judgments. But it makes no provision for validating and responding to the demands of groups who perceive their interests as separate from and in conflict with those of the nation, even though they are prepared to accept a smaller share of the proceeds than they would be entitled to as good members of the club. Can you even imagine an Official Languages Act in the United States guaranteeing the rights of those of its citizens who chose to conduct their business with the state in Spanish, and requiring post offices even in primarily Hispanic areas to be also designated with the word *"correos"*?

Even the newly emergent and militant liberation movements which might have been expected to adopt political positions emphasizing their unique identity have, instead, shackled themselves by their egalitarianism. The Women's Liberation Movement demands that women and men be treated equally. It does not demand that the apparatus of the state be used to meet the special needs of women, and it even resists the idea as politically counterproductive unless those needs can be ascribed to earlier discrimination rather than to innately feminine characteristics. The same is true, a fortiori, of blacks. Yet there do appear to be significant differences between either group and the dominant white male population, differences which only the most sophisticated research techniques suffice to obscure. Every self-conscious social group must choose, as a matter of policy, whether to define its distinctive characteristics as the results of injuries for which it requires compensation or as aspects of the self to be defended, whatever their origins, as vested interests. The question, ultimately, is whether assimilation or continued distinction on acceptable terms is the goal.

Where distinction is a politically realistic prospect, it would appear to be the more satisfactory choice. Advocates of liberty—a distinct minority—perhaps have no other choice, for their preference is indeed class-biased. And the institutions that promote liberty are often inimical to rapid economic growth; more responsive to the demands of cultural continuity than of equality of opportunity; and inherently, though not necessarily decisively, biased in favor of uniquely individual development rather than collective welfare. Whether this would ultimately lead to the greatest good of the greatest number is a highly subjective—as well as what Franklin Roosevelt used to call an "iffy" —question. It is iffy enough that the traditional, and Sisyphine, American effort to win majority support for civil liberty as a popular cause seems to me a little dishonest as well as fruitless. It is enough to maintain that it is a legitimate goal for a minority. Like blacks, gays, or the American Medical Association (women are not a minority) such a minority would possess no basis for a claim to innate superiority, and would advance none. It would note merely that circumstances alter cases, and generate specialized tastes and specialized needs. Liberty ranks high among these.

The maintenance of civil liberties does not, however, require the establishment of privileged social groups in the technical legal sense—that is, of categories of persons to whom special laws apply. This constitutional issue need not arise—though if it did, there are certainly enough precedents established in the treatment accorded corporations under American law to justify privilege in principle. These fictitious personages whose legal status as individuals was established a century ago by favorable judicial interpretations of the Fourteenth Amendment—which was intended, of course, to free the slaves—enjoy many specific privileges like variances on regulations governing pollution, zoning, or plant safety, exemption from property taxation for periods of years, and the like. But corporations, like upper-status individuals, also derive a measure of exemption from legal control from deference, influence, access to information and latent economic power; and these, if enjoyed openly, ought to be a sufficient source of freedom in themselves. According to a story— possibly apocryphal, but certainly mythic—which enjoyed wide currency in Louisiana at the height of Huey Long's power, his son, Russell, then an undergraduate at Louisiana State University, though for many years now a senator himself, was arrested by a state trooper for driving down the road to New Orleans at seventy-five miles an hour. The trooper was promptly fired, on the grounds that the safety of the people of Louisiana would surely be endangered by the operations of any policeman whose vision was so poor that he didn't know a Long when he saw one.

Meanwhile, there does indeed remain, as Mr. Koning justly observed, the privations of the starving Bengalis: a serious conflict of interest with the demands of the privileged West if ever there was one, and assuredly nothing to yawn over. In the next chapter I wish to consider certain aspects of the grossly inequitable distribution of wealth on this planet, the probable effect on this of the emergence of corporate power-structures that transcend the national state and may, indeed, eliminate it except as a folkloric vestige without independent authority like the Transkei or the Uzbek Soviet Socialist Republic; and finally, how this affects the prospects of liberty.

CHAPTER SEVEN

Liberty and the Giant Corporation

The national state is the guarantor of the conflicting claims of liberty and equality, to the extent that any guarantee is offered. It has undeniably supplied fertile ground for liberty, as it has likewise been liberty's chief adversary. Meanwhile, the national state has itself become the host of a form of economic growth that threatens to overpower it and, indeed, in smaller states frequently does so. In this case, the cancer is well enough organized to survive the death of the patient.

This flourishing economic organism is, of course, the multinational corporation. It is even more hospitable to the claims of privilege than the state is; or, more precisely, it has become the major source of such claims. Its effects on both liberty and equality are ambiguous, but they are not usually very positive. And the worst possible effects seem to occur from the combination of an "underdeveloped" state and a giant corporation directed from an imperial center, which therefore serves the imperial interests of its home state as well as its own economic interests. This is the source of the wastage that has proved lethal to so much of the "underdeveloped" world.

Governments that oppose the intrusion of intercontinental giants into their economies are overthrown, and replaced with others favorable to the giants' interests. Governments favorable to those interests are maintained beyond their term and contrary to the established constitutions that are intended to limit them. And these are almost without exception fascist governments which rely on the torture and imprisonment of hundreds of thousands of victims to relieve their apprehension even when there is very little evidence that they are seriously threatened by dissidence. The multinational giant, which in many cases has already demonstrated its power to overthrow the government if it wishes, never does so because that government is atrocious in its tyranny; it usually supports it, to avoid having to come to terms with a new and probably more difficult sovereignty.

These are still, to be sure, intermediate conditions. The corporate giant has not yet usurped or fully assumed the government of its hinterland. It merely controls the state well enough to insure that the state will not control *it* and place the public interest above the corporation's. From the viewpoint of liberty, this may well be the worst possible situation, for the government still maintains its hegemony over domestic institutions and the daily life of the citizens—who still retain at least *pro forma* the power to threaten its legitimacy at intervals and are therefore closely controlled. The Chase Manhattan Bank, if it were running the Union of South Africa as a wholly owned latifundium, would still have an interest in keeping wages low and labor docile and unorganized. But it would have none whatever in maintaining apartheid as a cultural norm, or in censorship of the arts. The present arrangement also adds to the constraint experienced by the residents of small nations by making the invading corporate giant the bearer of its home country's national interest along with the corporation's own economic ones. An example of this, in its crudest form, occurs when such companies provide cover for CIA men, or, less dramatically but more importantly, when they refuse to develop local facilities that would compete with established interests at home. The greatest damage done to Canada by patterns of American investment has probably not been the result of crude exploitation but of the refusal to allot to the Canadian subsidiaries any of the advanced functions like research and development which, being necessary to industrial autonomy, are retained in the United States. If however there were no border, and the continent were openly governed by an investment consortium which retained the idea of national differences only to promote tourism and a sense of the exotic, then some of these functions would normally be assigned to Canada. It would be no worse off than West Virginia or Arkansas, which, for years, were each allotted their own Rockefeller.

The thought, in any case, no longer quite boggles the mind. A few years ago a group of Californian investors were reported to have attempted to purchase outright an entire East African nation, which they hoped to use as an exclusive big-game hunting resort for themselves and their guests. The people who lived there would have been not only permitted but encouraged to remain and, as one might say, cook and help around the grounds; but not, I should imagine, to teach their children that any child may grow up to be like William Holden. The investors were unable to complete their transaction and withdrew from it. But it is interesting to speculate as to what the state of civil liberties would have been in their land—or should it be *on* their land? Clearly, the right to immigrate would have been carefully controlled, but what about to emigrate? Private property—at least, real property—simply would not have existed; only shares in the corporation. There would have been security guards and game wardens, whose duties their employers would have been free to prescribe. But what, if any, redress would have existed against their excesses? The corporation, presumably, could have been sued in the courts of California for civil damages attributable to its agents or employees. But what about criminal actions—would there have been any? The poorest and least articulate Chicano laborer on the King Ranch knows that he possesses, at least theoretically, the power to summon Texas Rangers and agents of the Immigration Service from the vasty reaches of empire, just as the Kings or Klebergs do. Is this knowledge comforting?

The obvious vulnerability of the East African people makes this fantasy nightmarish; and the fact that it was never realized an occasion for relief. But suppose we substitute in this fantasy a land and a people who have had their day repeatedly during the past two thousand years, and, when they had it, flaunted it. Italy is now said to be bankrupt and ungovernable. Essential services like the post office have broken down; the country, hit by the rise in oil prices and other inflationary factors, has not the resources to pay its bills under any government that would conceivably be lawful under its constitution. Even if it is bankrupt, nobody has the authority to force it into receivership. But what if there is simply no way to keep it going?

A plan emerges. Let the present government, as its final act, lease the country to Six Flags, Incorporated, the major operator of "theme" amusement parks in America. The entire country becomes a new theme park: Six Flags Over Rome. For an entrance fee of one hundred Swiss francs per day, visitors can ride and ride and visit any spectacle in the grounds: Settebello trains, leaning towers, catacombs, Stromboli erupting, anything. In the evening, for consenting adults and at a surcharge, the feast of Trimalchio re-created.

The fiscal problems of the Italian nation would finally be solved, having ended with the Italian nation itself, just over a century after it had been formed. Italy would be governed by the Directors of Six Flags, Incorporated, meeting in Atlanta or wherever the home office is—a bit further from Rome than Rome is from Eritrea, but not enough to raise a moral issue. Italian culture would be saved, the fifty million permanent staff members of Six Flags Over Rome would be paid to be even more Italian than they are now. Gucci, the cobbler, and Fellini, the director, would create their wares before admiring throngs, and these along with real frozen Italian pizza, would be made available to the public at every Six Flags theme park all over the world—even at the newest, Six Flags Over Estonia, which the Soviet Union, having finally gained confidence in détente, might be happy to accept by 1984. Those few Italians whose gifts for free enterprise prove difficult to accommodate within so totally planned an economy could be assigned rewarding though carefully limited roles as Mafiosi or, if too gifted even for this, transferred to the Home Office and allowed to make their way within the planet-wide corporate structure.

This, and worse, has already happened to the Indians and Esquimos of North America; the Iroquois, too, were once called a nation. Whether it helps any to keep your national façade like the Uruguayans, thus retaining traditional customs like picking Bordaberrys on election day—or to have all but the thinnest shell eaten away by a consortium of foreign investors—is hard to say. In either case, civil liberties are eroded to the vanishing point, with the added bitterness of discovering that really, not many people miss them. Such protest as does arise comes from social groups who rebel, and with good reason, against the stringent economic inequities the men in power propose to establish or continue, requiring, of course, the suspension of civil liberties needed to eradicate their opposition. But these liberties of themselves never command profound adherence among a majority of either left or right. Even if the American State Department, as it claims, used nothing more against the Allende government than severe economic sanctions designed to impoverish the country, it knew that this would be enough to prevent Allende's people from rallying to his support, despite the horror that must ensue if they did not.

At the root of the question of the relation of liberty to the national state is, I believe, the bitterest possible paradox. In the world as we know it, and as it has engraved itself upon our categories of thought, only the national state can be the guarantor of liberty. Americans think of liberty as derived from law and Britons from custom but both assume that it is meaningless unless ultimately it can be defended in court. The British common law has been regarded as a binding code only since the time of James I; and most people have regarded themselves as citizens of a national state only since a much later date—still only about a century ago. Many, of course, still do not. Many a perfectly competent Central African still does not know that he is supposed to be an Upper Voltaic and that the capital of his country is called Ouagadougou. It is, after all, a hell of a thing to admit. But for the citizen of the modern industrial state, the state is the only possible guarantor of freedom. This does not, of course, mean that he expects justice from its courts any more than he may expect a passport from its Passport Office. But he does know there is no place else to turn for either, except, perhaps, and dangerously, to his wits.

But the reason for this association between the state and freedom, as I have insisted earlier, is not that the state is an especially useful device for insuring freedom. Or, that any state, at any time, has a very good record for guaranteeing freedom to all of its citizens, most of whom, in any case, do not demand it, make very little use of it, and get nervous when other people do. It is rather that what we have come to accept as basic freedoms were those guarantees needed by an elite that was groping its way toward capital investment and industrial development.

This elite had very little reason to suppose, in a day of limited literacy, no mass media, and suffrage limited by property qualifications, that what it said about "the rights of man" would get back to the people and cause trouble. The philosophers of freedom for the most part doubtless sincerely wished that it might; but their own freedom clearly depended on the fact that few among the then ruling classes thought that it possibly could. When, as in England during and after the French Revolution, the ruling classes suddenly saw what happened when it did, a wave of repression set in. And even in America, where capitalist democracy first took formal shape, the authors of the Constitution found it unnecessary to stipulate that the rights of man applied to blacks and women, though they knew of course that without such specificity it would be assumed in the society of the time that they did not. Similarly it is still assumed that they do not apply to minors. Freedom, in the Western world, is an industrial by-product. Its captains of industry often acted—and still do—as if freedom were a form of industrial waste.

The state is the source of freedom in the same sense that it is the source of morphine—which is clearly not the same thing as saying there wouldn't be any if the state did not exist. In a larger sense, of course, there would not. Morphine and heroin are not natural substances, but rather are the products of a refined technology which could not have developed without a state to guarantee patents and property rights. But the state doesn't provide either liberty or opiates freely. It controls the traffic and punishes severely people who try to get it illegitimately; it designates the functionaries who decide how much you need; it operates the institutions in which those deemed to have abused it are confined for rehabilitation and kept from setting a bad example; and it surrounds the enjoyment of it with so much surveillance and paranoia that there is very little pleasure left in it. Perhaps as a consequence, though most people probably have fantasies about trying liberty, the addiction rate is really small.

Thus is the state both the guarantor of liberty and its enemy. Much of its hostility to liberty is, as I have indicated, a consequence of its commitment to equality; and this might be sufficient to reconcile many liberals to the compromises by which the state erodes their freedom, if the state's record with respect to equality were better. But it has also become the major instrument through which gross economic and social inequality is maintained in the world. It promotes inequality not only through its inevitable deference to established political and economic power but by its very nature and existence.

In a world in which class distinctions as well as ethnic discrimination have largely been declared illegitimate by the national state, the state itself provides the basis for the most egregious discrimination against the poorest and most helpless inhabitants of the earth. If it is wrong, as it surely is, to deny a man access to the goods, services, or social roles he needs to fulfill himself, simply because of his race or his tested scholastic aptitude, then it is surely even more arbitrary to do so because of his nationality. All these attributes are largely artifacts, reflecting as they do the complex interaction of social and genetic factors with legal definitions. But there is at least something more personal about race and IQ. Men do not become whiter or brighter as a result of either military victory or the absurdly named process of naturalization. But the economic consequences of the ensuing status change are enormous.

The injustice of discrimination against nationals of other countries was, of course, implicitly recognized for more than a century in the United States' open immigration policy; and explicitly in the effusive inscription on the base of the Statue of Liberty. Both these were part of the American commitment to the equality of man, though the inscription, which is certainly not intended to be insulting, did call upon the huddled masses, the wretched refuse of the teeming earth, to accept this designation of themselves, and may have discouraged those who did not from applying. But America repudiated this undertaking at the turn of the century by restricting immigration, largely at the instigation of American workers' organizations, whose distaste for unearned economic privilege did not extend to the privilege conferred by their citizenship. Samuel Gompers, generally recognized as the founding father of the American Federation of Labor, rose to prominence by successfully urging passage of the Chinese Exclusion Act, in the course of which he uttered some of the most racist vilification of the Chinese ever spoken of any racial group in the United States. Today, immigration into the United States proceeds at about a third of the rate that it did during its peak decade, 1901–10, when the population of the country was less than half the present figure. The rise of the multinational corporation has added a note of irony to these facts, since it is now common practice for American companies to take advantage of the low wages of workers in other countries, not only for the manufacture of goods to be sold in the hinterland of the branch plant but even in the manufacture of goods from American components intended for the American market. Examples of this include cameras or transistor radios assembled in Hong Kong or South Korea by workpersons who receive no protection from American labor legislation or collective bargaining agreements, and no benefits under American social legislation. Many of the Asiatic work force employed by the multinationals are unschooled juveniles as young as fourteen, earning as little as thirty cents an hour.[1] Whether this is a more exploitative practice than denying juveniles the right to work on any terms, and compelling them to attend schools often unsuited to their needs, interests, or ambitions for no recompense whatever, I would seriously doubt. But it does seem clear that an egalitarian nation, having made these young Taiwanese, Koreans, Malaysians and others functioning members of its economy, owes them the right to come to mainland America in search of a better job if they choose, even before they become recognized as refugees.

The legitimacy of the government of any democratic state depends on the consent of the governed as solicited and recorded by constitutionally prescribed processes. These processes are usually elections at established times and voting by elected legislative representatives in the interim. A democratic government's legitimacy is impugned by actions which seek to regulate the lives of persons who live beyond its borders. This argument cannot be applied merely because action occurring in one state affects the residents of others. We do, after all, live in one world and such problems as these do not affect the legitimacy of the state; they are the proper province of diplomacy and of international commissions. But whenever one state establishes policies *intended* to affect the lives of persons outside its borders, it has become an invader.

A state which assumes the function of governing vast numbers of persons who hold no franchise within it, whether through the agency of corporations chartered by it, through infiltration and subversion by intelligence agencies, or through military intervention, can no longer be regarded as legitimate even on its own terms. The refusal of the House Judiciary Committee to add to the articles of impeachment returned against President Nixon the unauthorized bombing of Cambodia has a fine note of irony. For who, indeed, could have authorized the bombardment of a small, helpless country remote from its adversary and incapable of furnishing it a *casus belli*. The Senate of the United States can authorize war. Nobody can authorize murder.

What the bombardment might logically be said to have done is confer American citizenship on the Cambodians, who surely have a right to be represented in actions of a democratic state that so strongly affect, when they do not terminate, their lives. Failing that, it strikes at the root of the legitimacy of American democracy, which requires that the American people accept responsibility for their government and control it through established political processes. Nobody would claim the right to keep even a dog that they could not re-strain from savaging their neighbors. How, then, can they possibly claim the right to maintain a government that has demonstrably become a dangerous nuisance to the rest of the world as well as, perhaps, to themselves? It will, of course, be maintained; there is no other political possibility. And it will retain considerable power. But its authority is largely lost. This loss of authority by the state cannot but enhance the legitimacy of the giant corporation. It operates from no democratic premise or reference to "the consent of the governed." It has certain responsibilities toward the community and the environ-ment which may leave people at its usually inadequate mercy. But being immediately responsible to no local constituency and never having promised anybody a rose garden or even a rice paddy, it is politically in a position to face demands based on rising expectations more coolly than a national state, which is bound by egalitarian and constitutional commitments that it then proceeds to flout (as the Philippines, South Korea and South Vietnam, Hungary, and other client states of the two great industrial minotaurs have regularly done).

What the starving Bengalis and their cohorts throughout the un-derdeveloped world need is the political means to assert the power that their numerical supremacy ought to give them if the world were a democratic state. It is not, however; and even if it were, democratic states, as we have seen, have great difficulty responding to the needs of their poorest citizens. Practically speaking, this would seem to leave the "third world" with no alternative except a revolution against the political power actually held by the industrially developed states. Such a revolution seems to me unquestionably moral and, indeed, long overdue; and it is the height of ethnocentric vulgarity for those of us in the more privileged parts of the world to repond to the threat of world revolution with moral indignation and hysterical fear.

Such a revolution would not, however, do the cause of bourgeois liberty any good; and I see no reason why it should not be resisted on grounds of pure self-interest. It certainly would be. There can be no such thing as a legal right to revolt; no society legitimates the means by which its structure is attacked from below, and one can only as-sume that efforts would be made to suppress it, no matter how justi-fied it might be economically or morally.

Of course, the third world forces might win their revolution. But if they did, they would be unlikely to raise their standard of living in the near future. One of the evil consequences of an advanced technology is that it may make a revolutionary redistribution of claims on the planet's resources impossible. Not because technology insures the victory of the giant who wields it—the Indochina war should have taught that lesson if no other. But technology does allow the giant to hold the world's resources hostage, and destroy them rather than yield them—or, as he would doubtless prefer to say, destroy them in the process of defending them. We still do not know the extent to which Indochina has been rendered sterile and uninhabitable, or for how long, by the American effort to protect the Indochinese from their autonomous socialist tendencies.

It also seems very clear that any effort to develop the rest of the planet industrially to the present Western or even Soviet level would be disastrous. It is one thing to argue, as I have done, that the resources of an industrially developed society would be sufficient to provide all its members with a decent guaranteed annual income, if expenditures for "security" functions and the propitiation of envy were sharply curtailed. It is quite another to insist that the same standard of living be made available throughout the world to peoples who have never become members of such societies. Such insistence, in any case, must come from them, not from us. Only they can judge whether the effort would be worth the risk.

But if the multinational corporation comes to be regarded as the legitimate basis for government in the future it will not, I think, be because it is a superbly efficient economic instrument—that is a truly absurd myth. Corporations are rife with deadwood and featherbedding. And it will certainly not be because it promises to promote the cause of social justice. It will be precisely because the corporation provides the only possible way of circumventing the burdens of egalitarian democracy and reinstating the honorable idea that conflict of interest is ineradicable from the world and should be not only recognized but institutionalized—as it is in collective bargaining agreements which do not start from the premise that management and labor complement each other as *yang* and *yin,* and compose one perfect whole. It is probably also an error to think of the multinational corporation and the national state as rival, or conflicting social institutions. What is happening is more simply evolutionary. For a period of a century or two, depending on the part of the world being considered, the interests of economic expansion and the emergence of new and powerful elites has been served by a peculiar form of sovereignty based on an ideological commitment to popular suffrage and the equality of man. This is an exhilarating vision, but no high lasts forever. Skillful administrators, whether in universities or the affairs of state, have long realized, however, that to challenge established and cherished forms of autonomy is a dangerous and provocative insult to a people who have been led to believe that they are self-governing. Instead of interfering with the parliamentary process itself, it is usually wiser to establish control over the funding of any program the legislature may adopt; and to establish other channels for the organization and funding of projects that have not been submitted to, or have been refused, legislative endorsement. Sometimes, as in the case of the establishment and maintenance of the Central Intelligence Agency, the legislature is happy and proud to act as its own betrayer. From the point of view of the electorate the interests of the multinational giant may be seen as in conflict with those of the state. To the ruling elite, it merely provides an alternative means of achieving ends that the state cannot or will not overtly adopt.

For the present, the corporate giant still needs the state to front for it, legitimate its exploitations, register its agreements, and torture its adversaries. But the relationship is shifting. The larger corporate giants now generate power directly and in such magnitudes that if connected to the state in the old way they may simply blow out its resistors and leave it a smoking ruin. The large corporation has proved itself to be more nearly immune to the democratic process than any other major social institution of our times—even, I should say, than the armed forces, which must be in some respects quite responsive to the will of Congress. It is much easier, for example, for a manufacturer to close a plant that has become unprofitable, even though this plunges a whole city in misery, than for the armed services to close a base on which a community has become similarly dependent. This irresponsibility to the needs of the community, which, as in the relationship of the soft coal industry to Appalachia, may amount to a war of attrition and impoverishment against an entire region, is of course one of the most compelling and familiar arguments for socialism. It would, I should judge, have been resolved in socialism's favor long ago if the growth of economic power in capitalist societies had not made the question largely moot. Once an establishment has successfully made a flexible tool of government, it is unlikely to be kept awake nights by the specter of government ownership—especially in America, where public enterprise and even government controls with real teeth in them seem antagonistic in principle to the ubiquitous commitment to private, personal success. Members of regulatory agencies, envisioning a career in the industries they are supposed to control, do not willingly antagonize the chieftains whose service they plan to re-enter, once their brief term of government office has ended.

For most people today, making it through some part of the corporate structure—or, in socialist countries, the state bureaucracies —is the only way to become successful. Even those institutions which have long been thought of as separate, like the private professions, the academy, or the traditional strongholds of independent enterprise like agriculture, are no longer separate in fact. Many young people find this condition intolerable, and try to find some way of supporting themselves, however modestly, "outside the system." But there are many more—and they may be shrewder—to whom the idea of mass society is equally repugnant, but who turn to the corporation because its inegalitarian and antidemocratic character promise them a distinction that they lack the resources, psychological or economic, to seek by separating themselves from the mainstream of society. At their worst, such young people may resemble Jeb Stuart Magruder. They may also be a lot better than that.

With all its constraints and often stifling conformity, the corporate world is the only one left that legitimates privilege and hierarchy. From the very begining it lets the flesh off the egalitarian hook and openly admits, without apology, not only that some people who are obviously not superior in character or intellect have more power, prestige, and affluence than others, but that they want these, prize them, feel entitled to them, do not propose to relinquish them to more worthy claimants, *and will be supported by the organization in their pretensions to them.*

All the egalitarian assumptions of the democratic process are openly negated in the conduct of the corporation; the negation is built into its structure. For many employees, the corporation is the basis of more community than any other institution—certainly more than their neighborhood or the city itself provides. Yet they have no voice in setting its policies and very little in determining its day-to-day operation. Moreover, this fact is accepted as perfectly legitimate, though increasingly subject to criticism as bad practice in that it leads to alienation and low productivity. It is being changed; management is changing it.

You can't be a citizen of a corporation—you can only be a stock-holder, and these would not be permitted past the gate by security if they came near the place, except on the date set by management for the annual meeting. This means, if you are a worker rather than an executive, that you are free to fight it, must fight it, there can be no bullshit about regarding it as a commonwealth. Conflict of interest is not only regarded as legitimate, it is institutionalized, along with the means of resolving it. There is an overarching interest, too, since excessive demands that would in fact bankrupt the company are not in the interests of a union even though it has the power to enforce them. But the very fact that conflict is legitimated means that the separateness of the two sides is, too; and so is their inequality of status. It isn't *guaranteed;* but it is defined as legitimate. The right to bargain collectively is recognized. And it may and does drive wages of highly skilled workers above those of junior executives. But it does not carry with it the right to dine in their dining room. In America, only a corporation may still lawfully segregate facilities by class.

In a setting of hierarchy and privilege, envy is a peculiarly disrup-tive force. The political institutions of democratic society tend to val-idate envy, while those of corporate life deny it legitimacy and weaken its political force. The lives of public servants are made mis-erable by demands for economy in government and the constantly reiterated suspicion that government officials or any beneficiary of public expenditure is getting something for nothing or more than he should. "A building doesn't have to be cheap to get by Sacramento," University of California faculty members used to say about the designs proposed for new campus construction, "it just has to *look* cheap." The expenditures of private corporations, however, cost the consumer as surely as government expenditures do. They are either passed on to him as rising costs, or they lessen the corporation's profits and hence its tax bills, and leave more for the private citizen to pay. Yet, there is nothing in American folkways that suggest that private citizens have a right to complain about the lavishness of cor-porate salaries or perquisites, or about the hierarchical way in which these are distributed. This remains largely true even though the real giants now subsist primarily on public funds, which of course is what the idea of a military-industrial complex means. Government spend-ing is a constant target; corporate spending is not. The gravity of this distinction, as has often been pointed out, is one of the things Pres-ident Nixon apparently forgot. He was the only boy in his chosen peer group for whom no legitimate way existed to divert funds from his enterprise into the maintenance of his home. Any candidate for a corporate presidency could simply have made this a condition for accepting the job.

Collective bargaining presents an especially clear example of the way an institution of the corporate economic sphere has evolved to cut off only the invidious aspects of the demands that riddle the political sphere. It is not only appropriate but customary for workers in one union to cite increases granted other unions to buttress their own wage demands; and if the officers of the corporation are known to be receiving salaries upward of one hundred thousand dollars a year, those demands are quite properly likely to be stiffened. But there will be no demand that the executives receive less. The bargaining machinery would hardly accommodate it. You can use another man to climb on; and you can seek to delay his ascent; but you can't legitimately pull him down to your level.

Most of these hierarchical characteristics of the corporation are mentioned today only by its detractors, as evidence of its inhuman and alienating, as well as its basically exploitive, character. And certainly it would be foolish to deny that most employees, from top to bottom, seem to find the corporate life basically frustrating in fundamental respects, among the most important of which is that corporations are notoriously unresponsive to ethical issues and to the need to work creatively. A General Motors executive earning, or at least receiving, more than a half million dollars per year was recently reported by the New York *Times* to have resigned because he found the position stultifying; it provided no scope for his creative interest. The proportion of men earning a half million dollars a year who feel personally unfulfilled may well be very high indeed; though I have suspected, since the days of *The Man in the Gray Flannel Suit,* that the alienated and stultified executive was a myth propagated precisely to diminish the envy to which such men were subjected. Kings used to try this, too, going around saying things like "Uneasy lies the head that wears the crown" until their subjects, no longer able to bear the sight of such distress, resorted to compassionate surgery. In the modern corporation, the king would have received severance pay as well.

I hold no brief for these organizations. And I have recapitulated some of their familiar characteristics here neither to praise nor blame them, but rather to suggest that one of the factors that give them their enormous power may well be precisely their hierarchical and

antiegalitarian mode of functioning. They are the only remaining legitimate citadels of privilege in the modern world; if you want to assert a claim to privilege and have it respected, you must do it within
some part of the corporate world—though the medical or legal professions will surely serve.

Corporations themselves, of course, do not assert such a claim.
While their legal divisions attempt with great acumen and corresponding success to establish a privileged position in the world, their
public relations divisions just as vigorously deny it. Consequently,
they too fail as models; even these fictitious personages attempt to
present themselves as folksy and drab. But they do acknowledge the
principle of privilege in their own operation; they depend on it. This,
I think, is one of the reasons why, though they are fairly responsive
to pressures to hire more members of discriminated social groups and
advance those already employed to higher staff (not line) posts, they
are resistant to admitting blacks, women, or Jews to the highest policy levels—the Chairperson of the Board is still almost always a male
WASP, or drone. This is unlikely to be due to sheer defense of their
own status, because the first members of a discriminated group to
gain a coveted status are almost always *plus royaliste que le roi.* I
think, perhaps, it may be resistance to any further extension of the
concept of fairness and restitution as social forces; a felt conviction
that democracy has no place in the great board rooms of the nation,
rather than any pejorative view of the excluded peoples themselves.
This innermost dynamic of modern society may be clinging to a certain hangdog determination to be the last mechanism in which the
wrench replaces the screw.

Granted the choice between being governed by the demands of a
corporation and those of a democratic state whose policies are, in
any case, largely determined by corporate demands, I would still
choose the national state. Corporations are probably too lacking in
diversity and moral commitment, too rational to be trusted to en-
compass the whole of life, as the state must. The corporation does,
however, promise to treat those subject to its control with much less
ressentiment than the state does. Corporations violate and exploit
people for their own ends, but they seldom set out to punish, humiliate, or make examples even of their adversaries. They are not *spiteful.* Their posture in interpersonal encounter is defensive rather than
aggressive: aggression is reserved for acts of economic aggran-

dizement. And greed, even towering greed, is not nearly as ugly an emotion as spiteful envy. The masses are powerless, among other reasons, because their spite divides them; and the democratic state has become spite incarnate.

So it would not be a happy choice. But the issue of choice does not arise. The drama of history is not released in alternative versions to suit the tastes of different audiences; and we are not spectators but participants. Some of us have a very limited choice of roles, but nobody has any choice about what is to be presented; though all the Playwright's recent work justifies our suspicions that Her next piece will be no less vulgar. But we do seem to be present at a time when new and very different conventions of plot and staging are about to be adopted.

If the next stage in history does turn out to be the era of the multinational corporation, it is possible that neither the cause of liberty nor of opportunity might be worsened. An exploited class that thought of itself as composed of workers rather than citizens ought to find itself much less hampered by its own loyalties in seeking opportunities to turn against its oppressors and seek substantial social and economic gains. It is not drink, as the old saw has it, but patriotism, that has proved to be the workingman's curse in his continued struggle for a fair economic shake. But the open triumph of the corporation should place that intoxicant safely out of reach. No workingman busts his ass for a corporate employer, though executives often do. Neither, however, are workingmen consumed with envy because the corporation gives some of its employees who don't even work as hard much more than it does them; or with indignation because there is not even a pretense that management is recruited from among the ablest workers. In the corporation, in contrast to the state, differential rewards may be legitimated by differences in status.

In a world governed by multinational corporations in which the state had become a vestigial occasion for regional folklore rather than a political entity, a realistic class-conflict based on mutual respect rather than a sentimental and misleading identification of one class with the interests of the others might well become established; and this, I think, would be a very welcome clarification of everybody's relationship to reality, as well as to the means of production. What I would hope would develop would be a modern equivalent of the system of estates which governed France until the French Revolution: an unhappy series of events which I am pleased to have been unable to attend, and which did indeed lead toward, in the words the playwright Peter Weiss gives to the Marquis de Sade:

> the withering of the individual man
> and a slow merging into uniformity
> to the death of choice
> to self denial
> to deadly weakness
> in a state
> which has no contact with individuals
> but which is impregnable.[2]

But it is unlikely that anything quite so agreeable will happen. For fifty years or more, wherever political liberalism holds sway, we have accustomed ourselves to seeing democracy and fascism as polar opposites and alternative political arrangements vying for control of the national state. It now seems to me evident that this was always an error. Democracy is not an alternative to fascism, but a stage in its development, an earlier form of populism. Granted the pressures of population, the current fragmentation of culture, and the technological possibilities for oppression, the rise of the multinational corporation may well be another bend in the same road, slightly more scenic and on higher ground. Fascism, after all, is not a static concept either; it may be expected to lose some of the crudity associated with Hitler, Stalin, or Joseph McCarthy—all of whom, be it noted, gained power by lawful means. Corporate executives are almost always smoother and the rise of the multinational corporation may simply turn the world into something like the asylum at Charenton. There is only one really scary character in *Marat-Sade,* and that is Coulmier, the bureaucrat who runs the place.

A populist government can hardly be favorable to liberty; but it certainly does not follow that an elitist one will be. It depends on the quality of the elite and the strength of its commitment to humane respect for other persons and to culture, both broad and deep. The twentieth century has not dealt kindly with these commitments. One must recall the Krupp von Bohlens, perhaps Germany's greatest industrialists, who already during World War I directed a munitions cartel so highly respected that Allied bombers were ordered to spare their plants; and who, during World War II, used Russian prisoners of war on death-camp rations to run them—a war crime for which Alfred Krupp von Bohlen was incarcerated after the defeat of Germany. The Krupp von Bohlens can hardly have been as tense and peculiar a family as they appear to be in Visconti's film *The Damned*. But their contribution to human dignity and freedom has nevertheless been less than might have been expected.

The Krupps, like Fritz Thyssen, who helped Hitler consolidate his position of power, were industrialists, not Junkers, the landed Prussian aristocrats who occupied the top position on Germany's social scale, but who were already becoming atavistic by the time of Hitler's rise. These did finally rise to a noble and tragic occasion, in the "Officers' Plot," to assassinate Hitler on Saturday, July 20, 1944—though their action may be dismissed as too little, too late and, especially, too incompetent. It was more than anyone else did, however; President Roosevelt, who had earlier been approached for support to mount a more promising attempt, dismissed this feeler contemptuously as coming from archconservatives who, he assumed, must all really be supporters of Hitler—a common enough liberal assumption. Two hundred persons—which, to be sure, is less than one-tenth of one per cent of the victims of the fire-bombing of Dresden—were executed for this attempted assassination. One of these, Ulrich Wilhelm Graf Schwerin von Schwanenfeld, had a son, Christof Schwerin, now political correspondent of *Die Weltwoche* of Zurich. I have extracted the following passage from an article Herr Schwerin wrote for that paper and the New York *Times* of July 20, 1974, in memory of the thirtieth anniversary of the plot, because it illuminates clearly and movingly the factors that make me fear that the plight of Western man in industrial democracy is not even a dilemma:

What happened July 20 created nothing but indifference.

. . . .

From documents on hand today we know that the motives behind the Officer's Plot were more moral than political. The risk of self-liberation had to be undertaken to save Germany's honour.

It was amazing that both high officers in the German Army and members of the Prussian—the so-called Junker—aristocracy, realizing the political futility of the attempt to assassinate Hitler, risked their lives. Indeed, not one of the great aristocratic names of Prussia is missing from the death list.

It has been said that only the military was in the position to organize a revolution and that only the aristocrats who held

high civil-service jobs were aware of the illegality of the Nazi
regime. In reality, the resistance was composed of an elite from
all classes, traditions, and regions of Germany.

. . . .

Now, thirty years later, the German resistance has become a
historical matter. And in West Germany, with its so-called economic miracle, where people are obsessed by the luxuries of the
boom, it is an unwelcome memory.

. . . .

In our times there are conflicts between what the state demands and our democratic ideals under which each individual is
supposed to act as if he alone is responsible for the perpetuation
of rights and justice in society.

There are indeed. And when democratic ideals have been sufficiently corrupted in practice, the rule is no longer very helpful in
telling us how each individual is supposed to act. Mr. Nixon, too,
acted as if he alone were responsible for the perpetuation of rights
and justice in society, though not quite in the sense that Mr.
Schwerin means. So did Hitler. The difficulty is that neither of these
heads of state, in the course of their extraordinary rise from humble
origins, became a devotee of these concepts. These were not matters
with which their constituencies were greatly concerned, or demanded
much expertise.

It would be unfair and cynical to say that men get the kind of government they want; in an age of torture and mass executions they
clearly do not. But they do get the kind of government, and only the
kind of government that within the limits of their culture, they can
imagine. Government cannot transcend their hopes or values, or
safeguard what they do not cherish. Its form, then, may be less important than we suppose. National state or corporate giant; in 1975,
all roads lead to Six Flags—or promise to. After all, where else is
there?

NOTES

INTRODUCTION

1. New York, Alfred A. Knopf, 1967.
2. New York, Schocken Books, 1964.

Chapter 1

1. Miriam Wasserman's *The School Fix: NYC: USA* (New York, Outerbridge and Dienstfrey, 1970) and Colin Greer's *The Great School Legend* (New York, Basic Books, 1972) are among the best and most scholarly studies of the function of the schools, especially the urban schools, present and past, in identifying the children of the poor as failures and removing them from the economic mainstream; while Christopher Jencks, et al., *Inequality: A Reassessment of the Effect of Family and Schooling in America* (New York, Basic Books, 1972) provides a less convincing but more generalized and theoretical rationale for supposing that the schools cannot, in principle, be expected to have much influence on the distribution of economic opportunity in America.

2. The Canadian budget for public education, which was around 8 billon dollars per year, is quite comparable in magnitude to the American.

3. Andy Logan, "Around City Hall: A Hail of Bullets," *The New Yorker,* March 24, 1973, pp. 76–95.

4. "The Place of Private Police in Society; An Area of Research for the Social Sciences." *Social Problems* 21, 3, 1974, pp. 438–53.

5. T. Scott and M. McPherson, "The Development of the Private Sector of the Criminal Justice System," *Law and Society Review,* 6 (November 1971), p. 272.

6. Cf. Marvin E. Wolfgang and Marc Riedel, "Race, Judicial Discretion, and the Death Penalty," *The Annals,* Vol. 407, May 1973, pp. 119–33.

7. New York, Random House, 1965, *passim.*

8. New York, Schocken Books, 1964.

9. Cf. especially Colin Greer, *The Great School Legend* (New York, Basic Books, 1972), *passim;* and Clarence J. Karier, Paul Violas, and Joel Spring, *Roots of Crisis* (Chicago, Rand McNally, 1973), pp. 6–39 and 84–137. Together, these works heavily document the historical roots

of the public school system in the demands of an evolving industrial society, and the molding of the school practice by the needs of industry as perceived by its spokesmen and leaders.

10. Cf. Charles C. Moskos, Jr., "Why Men Fight," in Edgar Z. Friedenberg, Editor, *The Anti-American Generation* (New Brunswick, N.J., Transaction Books, 1971), pp. 217–38.

11. New York, Harper and Row, 1971.

12. D. L. Rosenhans, "On Being Sane in Insane Places," *Science, 179,* 4070, pp. 250–58, January 19, 1973.

13. Cf. T. J. Cottle, "Life Study: Wind" in T. J. Cottle, Editor, *The Prospects of Youth: Contexts for Sociological Inquiry* (Boston, Little, Brown, 1972), pp. 344–47.

14. Indianapolis, Bobbs-Merrill, 1963.

15. New York, Simon and Schuster, 1971, Part 2, pp. 88–119.

16. For a full discussion of the moral implications of the problem of obtaining blood for surgical use, as well as of existing variations in practice in the nations of the world—and a bloodcurdling account of the use of the courts to prevent hospitals of the city of Kansas City from setting up a hygienic, blood-donation system to replace the skid-row enterprise of the plaintiffs, see Richard Titmuss, *The Gift Relationship: From Human Blood to Social Policy* (New York, Pantheon, 1971).

17. New York, Doubleday, 1974.

Chapter 2

1. *Science, Technology and Society in Seventeenth Century England* (New York, Fertig, 1970). First published in *Osiris,* 4, Part 2, 1938.

2. See Barrington Moore, Jr., *Social Origins of Dictatorship and Democracy* (Boston, Beacon Press, 1966), pp. 16–20. Moore maintains, on the basis of convincing evidence, that if violence be measured in terms of human deaths occasioned by starvation and disease as well as by direct assault, the urbanization of England was a more violent process than the French Revolution, which later served the same end of modernization.

3. Cf. Colin Greer, op. cit., *passim.*

4. Arthur R. Jensen, "How Much Can We Boost IQ and Scholastic Achievement?" *Harvard Educational Review 39,* Winter 1969 (reprint C-113, 123 pp.).

5. R. F. Herrnstein, *I.Q. in the Meritocracy* (Boston, Atlantic Little, Brown, 1973), especially the preface and Chapters IV and V.

6. "Pay of Fat Executives Is Found Leaner than Checks of Others," the New York *Times.* January 2, 1974. The article concludes with a statement that "the overweight have become America's largest, least protected minority group."

7. New York, Doubleday, 1968, pp. 146–54.

8. Christopher Jencks, et al., *Inequality, A Reassessment of the Effect of Family and Schooling in America* (New York, Basic Books, 1971).

9. "The World Behind Watergate," New York Review of Books, XX, 7, May 3, 1973, pp. 9–15.

10. In *Wampeters, Foma, and Granfalloons* (New York, Delacorte, 1974), p. 194.

11. Kirkpatrick Sale, *SDS* (New York, Random House, 1973), p. 643.

12. *Ibid.*, p. 644, et seq.

13. John Roemer, "Gordon Liddy: He Bungled into the White House," *Rolling Stone*, 139, July 19, 1973. Aldrich left Buffalo after receiving his Ph.D. in English, and moved to San Francisco, surely an equally fertile base for his study. Few if any locations could have displayed the phenomena he has chosen to investigate as sharply as Buffalo from 1967–71.

14. Sale, 1973, op. cit., pp. 566–67.

15. *Ibid.*, p. 590.

Chapter 3

1. "Presumption of Innocence: Bail & Politics," by Nat Hentoff. *Civil Liberties*, 294, March 1973, p. 2.

2. Boston, Beacon Press, 1970, pp. 169–70.

3. New York, Vintage Books, 1945, Vol. II, p. 307 (first published in 1840).

4. William J. Blowers, *Executions in America* (Lexington, Mass., Lexington Books, 1974), p. 168.

5. E. Z. Friedenberg, *Coming of Age in America* (New York, Random House, 1965, *passim*); Carl Nordstron, E. Z. Friedenberg, and Hilary Gold, *Society's Children: A Study of Ressentiment in Secondary School* (New York, Random House, 1966, *passim*); E. Z. Friedenberg, "The Gifted Student and His Enemies," *The Dignity of Youth and Other Atavisms* (Boston, The Beacon Press, 1965), pp. 119–35.

Chapter 4

1. A useful and perceptive discussion of this issue as a methodological problem in sociology is Alexander Liazos, "The Poverty of the Sociology of Deviance: Nuts, Sluts, and Preverts," *Social Problems*, 20, 1, Summer, 1972, pp. 103–20.

2. Cf. Howard F. Stein, "The Silent Complicity at Watergate," *American Scholar*, 43-1, pp. 21–37, Winter, 1973–74, for a much more complete analysis reaching parallel conclusions.

3. Howard S. Becker, *Outsiders* (Glencoe, Illinois, The Free Press, 1963). Quoted in David Solomon, Editor, *The Marihuana Papers* (Indianapolis, Bobbs-Merrill, 1966), p. 59.

4. U. S. Treasury Department, *Traffic in Opium and Other Dangerous*

Drugs for the Year ended December 31, 1931 (Washington, Government Printing Office, 1932), pp. 16–17.

5. Bureau of Narcotics, U. S. Treasury Department, *Traffic in Opium and Other Dangerous Drugs for the Year ended December 31, 1932* (Washington, Government Printing Office, 1933), p. 13.

6. Bureau of Narcotics, U. S. Treasury Department, *Traffic in Opium and Other Dangerous Drugs for the Year ended December 31, 1933* (Washington, Government Printing Office, 1934), p. 61.

7. Bureau of Narcotics, U. S. Treasury Department, *Traffic in Opium and Other Dangerous Drugs for the Year ended December 31, 1935* (Washington, Government Printing Office, 1936), p. 30.

8. Solomon, op. cit.

9. Mayor's Committee on Marijuana, *The Marijuana Problem in the City of New York* (New York, Jacques Cattell, 1944). Substantially reprinted in Solomon, op. cit., pp. 227–360.

10. George Morris Carstairs, "Bhang and Alcohol: *Cultural Factors in the Choice of Intoxicants,*" *Quarterly Journal of Studies on Alcohol,* Vol. 15, 1954, pp. 220–37. Available in Solomon, op. cit. Carstairs, a British psychiatrist, reports observations made throughout the year 1951, as a resident of a village of 2,400 including 93 Rajputs and 85 Brahmins, in the state of Rajasthan in Northern India.

11. And one white superstar whose Dionysiac drumming made him a kind of dishonorary black—Gene Krupa.

Chapter 5

1. New York, Harper and Row, 1974.

2. *Ceremonial Chemistry* (New York, Doubleday, 1974), *passim.*

3. New York, Praeger, 1970, *passim.*

4. "Children, Schools, and Utopias," in Satu Repo (ed). *This Book Is about Schools* (New York, Pantheon Books, 1970), p. 171.

5. *Between Two Ages* (New York, The Viking Press, 1970), pp. 222–36.

6. Sale, op. cit., p. 64.

7. *Push Comes to Shove: The Escalation of Student Protest* (Boston, Houghton Mifflin, 1970), p. 145.

8. *Ibid.,* p. 146, italics in original.

9. Anon. (New York, Dial Press, 1967), *passim.*

10. Anon. (New York, Dial Press, 1967), pp. 20–30.

11. "U. S. Journal: Imperial County, California: The Glamis Run," *The New Yorker,* L, 3, March 11, 1974, p. 111.

Chapter 6

1. The annual Encyclopaedia Britannica Lecture, Edinburgh, April 26, 1974 (CIDOC, Cuernavaca, Doc. 1/V, 74/62).

2. Tocqueville, *Democracy in America,* Vol. 7, Chapt. XIX.

Chapter 7

1. Richard Barnet and Ronald Miller, "Global Reach—II," *The New Yorker*, L, 42, December 9, 1974, p. 131.

2. Peter Weiss, *The Persecution and Assassination of Jean-Paul Marat as Performed by the Inmates of the Asylum of Charenton Under the Direction of the Marquis de Sade* (New York, Atheneum, 1965), p. 75. Pocket Book Edition.

"consent of the governed" in, 74–77; in modern industrial society, 62–82; as a political liability, 62–63; ressentiment and, 72–76; unpopularity of, 56–62; will of the people, 84, 85

Liddy, G. Gordon, 51, 52, 53
Lifton, Robert Jay, xv
Lincoln, Abraham, 82
Lindsay, John, 62–63
Liquor industry, xiv
Locke, John, xv, 56
Lockheed Corporation, 41, 140
Logan, Andy, 7
Long, Huey, 160–62, 165
Long, Russell, 165
Long Goodbye, The (Chandler), 89
Long Goodbye, The (motion picture), 126–27
Lord Jim (motion picture), 127
Lysergic acid diethylamide (LSD), 108

McCarthy, Joseph, 182
McDonald's (restaurant chain), 157
McGovern, George, 86, 130
McPherson, M., 8
McQueen (motion picture), 125
Madness and Civilization (Foucault), 14
Magruder, Jeb Stuart, 177
Maliczewen, Reck von, 139
Mao Tse-tung, 48, 136, 146
Marat-Sade (Weiss), 182
Marcuse, Herbert, 3
Mardian, Robert, 52, 53
Marijuana, 91, 100–10, 112; penalties imposed on users, 109–10; pharmaceutical preparations of, 100
Marijuana Tax Act of 1937, 100, 103–4
Marine Hymn, 145
Marx, Karl, xv, 29, 34, 36, 88, 136–37, 141
Massachusetts Bay Colony, 15
Measure for Measure (Shakespeare), 119
Medici, Lorenzo de', 155
Mental hospitals, 19–20
Mercantilism, 31, 34
Merchandising appeals, specialized market, 4–5

Merchant of Venice, The (Shakespeare), 155
Merton, Robert K., 31
Michelin, 139
Milgram, Stanley, 118–20, 121, 125
Military-industrial complex, 178
Military Justice Is to Justice as Military Music Is to Music (Sherrill), 17
Mill, John Stuart, x, 4
Mitchell, John, 48, 53
Moltke, Helmut von, 130
Montezuma, Emperor, 145
Moore, Barrington, Jr., 70
Moral Indignation and Middle Class Psychology (Ranulf), x, 15
Moravian Theological Seminary, 51
Morphine, 171
Morris, William, 36
Mossadecq, Mohammed, 27, 86
"Mother's Little Helper" (song), 26
Multinational corporations, liberty and, 166–84; collective bargaining, 175, 179; discrimination, 171–73; government of the state, 166–70, 176–77; legitimacy of democratic state, 173–74; privilege and hierarchy, 177–80; third world forces, 174–75
Muskie, Edmund, 130

Napalm, 6
Napoleon I, 32
Narcotics Control Act, 105
National Commission on Marijuana and Drug Abuse, 105
National Lampoon, 132
Nazi Party, 54, 139–40
New Democratic Party, 63
Newton, Sir Isaac, 32
New York Academy of Medicine, 105
New York City police strike (1971), 8
New York *Daily News,* 62, 65
New Yorker, The, 142
New York Review, 81
New York Stock Exchange, xvi
New York *Times,* 63, 112, 131–32, 147–48, 179, 183–84
Nicotine, 106–7
Nietzsche, Friedrich, x–xi, 76, 126, 136
Nixon, Richard, 48–55, 71, 72, 89,

194   INDEX

90, 105, 122, 135, 157, 159, 163,
173, 178–79, 184; attitude toward
the presidency, 48; Vietnam War,
49, 50, 51, 58. *See also* Watergate
affair
Nova Scotia Liquor Commission, xi

Obedience to Authority (Milgram),
118
Offenbach, Jacques, 145
Officers' Plot (1944), 183–84
Official Languages Act, x
Ohio National Guard, 85, 130–31
Oil industry, 91–92
"On Liberty" (Mill), x
Ophuls, Max, 156
Opportunism, equality and, 28–55,
153; discrimination, 28–29, 42;
economic productivity, 34–35, 37;
ethnic and racial groups, 41–47;
industrialism, 31, 33, 34;
inegalitarian state, 29; modern
political thought, 29–33; Nixon
administration, 48–55; practice
of torture, 28; public school
system, 39, 47; public subsidies,
40–41; Victorian morality, 35–37;
Vietnam War, 37–38, 49, 50, 51;
working classes, 38–39
Ortega y Gasset, José, 50
Oughton, Diana, 38

Packard, Vance, 3
Pakistan, 116
Pan American World Airways, 96
Pascal, Blaise, 154
Patrolmen's Benevolent Association,
62, 63
Peel, Sir Robert, 14
Penal system, 9–14
Pentagon, 6
Pericles, 82
Petition of Right (1628), 32
Pfeiffer, Jules, 73
Philippines, 116, 174
Plato, 156
Plessy v. Ferguson, 152
Political Illusion, The (Ellul), ix
Populism, 147–65, 182; abortion of
ideological conflict, 162–64;
FDR and, 159–62; liberty and,
150–52, 164–65
Pornography, 6, 110
Portugal, 132; *coup* of 1974, 156
Prison physicians, 17

Prison reform, 11–12
Privilege, redistribution of liberty
and, 150
Professional police, establishment of,
14
Progressive Conservative Party, 63
Progressive Labor Party, 136
Prostitution, 21
*Protestant Ethic and the Spirit of
Capitalism, The* (Weber), 31
Psychedelic drugs, 91
Public education, clientele for, 6–7
Public school system, 2, 6–7, 15–16;
equality and, 39, 47

Qadaffi, Muammar el-, 145

Rajputs (caste), 108
Ranulf, Svend, x, 15
Raza, La, 95
*Readers' Guide to Periodical
Literature, The,* 103
Reagan, Ronald, 37–38, 140
*Reflections on the Causes of Human
Misery* (Moore), 70
Reformation, 31
Reification of clienteles, 1–27;
institutional symbiosis, 18–21;
law enforcement industry, 7–15;
meaning of, 1; medicine and law,
16–18; operators and clients
(in their own interests), 21–27;
politically powerless and, 1–2;
public school system, 2, 6–7,
15–16; public-welfare system,
1; specialized sales markets,
4–6
Religion and the Rise of Capitalism
(Tawney), 31
Report of the Committee on Youth
to the Secretary of State
(Canada), 105–6
*Report of the Indian Hemp Drug
Commission,* 105
Report from Iron Mountain, 140–
41, 146
Ressentiment, defined, xi–xii
Revolt of the Masses (Ortega y
Gasset), 50
Revolutionary Party (Mexico), 64
Rhodesia, 29
Rickenbacker, Eddie, 99
Riesman, David, 47
Rise of the Meritocracy, The
(Young), 44

R.